McDonald's drinkware

IDENTIFICATION & VALUE GUIDE

MICHAEL J. KELLY

COLLECTOR BOOKS

A Division of Schroeder Publishing Co., Inc.

Upper right corner: 1981 brandy snifter from Cromwell, Connecticut, 1981. $20.00 – 25.00.
Left middle: Ronald McDonald plastic mug with red shoes, 1985. $5.00 – 9.00.
Bottom of page, left: Ronald McDonald tumbler from 1976 – 1977 Collectors series. $2.00 – 3.00.
Bottom of page, center: Amber Chicago Operations and Training mug. $15.00 – 20.00.
Bottom of page, right: Cinderella tumbler from Canadian Disney Animated Film Classics set of four. $8.00 – 10.00.

Cover design by Beth Summers
Book design by Lonna Bradford & Allan Ramsey

COLLECTOR BOOKS
P.O. Box 3009
Paducah, Kentucky 42002 – 3009

www.collectorbooks.com

Copyright © 2005 Michael J. Kelly

Searching For A Publisher?

We are always looking for people knowledgeable within their fields.
If you feel that there is a real need for a book on your collectible subject
and have a large comprehensive collection, contact Collector Books.

The current values in this book should be used only as a guide. They
are not intended to set prices, which vary from one section of the country to another. Auction prices as well as dealer prices vary greatly and
are affected by condition as well as demand. Neither the author nor
the publisher assumes responsibility for any losses that might be incurred
as a result of consulting this guide.

CONTENTS

Acknowledgments 4

About the Author 4

Introduction 5

This Book's Organization 6

A Brief History of McDonald's Drinkware 6

McDonald's Collecting Resources 9

Pricing 9

McDonald's Drinkware

Anniversaries...11

Bar Drinkware 13

Breakfast Mugs 15

Camp Snoopy 18

Charity and Community Involvement......................19

Christmas...20

Classic Fifties Milkshake Glasses 24

Commuter Mugs 26

Conventions and Meetings 27

Cup Holders 30

Disney 31

Dukes of Hazzard 37

French Issues 38

Garfield Glass Tumblers................................39

German Issues 40

Grand Openings and Groundbreakings.................41

Hamburger University and
     Achievement Awards 43

Hawaii 46

Hong Kong Christmas 47

The Hunchback of Notre Dame...........................48

In-House Employee Premiums
     and Catalog Order Items 49

Insulated 52

Japanese Issues 61

Kuwait Issues Celebrating First Store
     Openings in the Middle East 62

Mac Tonight 63

McDonaldland Characters 65

Miscellaneous Drinkware 78

Monopoly Glassware, Plastic,
     and Paper Cups with Wax Coatings 90

Mug Sets 98

Muppet Caper 102

Netherlands Issues 104

Paper Cups and Wax-Coated Paper Cups 105

Pitchers 136

Plastic Cups 137

Puerto Rico Issues..200

Radio and TV Stations 201

Red Wing Pottery Mugs...............................203

Ronald McDonald House 204

Specific Locations 208

Sports Glassware 218

Stemware and Carafes.................................232

Styrofoam Coffee and Hot Beverage Cups 243

Sundae, Mocha, and Parfait Cups 246

Thailand Issues 247

Toy Cups 248

Travel Mugs (USA)/Port-A-Mugs (Canada) 249

Workshops, Conferences,
     Picnics, Training, Reviews, and Rallies 252

Index 254

ACKNOWLEDGMENTS

An ancient Asian saying, "He who rides a tiger fears to dismount," summarizes the relationship I have had with this book over the past five years. This book has been my tiger, and the ride has been interesting, long, and challenging. Having dismounted, I now confess that it has also been largely a solitary and not always comfortable ride. Fortunately, various people have helped to make the ride easier. First, a blanket thank-you for all the McDonald's counter employees I have assaulted with requests for the latest promotional drinkware. They may possibly remember the strange guy who walked up to the counter and asked for one of each of all the latest drinking containers. The Slippery Rock, Pennsylvania, store has been especially understanding, but I have left many puzzled counter attendants in my wake all around the United States and certain parts of Europe. For other kinds of contributions I would like to thank the following people: Pat Lonergan, Tony McGaha, Robert Wilson, Lance Golba, John and Eleanor Larsen, Meredith Williams, and Kathy and David Clark. My wife, Priscilla, deserves special mention for being so very patient and consistently supportive even though she often wondered what it was I found so fascinating about the tiger. If I have forgotten to thank anyone who has helped, I apologize here and thank them now. They know who they are.

ABOUT the AUTHOR

Michael J. Kelly has co-authored with Mark Chase two previous books on collectible drinking glasses: *Contemporary Fast-Food and Drinking Glass Collectibles* (Wallace-Homestead, 1988) and *Collectible Drinking Glasses: Identification & Values* (Collector Books, 1996; Values Updated Edition, 1999). He is the co-founder of Collector Glass News and has published numerous articles on collectible drinking glasses in *The Antique Trader, Collectible Toy Values Monthly*, and other publications. On the subject of collectible drinking glasses he has been interviewed by and quoted in *Martha Stewart Living Magazine, Kiplinger's Personal Finance Magazine*, and *The Youngstown Vindicator*, and a syndicated radio talk show. Another highlight of his glass collecting career occurred on June 8, 1995, when Fox Television Network's *Personal fX Collectible Show* featured a segment on glass collecting and featured his collection in a broadcast from the basement of his home in Slippery Rock, Pennsylvania.

Michael Kelly holds a Ph.D in English from the University of Massachusetts (1968) and a post doctorate Master of Arts in Professional Writing from Carnegie Mellon University (1989). He retired in 2002 after teaching writing and literature at Slippery Rock University in Pennsylvania since 1967. He and his wife Priscilla reside in Mill Valley, California.

Questions, comments, and inquiries about the contents of this book will be acknowledged by the author who is anxious to continue collecting information on the history of McDonald's drinkware. Correspondence should be addressed to Dr. Kelly in care of Collector Books, P.O. Box 3009, Paducah, KY 42002-3009.

INTRODUCTION

Today's collectors are sophisticated and want solid information about the things they collect, and that has been the motivating force behind this book. Collectors want more than one-line descriptions and listings and values. They want specific, reliable facts and dates, and historical, contextual information. They are well aware that information is precious, often very difficult to come by and totally necessary for intelligent and efficient collecting. They are equally aware that there is a lot of misinformation making the rounds in print and on the electronic media. Filling knowledge gaps and (when necessary) correcting received opinion have been my goals.

My intention in writing this book was to create a safe haven for collectors of McDonald's drinkware. A collector myself and the co-author of two previous books on collectible drinkware, I realize intensely the importance of accurate and relevant information within collecting fields. Assembling this book has confirmed my suspicion that confusion and uncertainty are more likely the rule than the exception. My goal was therefore to set the bar high with regard to the integrity and comprehensiveness of the information presented.

Thus the guiding principle of this book was to provide as much useful, interesting, and accurate information as I could assemble. I have examined each of the drinkware items listed in this book with my own eyes, and I have described them precisely. I have taken extra pains to research, verify, and select the information presented here. It has not been easy. If you don't look closely enough at the drinkware item you are holding in your hand, you have an excellent chance of missing a detail, a difference, an important feature. Background information is another evasive thing. The knowledge is out there, but it's extremely difficult to find the knowledge epicenter, if there is one.

Why? Well, many collectors are too busy collecting or selling or trading to take the time to investigate and pass on information. They tend to be so absorbed by their collecting that they are sometimes reluctant or unable to share their knowledge. It's common for collectors to forget the detail, the anecdotal information, the place or date in time. The satisfaction of ownership or possession without detailed information about the collectible in question is

enough for many collectors. Overlooked are the facts that make the collectible worth collecting in the first place. Collecting without knowledge seems purposeless to me. I hope this book will provide meaningful guidance and direction.

Another major obstacle to McDonald's collectors trying to pin facts down is the fact that McDonald's has not kept very good records on their drinkware promotions, especially during the early years of the franchise. The central record keeping was not very good, nor was it of much interest to the rapidly growing franchise. Selling hamburgers, fries, and milkshakes took precedence. Widely scattered regions could pretty much do what they wanted to do when it came to promotions. It's therefore quite difficult in many cases to say with certainty who issued what drinkware when and where. Ironically, this fact is what makes collecting McDonald's drinkware so interesting and exciting.

In this book I've assembled enough drinkware and arranged it in such a way that collectors should be able to get a good overview of the great variety of drinkware McDonald's has issued over the years. I do not make the claim that my listings are comprehensive, but I can say with confidence that the listings in this book go far beyond anything on the same subject published to date. When you go out drinkware hunting or when you browse the online auctions, you will find drinkware not listed in this book. My reaction to that is, wonderful! There is no way to nail this collecting category down, not with approximately 30,000 McDonald's stores in the world promoting their food offerings every day of the year. This abundance of drinkware means that there is more to collect and more to discover about McDonald's drinkware and that your collection will never be finished as long as McDonald's is in business and you have the desire to collect.

I find collecting McDonald's drinkware quite challenging and interesting. I strongly believe that information about the drinkware deserves to be preserved. My hope is that McDonald's collectors will feel that I have built a solid base here and that I have given them a good point of departure. Finally, I hope that collectors will find and enjoy their own niche within this special universe of drinkware and that they will come to their own conclusions about the importance, desirability, and value of this drinkware.

THIS BOOK'S ORGANIZATION

I've tried to choose heading names that are logical and intuitive so that users of this book can find what they are looking for easily. I've chosen to organize the drinkware entries in this book alphabetically by category, promotion name, drinkware type or composition, promotion occasion, or country (or state) of origin. Several major categories or headings include two or more categories or kinds of drinkware, as for example "Hamburger University and Achievement Awards" or "Miscellaneous McDonald's Mugs with Logo or McDonald's Name Alone." Such combinations seem to be justified by the similarity or relatedness of the drinkware types paired in the category.

Within major categories that have no sub-categories I most frequently arrange the entries according to date of issue, proceeding from earliest to most recent. Undated issues are listed below (after) dated issues and arranged either alphabetically or by category. Exceptions to this method of organization occur under several major categories including "Specific Location Promotions" where drinkware is arranged alphabetically by state or country and within states or countries by date from earliest to most recent; "Plastic Cups, Miscellaneous, No Date" where the cups are listed in no particular order; and "Plastic Cups — States" where cups are arranged alphabetically by state and within states by date.

Within major categories that contain sub-categories, for example, "Paper Cups and Wax-Coated Paper Cups," I arrange the sub-categories alphabetically and the drinkware within those sub-categories by date from earliest to most recent. Undated items appear below (after) dated issues.

My original intention was to attempt in the listings to keep glass, ceramic, plastic, and paper drinkware separate. However, as the listings grew and the categories became more complicated to manage, I discovered that I could not conveniently or logically sustain such clean divisions. Users of this book will therefore find that under some major categories several kinds of drinkware will be included. It made sense to me, for example, under the "Monopoly" heading to include glass, plastic, and paper examples since there are too few glass and plastic issues to warrant separate categories. Likewise it seemed best to me to combine glass, ceramic, plastic, and paper "Mac Tonight" drinkware under one heading since there are too few paper and plastic examples to flesh out two additional viable stand-alone categories.

I am confident that users will find my organization of drinkware clear and easy to use. The Table of Contents provides a visual view of the book's structure, and the Index will help users locate specific drinkware items quickly.

A BRIEF HISTORY of McDONALD'S DRINKWARE

Fortunately we can say that we know precisely when the history of McDonald's drinkware began, in 1955 in Des Plaines, Illinois where Ray Kroc built his first McDonald's restaurant. If we want to include the original McDonald brothers' restaurants in southern California from the late 1930s to the early 1950s, we can push the date back further. But since the McDonald's we are all familiar with today was launched in 1955 by Ray Kroc, I'm going to keep things simple and convenient and stick with that date. Therefore, we can conclude that when it comes to the matter of McDonald's collectibles, there isn't anything older than 1955, nothing older than 50 years. If you saved some of the original paper cups from the Des Plaines restaurant the day it opened, and if you saved the cup, mug, or glass you just bought yesterday from a twenty-first century McDonald's franchise, you certainly have the earliest and the latest drinkware. But as we shall see, there is a lot of drinkware in between!

McDonald's drinkware is as old as the company. It could be argued that it is the oldest, longest running significant McDonald's collectible. Sure, someone could argue that there were napkins and straws and tray liners and hamburger wrappers and salt and pepper packets and counter displays in those days and that they should be granted a certain privileged status; no one could deny the historic importance and interest of such memorabilia. But I am making the claim that the drinkware constitutes the biggest and most important continuous category of collectible McDonald's artifacts. Everything else distributed by McDonald's is a more recent development, and people are collecting those things too. Happy Meals, which were introduced in 1979, have generated a virtual toy collecting industry, but the drinkware is a constant and has been there since the beginning, and more and more collectors are beginning to appreciate this fact. Quite frankly, I'm amazed that it took all but a few serious collectors so long to figure this out.

The earliest McDonald's drinkware served a strictly utilitarian function, it held fluids: coffee, soft drinks, and shakes. It was ephemeral and disposable and had no special appeal. It wasn't much different from the drinkware other hamburger joints and drive-ins put on the counter. It was not meant to be saved. It was not a vehicle for advertising or an incentive for worker excellence or a souvenir given out at special gatherings. The thought of saving it or collecting it or writing a book about it would have puzzled customers, employees, and management. After all, it was only paper cups.

However, as the franchise grew under the entrepreneurial genius of Ray Kroc and the innovativeness of individual franchise owners, its needs changed and the drinkware gradually began to assume a special extra function, advertising and promotion. McDonald's was not alone in the race to establish a chain of restaurants to serve the needs and changing tastes of Americans in the late 1950s. This rapidly expanding upstart company was always looking for ways to differentiate itself from its numerous competitors and to capture the loyalty of its customers.

I do not mean to imply that the franchise suddenly decided that drinkware would be its most effective advertising medium. There are many ways to advertise, and McDonald's was well aware of this with advertising tentacles of every kind everywhere. Logic and good business sense eventually led to the conclusion that no matter what the entree, each meal included a drink, and drinks are contained in containers. Most are discarded after the meal either in the restaurant or in the parking lot's trash can, but it eventually occurred to owners and operators that these containers could (and would) be kept if they were neat enough and had collectible appeal.

In the early years of the franchise, there was not a lot of extra money to pour into advertising or company-wide promotions. Individual franchisees used their imaginations and their best business sense to promote the McDonald's name brand. Drinkware was not on the corporate radar screen. Everyday matters like franchise expansion, market share, corporate finances, and food quality had to come first. Drinkware as an aid to all of these efforts was an idea waiting to happen. Because no single source that I know of has ever attempted to explain how the collectible drinkware phenomenon developed, I will try to make a couple of connections here.

In the early 1960s it became apparent that the young and growing company needed a national advertising campaign to boost public awareness and break into the fast food market and gain the momentum that Kroc envisioned. This momentum materialized when Willard Scott, a young announcer for WRC-TV in Washington, D.C., put on a Bozo type clown suit and became Ronald McDonald in a series of television commercials. The year was 1963, and collectors who want to know more about the evolution of

Ronald's debut and its astounding success as a marketing device meant to appeal especially to children, can read all about it in John Love's *Behind the Arches*. By 1965 Scott had become immensely successful as Ronald McDonald, working for a large Washington McDonald's franchise called the Gee Gee Corporation and the Kal, Ehrlich, and Merrick Advertising Agency. Ronald had become "the perfect national spokesman for the chain" (Love, 221), and franchise owners not only spent much larger amounts of money on advertising but saw their store revenues surge. By 1965, as Love points out, Ronald McDonald made his first national television appearance and became "the only commercial character in the United States with a recognition factor among children equal to that of Santa Claus" (222). The "other" franchises, it turns out, had badly "miscalculated the importance of the children's segment" (222).

Ronald McDonald's success in national television commercials had everything to do with children who in most cases (then and now) determined which restaurant the family would patronize. Lovable Ronald did what kids like to do, play with friends, so the late 1960s and early 1970s saw the development of the first McDonald's playgrounds in Pennsylvania and California. These McDonaldland play areas actually constituted a fantasy world for children, especially after the additional Playland characters and creatures were soon added as companions for Ronald McDonald. Local and national television campaigns ensured that children both recognized and loved these characters as certainly was the case by the late 1960s and early 1970s when the company's new advertising arm began to spend more money on promotions. As John Love remarks in *Behind the Arches*, "...Playlands soon became the new centerpiece of McDonald's strategy for dominating the children's market" (308).

With the characters in place in their playground setting, it was time to put them to another use inside the restaurants on packaging and premiums. At some point in the early 1970s, someone, Love does not cover this subject, came up with the idea of putting Ronald and the Playland characters on glasses that could be sold with menu items. Thus evolved the set of six clear glass figurals that I show on pages 65 – 67. This turned out to be a false but very significant start for reasons I cover in my discussion of this set. Management was not deterred for long, however, and another set of McDonaldland characters appeared on glass tumblers which I show on page 68. Even though this second early 1970s attempt at a set of character glasses also failed, it was closer to what the company had in mind than the first set. It was not until 1975 – 1976 that McDonald's was able to get a set of six acceptable glasses (see page 69) into some of its stores, and this set paved the way for the very successful system-wide 1976 – 1977 promotion (page 70) of the six major and by now established McDonaldland characters. At this point, it is safe to say, the glass juggernaut was well underway.

McDonald's efforts to get plastic cups to market appear to have been successful slightly earlier than their efforts to market glassware. Here I allude to the yellow cups shown on pages 139 – 140. These cups feature the same images of the McDonaldland characters that the 1975 – 1977 sets featured and can be identified as 1973 issues since the fifth anniversary Hawaiian cups appeared five years after McDonald's established their presence there in 1968. By 1978, as page 141 (top) shows, the plastic juggernaut was well established in its own right and running parallel to the glassware.

We know that in 1975 McDonald's introduced its famous "two all-beef patties special sauce lettuce cheese pickles onions on a sesame seed bun" commercial jingle and had some fun with it on national television by turning it into a contest. They also put the jingle on a glass which I show on page 88. This early glass with no Playland characters on it is proof that the McDonald's advertising machine clearly saw the potential for conveying product oriented messages on its drinkware. It was inevitable that all kinds of drinkware would now be used to serve a wide array of the company's promotional needs. In addition to the Playland characters which survive to this day and have even been added to (Birdie the Early Bird), McDonald's began to court the sports audiences with football and baseball and soccer glass sets in the late 1970s and early 1980s, to commemorate conventions and meetings and store openings and workshops with numerous kinds of souvenir drinkware, and to reward hard working employees with personalized drinkware for excellence on the job. Other streams of drinkware from Hamburger University which opened in 1961 to Ronald McDonald House which opened in 1974 merge with dozens of other opportunities for promotional drinkware to bring more people into the stores including alliances with Disney, NASCAR, the Olympics, and popular cartoon characters such as Garfield, Flintstones, the Peanuts characters, and the Muppets, just to name a few. The bottom line: by the late 1970s McDonald's was fully aware that of all the ways they had to establish the brand, create customer loyalty, boost employee morale, reward employees for performance, and commemorate the franchise's landmark accomplishments, drinkware was its most effective and versatile vehicle. The drinkware had, and continues to have, an undeniable appeal to customers, employees, management, and collectors. I'm confident that people who use this book will agree with me.

That's the good news. Now for the other kind. The rich stream of glassware that dominated promotions in the 1970s and 1980s has been reduced to a trickle, at least in the United States. Of course there are occasional promotions, but paper and plastic cups now are the preferred means for carrying McDonald's promotional messages. The reasons are no doubt economic with Oak Brook carefully watching the bottom line. Paper and plastic are cheaper than glass, unbreakable, and easier to store. Collectors will just have to get used to this reality and hope that interesting glass and ceramic issues will be available from time to time as they seem to be in various countries around the world. All things considered, the outlook for collecting drinkware is a positive one, especially when online auctions are taken into account. And I am confident that there will continue to be enough previously undiscovered drinkware as well as contemporary in-house offerings to satisfy today's collectors.

McDONALD'S COLLECTING RESOURCES

Collectors of McDonald's drinkware will find the following resources helpful for learning more about McDonald's collectibles, meeting other McDonald's collectors, and using the Internet to locate items for their collections.

www.mcdonalds.com

The corporation's website contains a number of useful features and resources. A good site for both beginning and advanced collectors to visit.

McDonald's Collectors Club

Quarterly Newsletter
mcdclub.com
Membership Director
Barbara Hunt
1001 Sullins Ct.
Virginia Beach, VA 23455
Membership ($25.00 per year for an individual, $30.00 for a family) is a must for collectors who want to stay in touch with McDonald's collecting in the U.S. The club was founded in 1990 and now has about 1,300 members and seven regional chapters. The club's annual convention is a must-attend event for anyone interested in McDonald's collectibles.

Collecting Tips Newsletter

Meredith Williams
A Monthly Publication, $25.95 per year
P.O. Box 633
Joplin, MO 64801
willictn@clandjop.com or wiLLictn@jopLin.com
This newsletter primarily keeps subscribers current on Happy Meal promotions and other McDonald's collectibles. Drinkware is not a special emphasis, but you can't overlook the possibility that there could be news you could use.

McDonald's Collectibles: Identification and Value Guide

Gary Henriques and Audre DuVall
Collector Books, Values Updated, 1999
This book covers a wide variety of McDonald's collectibles and has a lot of other useful franchise information. Pages 313 – 338 show an interesting variety of McDonald's drinkware, some of which does not appear in my book.

www.eBay.com

An increasingly popular venue for buying and selling all McDonald's collectibles. There's a lot of drinkware listings and spirited bidding for rarer items. Bidders and collectors need to be careful, however, because there is abundant misinformation. Often sellers make inaccurate claims about the age, value, condition, or nature of their offerings. It's also easy to get carried away and pay too much for items.

Fast Food Fun!

3381 W. 130th St.
Cleveland, OH 44111
216-941-7127
ffoodfun@aol.com
This is an auction site run by Ken Brady. It is hosted by eBay and features collectibles from all the major fast-food franchises. You'll find some interesting drinkware here.

Behind the Arches by John F. Love:

Love, John F. Behind the Arches. Rev. Ed. New York: Bantam Books, 1995.
This history of the McDonald's franchise is necessary reading for anyone interested in the founding and building of the franchise. While there is not much information about collectibles and promotions, it's full of information which will help the collector put McDonald's rich and historically significant history into perspective.

PRICING

The price ranges I have assigned to the drinkware in this book are based on average selling prices of McDonald's drinkware in online auctions, private auctions, and private transactions, as well as prices at McDonald's conventions, collectible shows, antique malls, and flea markets. Collectors may pay more or less for the drinkware I list. I would not presume to insist that these prices are firm and final. Every collector has a good day and gets the prized item for practically nothing by chance or vendor ignorance, and all collectors pay too much at times. I know I have had to pay more than I wanted to pay to secure important glasses I have shown in this book, and I have bought many unusual pieces of McDonald's drinkware at bargain basement prices. Like most collectors I fall back on the time-honored

expression: "win a few, lose a few!" If that doesn't help, here's another one: "It'll all average out in the end."

Collecting trends, family budgets, market conditions, and a whole host of sociological factors subtly combine to determine prices. In fifteen years of glass collecting I have learned that collectors attach varying degrees of value to various collectibles and that price spikes can be caused by any number of factors. "On any given day..." is a phrase that comes to mind. Collisions of egos at auctions result all too often in abnormally high prices, and collectors who wish to fill gaps in their collections or who just have to have "right now" an item "no matter what it costs" are also partly responsible. But on the whole I believe that over time collectors will sense that most McDonald's drinkware is reasonably priced when all these various constraints are considered.

Obviously, some drinkware is worth more than other drinkware because of age and rarity. Supply and demand is another self-explanatory phenomenon. Prototypes, sample glasses, production variations, error glasses, early paper and plastic pieces, and regional issues tend to command proportionally higher prices, as perhaps they should. Informed collectors know about these collecting areas, and prices ultimately fall in line with such market realities.

Some drinkware, because of its uniqueness, should bring lofty prices, and we appreciate this fact when it comes time for a decision. In general, the earlier the piece, the higher the price. Foreign issues tend to command premium prices because of the lack of knowledge about them and the difficulty of obtaining and shipping them. Collectors need to be mindful that McDonald's, as this book goes to press, is only fifty years old, so we are not talking about ancient artifacts. Most of the drinkware collectors are presently collecting fails to qualify as bona fide collectibles because they are not, as some pundits insist they be, at least twenty-five or thirty years old. Obviously, items from the fifties and sixties are rare and desirable. In the early years of the franchise, paper cups were the order of the day; other kinds of promotional drinkware were unthought of. It should come as no surprise, therefore, that today they are highly prized because of their rarity. (Who would have thought of saving those first paper cups?) Early plastic issues command similarly high prices for the same reasons. (Why would anybody have had the impulse to save them?)

In the mid-seventies when glass promotions went into full swing, quantity and durability problems were solved by massive national promotions. Mugs and glasses from these promotions have survived in great quantity, and as a result, they are worth a dollar or two at best, what we would gladly pay at any retail store for a generic mug or tumbler. Prices are very brisk, as we might expect, for limited production in-house and convention issues. Regional meetings, conventions, anniversaries, groundbreakings, holiday and special occasion issues, and charity issues are exciting collecting areas to get into because there's no knowing what you might find. Operators and owners in the early days of the franchise launched all kinds of promotions. Many were regional and extremely limited to the employees and sometimes to the patrons of a small group of stores. The drinkware these promotions generated is therefore of great interest and highly collectible. Collectors will also find that a lot of McDonald's drinkware has been available to employees and operators for many years through the corporation's central marketing offices and internal divisions. This drinkware is out there and on the market along with all of the other drinkware.

Drinkware made specifically in extremely limited quantities for owners and operators is the most prized because of its scarcity, so much so that I find it difficult to assign prices to it. It seems to me, for example, that owner/operator convention drinkware, especially from the early days of the franchise, should be highly desirable because of its limited production. Collectors with means will pay whatever they have to to get what they want for their collections. My feeling, after taking all of these factors into consideration, is that all of McDonald's drinkware is inherently interesting and worth collecting, but collectors would be well advised to specialize since collecting it all is an overwhelming undertaking which involves not only considerable financial outlays but huge amounts of storage space. There is enough drinkware in many of the categories I list in this book to challenge almost any collector. With persistence and luck and the information this book contains, collectors can assemble for not too much money an impressive, interesting collection or display of McDonald's drinkware. Good luck!

McDONALD'S DRINKWARE

ANNIVERSARIES

ANNIVERSARY TANKARDS

1. McDonald's 20, April 20, 1975, a 6" clear glass mug with red, yellow, and black decoration. $25.00 – 35.00.
2. McDonald's "Q(uality) 20 Years" tankard, 5$\frac{1}{8}$" black pottery with gold decoration dating from 1975. $50.00 – 75.00.
3. McDonald's 25th Anniversary April 15, 1980, a 5$\frac{5}{8}$" oatmeal-colored Pfaltzgraff pottery stein with 2" diameter applied metal plate. A Pfaltzgraff imprint appears on the bottom along with these numbers: 6 – 286. $15.00 – 25.00.

ANNIVERSARY MUGS

1. 25th Anniversary, 2814 Post Road, Warwick, Rhode Island, December 18, 1988, a 3$\frac{3}{4}$" white ceramic mug with red decoration. $15.00 – 25.00.
2. McDonald's 30th Anniversary, a 6" mug with Speedee and old arches on front and new logo with "Celebrating 30 Years with You" on reverse, red and yellow decoration. $20.00 – 25.00.
3. 30th 1985 Birthday, a 3$\frac{1}{2}$" clear Luminarc glass mug with frosted decoration. $10.00 – 15.00.

ANNIVERSARY MUGS

1. Celebrating Thirty Years With You! East Hanover, New Jersey, April 15, 1985, a 4½" white ceramic mug with black decoration showing the East Hanover store. On the bottom: "Made in England." $20.00 – 35.00.
2. McDonald's 1985, a 5³/₁₆" heavy lead crystal clear glass mug with the McDonald's logo and the 1985 date. This finely crafted mug has impressed bands around the top and the bottom and was obviously not an over-the-counter premium. This is a 30th anniversary mug available only through the McDonald's catalogs or at regional meetings and conventions. $20.00 – 40.00.
3. McDonald's First Anniversary Norwalk (North), 199 Milan Ave., Norwalk, Ohio, 668 – 1487, a 5½" clear glass mug with red and yellow decoration. "Canada" is embossed on bottom in small lettering. $15.00 – 20.00.

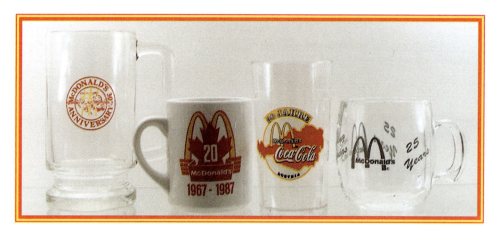

THREE ANNIVERSARY MUGS AND A TUMBLER

1. McDonald's 30th Anniversary with Speedee and slashed arch and new logo in circle/McDonald's logo and "Celebrating 30 Years with You," 3³/₄", with red and yellow decoration. $8.00 – 12.00.
2. McDonald's 20 years in Canada 1967 – 1987, a 3⁵/₈" white ceramic mug with red and yellow decoration featuring a large red maple leaf with a number 20 in it in front of a large McDonald's arch. The reverse features a drawing of an early "slashed arch" McDonald's restaurant, early golden arch sign, and Canadian flag on flagpole. $20.00 – 30.00.
3. McDonald's 20th Anniversary in Austria, a 5" clear acrylic tumbler co-sponsored by Coca-Cola. Red, white, yellow, and black decoration. $10.00 – 15.00.
4. McDonald's "Serving Kansas" for "25 Years," a 3⁵/₈" clear acryllic mug with gray decoration. On either side of "Serving Kansas," which appears opposite the handle, there's a gray McDonald's logo and "25 Years." This is a thick acryllic mug which could easily be mistaken for glass. It probably dates from the early 1980s, assuming that Ray Kroc got a store into that state not too long after he launched his new company in 1955. $15.00 – 25.00.

CANADIAN OLD FASHIONED TUMBLER SETS

Row 1.

This five-piece Canadian McDonald's decanter set was marketed (as its original shipping box informs us) by Cutler Brands and Designs Inc., 136 Geary Avenue, Toronto, Ontario M6H 2B7. It includes one 26½ oz. 753 ml. decanter and four eight-oz. 227 ml. 3¼" "on the rocks" tumblers. "Italy" is stamped on the bottom of the 8" decanter. The decoration on these pieces is wonderful. The neck of the decanter has a gold band, and each of the tumblers has a half-inch gold band at the top with the Canadian McDonald's logo and McDonald's name. The set was available to owners and operators and probably to certain employees. Set: $100.00 – 150.00; Decanter: $30.00 – 50.00; Tumblers: $10.00 – 15.00.

Row 2.

3¼" old fashioned set of four. Each glass has a gold rim and gold Canadian McDonald's logo. Very simple and elegant. Probably available only to owners and management through the in-house catalog. This set probably comes with a decanter. $15.00 – 25.00 each.

MISCELLANEOUS BARWARE

1. 3³/₈" smoke-colored old fashioned glass with dimpled bottom and large McDonald's logo in gold. This glass is undoubtedly part of a larger set available to owners and operators; there may even have been a matching decanter. $10.00 – 15.00.

2. Shot glass with McDonald's logo in red and yellow, 2¹/₄". McDonald's is definitely not known for distributing shot glasses as premiums or for using them in promotions, so these items are quite rare. This one, with the McDonald's logo alone, is especially desirable. $30.00 – 40.00.

3. Shot glass, 2⁵/₁₆" with black decoration showing a piano with a McDonald's logo just above the keyboard and with "New York 160 Broadway" below the piano. An unusual shot glass probably given as a special occasion gift to management at the 160 Broadway location. $30.00 – 40.00.

4. 1981 Rheingauer Weinwoche wine glass from Germany. This 3³/₈" mini tumbler has yellow decoration showing grapes on the vine along with the Golden Arches logo near the bottom. On the reverse there's the metric measurement telling us that this glass holds ¹/₁₀ of a litre. Glasses like this are quite rare. $40.00 – 60.00.

5. Beer glass with large yellow McDonald's logo, 9¹/₈". This wonderfully bold glass was probably a convention or workshop gift. McDonald's beer glasses are uncommon. $30.00 – 50.00.

6. 5¹/₂" clear glass mug with deeply etched bull elk standing amongst tall evergreens and a snow capped mountain on the front and an etched Golden Arches logo on the reverse. This unusual and beautiful mug was found in Michigan, and I'm told that it may have originated there, perhaps as a convention or regional meeting gift. I'm also assured that there are elk in Michigan. I'm classifying this mug as barware because it has a very unusual recessed bottle cap opener in the center of its bottom. The cap is twisted off the bottle when the cap is inserted into the recessed cavity and either the bottle or the mug is turned. This mug was made in France by Luminarc as the bottom indicates. It probably dates from the mid to late 1980s. I say this because the only other mugs like this that I know of are a set of four Pizza Hut mugs featuring Buffalo Bills' helmets which was issued in 1987. $35.00 – 50.00.

MISCELLANEOUS SINGLE BREAKFAST MUGS

Row 1.

1. McDonald's "Good Morning" milk glass coffee mug with orange happy smile sun and McDonald's logo in black and yellow on one side. This is the all-time most common McDonald's mug, and they are plentiful on eBay. These mugs were made by Anchor Hocking. There appear to be at least two different versions of bottom information. The information on one of the mug types is as follows: "Oven-Proof (with a number below, and an Anchor Hocking anchor logo with a frame around it and the number 312 beneath it) Made In USA." The numbers on the bottoms of these mugs vary considerably, and some of the mugs have five little pimply dots under "Made In USA." The information on the bottom of the other mug type appears to be more modern and is as follows: "ANCHOR HOCKING (unframed anchor logo with an H) Fire-King Oven-Proof (number below) Made In USA." The numbers under "Oven-Proof" on this mug type vary considerably and may be company codes for the mug run. Both bottom configurations are easy to find, and my guess is that the simpler bottom is the earlier of the two. In describing other Fire-King "Good Morning" mugs below, I will refer to their bottom designs as "earlier" or "newer." $1.00 – 2.00.

2. McDonald's "Good Morning, Pittsburgh" milk glass coffee mug with orange happy smile sun and McDonald's logo in black and yellow on one side. Uncommon. "Newer" bottom design. $10.00 – 25.00.

3. McDonald's "Good Morning Fairmont" milk glass coffee mug with red-lined happy smile face and McDonald's logo, red and yellow decoration. On the reverse: "'You're the reason we do it.' East Fairmont Grand Opening April 19, 1980 Fairmont, West Virginia." Regional mugs of this type are fairly rare. Uncommon. "Earlier" bottom design. $15.00 – 25.00.

4. McDonald's "Good Morning Canada" milk glass coffee mug with orange happy smile sun and Canadian McDonald's logo in red and yellow on one side. "Newer" bottom design. $8.00 – 12.00.

Row 2.

1. McDonald's Canadian Good Morning style milk glass breakfast mug without "Good Morning Canada" on it. It is not known whether this mug is a lesser known regular issue or a mug that somehow went through the production process without having "Good Morning Canada" applied to it. In any case, it is rare. "Newer" bottom design. $12.00 – 20.00.

2. McDonald's "Breakfast" milk glass coffee mug with large orange happy smile sun and McDonald's logo in yellow and red on both sides. Unfortunately, the happy smile face on the orange sun is nearly the same color as the sun and cannot be seen from any distance. In addition, the fact that "Breakfast" appears alone strongly suggests that this mug may be a prototype for subsequent "breakfast brigade" mugs. "B – 47" appears in raised lettering on the bottom. $25.00 – 50.00+.

3. McDonald's "breakfast brigade" milk glass coffee mug with orange happy smile sun and McDonald's logo in yellow and black on both sides. $7.00 – 10.00.

4. McDonald's "breakfast brigade" milk glass coffee mug with McDonald's logo in yellow and red on both sides. $9.00 – 12.00.

MISCELLANEOUS BREAKFAST MUGS

Row 1.

1. McDonald's clear glass 3³/₈" breakfast mug with red and yellow block logo and yellow smiling sun at upper right. $4.00 – 8.00.

2. "Guaranteed Breakfast promotion sure to please your customers" along with McDonald's logo and happy smile sun image in red, and on the other side "Sun-Times More News *You* Can Use," a 3³/₄" white ceramic mug with red decoration. "Made in England" appears on the bottom. Mugs like this were sent by marketing groups to McDonald's owners and operators to encourage them to participate in various focused promotions. Items like this are unusual since they were produced in very limited numbers. $25.00 – 40.00.

3. "My Morning Mug," a 3⁵/₈" white ceramic mug with large yellow and red McDonald's logo and yellow line drawing of happy smile sun, design on one side only, made in Staffordshire, England, by Kiln Craft. $15.00 – 20.00.

4. "McDonald's The Plaza Food Court Palmerston North My Morning Mug," a 3⁵/₈" mug with red lettering and yellow arches and smiling sun. This unusual mug is from New Zealand. There's a sticker on the bottom that says "Ken Griffiths Imports Ltd. Fax (04) 297-3398." $35.00 – 50.00.

Row 2.

1. "Buenos dias!!" a 3³/₈" white pottery mug from Mexico with orange smiling sun and large Golden Arches. Graphics on one side of the mug. $12.00 – 20.00.

2. "Many Happy Returns," a milk glass coffee mug with various nature icons and small Golden Arches on either side of the word "Returns" (same design on both sides of mug). $6.00 – 9.00.

3. "Taking Breakfast by the Hand All Over the Land," a 3³/₄" white ceramic mug showing a happy smile sun rising over an idyllic country setting with multicolored decoration. $7.00 – 11.00.

4. McDonald's logo and happy-faced sun above tri-colored bar on 5¹/₂" white milk glass pedestal mug. $5.00 – 9.00.

5. McDonald's logo in yellow and black on 5¹/₂" white milk glass pedestal mug. $5.00 – 8.00.

Row 1: Office coffee mug set of four (mid to late 1980s).
These mugs feature office motifs and the standard jokes about how tough it is to function on the job early in the morning before that first cup of coffee. $3.00 – 6.00 each.

1. a.m. with international "No" symbol and "I'd like mornings better if they started LATER."
2. Black and yellow caution sign and "Warning: FIRST CUP Talk to me at your own risk!"
3. "While You Were Out" telephone message form with "Gone for the Morning!" written on it.
4. "It's much too early to start talking…LEAVE A NOTE!" written on yellow note paper.

Row 2: International coffee set of three mugs (1989).
Each of these black ceramic mugs features motifs which are characteristic of each country and, presumably, its coffee. Originally the mugs came with a small foil packet of international coffee and were "Available at breakfast only" according to the table display. $5.00 – 8.00 each.

1. McDonald's French Roast
2. McDonald's Irish Cream
3. McDonald's Vienna Roast

CAMP SNOOPY COLLECTION SET OF FIVE (1983)

These five 6" round-bottom glasses feature Charles Schulz's popular cartoon characters in colorful wraparound action and generous color in a camping context. The title of each glass appears in a bubble spoken by Schulz's characters. These glasses are undated, but they have a hodgepodge of copyright dates going back to 1950; they were issued in the summer of 1983 with the actual rollout of glasses beginning on July 1, so ignore flea market and eBay vendors who (wrongly) insist on the earliest date. These glasses were heavily and widely distributed, so they are plentiful and inexpensive. $.50 – 1.00 each.

Row 1: Set of five glass Camp Snoopy tumblers.

1. There's no excuse for not being properly prepared (Lucy).
2. The struggle for security is no picnic! (Linus).
3. Civilization is overrated! (Snoopy).
4. Rats! Why is having fun always so much work? (Charlie Brown).
5. Morning people are hard to love (Snoopy).

Row 2: Set of five plastic Camp Snoopy cups.

Ironically, these plastic cups are not well-known in spite of the fact that their glass counterparts have achieved international fame as the quintessential over-distributed glass. The graphics on these cups are identical to those on the glasses, but these cups are almost impossible to find in excellent condition. Vindication for plastic? I think so! $7.00 – 12.00 each.

1. There's No Excuse For Not Being Properly Prepared (Lucy).
2. The Struggle For Security Is No Picnic! (Linus).
3. Civilization Is Overrated! (Snoopy).
4. Rats! Why Is Having Fun Always So Much Work? (Charlie Brown).
5. Morning People Are Hard To Love (Snoopy).

Camp Snoopy Collection Owner-Operator Glass — Camp Snoopy Special Edition (1983).

This glass, regarded by many as the ultimate McDonald's collector glass, was sent as an incentive or reminder to selected McDonald's owner/operators to commit their stores to participation in the Camp Snoopy Collection promotion. It is thought that only one of these glasses was sent to each McDonald's store owner/operator, so as few as 1,500 to 2,000 of these glasses may have been made. Therefore, this glass is in extremely limited supply and quite sought after by glass, and McDonald's, collectors. Since the text on this glass is not well known, I include it here: Snoopy saying "Happiness Is Starring in Peanuts For Over Thirty Years," Charlie Brown saying "Good Grief! McDonald's 'Camp Snoopy' Glasses Are Coming!," Lucy saying "Five Great Glasses…And Mine's The Best," and Linus saying "Hurry! Commit By March 15, 1983." $400.00 – 600.00 +.

"Good Grief! McDonald's 'Camp Snoopy' Glasses Are Coming!"

"Five Great Glasses…And Mine's The Best!"

"Hurry! Commit By March 15, 1983"

"Happiness is starring in Peanuts for over thirty years."

CHARITY and COMMUNITY INVOLVEMENT

CHARITY AND COMMUNITY INVOLVEMENT

Row 1.

1. McDonald's Charity Golf Classic 1992, a 6¹/₈" mug shaped like a golf bag, red decoration. $15.00 – 20.00.

2. McDonald's San Joaquin County (California) 1984 Senior Tennis Tournament, a 5¹/₂" mug with red and yellow decoration. $15.00 – 20.00.

3. Wabash Valley Golf Club, Geneva, Indiana, Pro-Am Charity Shoot-Out sponsored By: CTS, McDonald's, Coca-Cola, a 4¹/₈" old fashioned glass with frosted decoration. $8.00 – 12.00.

4. McDonald's Salutes Our Adopted School, a 5¹/₂" mug with red and yellow decoration. $10.00 – 15.00.

Row 2.

1. McDonald's 1988 McBingo Winner, a 5¹/₂" clear glass mug with red and yellow decoration. $10.00 – 15.00.

2. Saint Mary of Nazareth Hospital Center, a 5¹/₈" pedestal mug with red and yellow decoration. $10.00 – 15.00.

3. McDonald's Restaurant, "Team Up To Save Lives," Fire Department, Borough of Old Forge (Pennsylvania), a 3³/₄" white ceramic coffee mug with red decoration. $15.00 – 20.00.

4. "Michael Jordan R.M.C.C. Celebrity Golf Championship Benefitting Ronald McDonald Children's Charities And The Michael Jordan Foundation," a 3⁵/₈" white ceramic mug with multicolored decoration showing Michael Jordan swinging a golf club. On the bottom: "MAdeINCHINA." $5.00 – 8.00.

MISCELLANEOUS CHRISTMAS MUGS

Row 1.

1. McDonald's Christmas 1979, a $5\frac{1}{2}$" clear glass mug with red decoration. $20.00 – 30.00.

2. McDonald's Christmas 1981, a $5\frac{1}{2}$" mug with red decoration. $15.00 – 20.00.

3. Merry Christmas 1983, a $5\frac{3}{4}$" green ceramic pedestal mug with gold decoration. $15.00 – 25.00.

4. McDonald's Bloomington, Indiana, Christmas 1983, a $5\frac{1}{2}$" clear glass mug with red and yellow decoration. $15.00 – 20.00.

5. McDonald's 1983 Crew Christmas Party, Troy, Sidney, Piqua East, Piqua West, Tipp City, a $5\frac{1}{2}$" clear glass mug with red and yellow decoration. The locations listed on this mug are in west central Ohio. $15.00 – 20.00.

Row 2.

1. "Merry Christmas McDonald's of Newark, New York 1984," a $5\frac{1}{2}$" mug with red and yellow decoration. $15.00 – 20.00.

2. McDonald's of Piqua, Troy, Tipp City, Sidney 1985 Christmas Party, a $5\frac{1}{2}$" clear glass mug with red and yellow decoration. These stores are located in west central Ohio. $15.00 – 20.00.

3. "Merry Christmas 1986," a $3\frac{1}{2}$" milk glass mug with red and green decoration which features three snowmen and two Christmas trees. Red arches appear over one of the Christmas trees. Embossed on the bottom: "Oven-Proof/Galaxy/Made In/Mexico." $15.00 – 25.00.

4. McDonald's 1986 Christmas Party, McDonald's Of: Piqua, Troy, Sidney, Tipp City, Greenville, Ohio, a $5\frac{1}{2}$" clear glass mug with red and yellow decoration. The stores listed on this mug are in west central Ohio. $15.00 – 20.00.

5. McDonald's South Bend (Indiana) Market Christmas 1986, a $5\frac{1}{2}$" clear glass mug with red and yellow decoration. $15.00 – 20.00.

Row 1.

1. McDonald's of Clarion, Christmas 1987, 7th and Main Streets, Clarion, PA, 16214, a 5¹/₂" mug with red and yellow decoration. $15.00 – 20.00.

2. McDonald's of Dana Point, #1 Team, Christmas 1987, a 5¹/₂" clear glass mug with red and yellow decoration. Dana Point is in California between Los Angeles and San Diego and is often referred to as the "California Riviera." $15.00 – 20.00.

3. Christmas mug given to the crew in Bay City, Michigan, in 1987. I got this mug from the crew member who still works for McDonald's. This is a temperature sensitive mug which shows a Christmas winter village below a crescent moon. There's a black panel above the village scene. When the mug is filled with hot or boiling water, Santa and his reindeer appear along with "Merry Christmas" and a large red McDonald's logo. On the bottom: "Made in Brazil." $15.00 – 20.00.

4. Season's Greetings from South Dartmouth (Massachusetts) 1988, a 3¹/₄" white ceramic mug with green decoration. $15.00 – 25.00.

5. Season's Greetings, McDonald's of Burien (Washington) 1990, a 5¹/₂" mug with red and yellow decoration. $15.00 – 20.00.

Row 2.

1. McDonald's Westgate Christmas 1990, a 5¹/₂" clear glass mug with red and yellow decoration. $15.00 – 20.00.

2. "McDonald's Christmas 1992" on one side of a white 3¹/₂" ceramic mug with red and green decoration and "Merry Christmas from Lee & Mary Wagy Owner/Operators" on the other. The Wagys are owners of several McDonald's stores in North Kansas City, Missouri. Mugs like this are extremely rare and desirable because they are so unusual and personal. $15.00 – 45.00.

3. "Happy Holidays," a 3³/₄" gray ceramic mug with red and white decoration featuring Ronald's face on a postage stamp. The postmark says "North Pole Dec. 199-," so we know that the mug was issued during the 1990s. On the bottom: "Linyi Headwind Made in China." $8.00 – 12.00.

4. Merry Christmas From Macamerica, a 4" Anchor Hocking oven-proof white milk glass mug with black decoration. $15.00 – 25.00.

5. Happy Holidays, a 5¹/₈" Mason jar mug featuring a stocking stuffed with presents and the McDonald's logo all in green decoration. Probably came with a lid. $10.00 – 15.00.

MISCELLANEOUS CHRISTMAS ISSUES

Row 1.

1. McDonald's Italia, a 5³/₄" fountain glass sponsored by Coca-Cola with pine cone and holly berry wreath border encircling top of glass. Shown with gift box it came in. $15.00 – 20.00.

2. Italian fountain glass gift box.

3. Season's Greetings, a 3¹/₂" red ceramic mug (white inside) with gold decoration showing a reindeer's head. Two sets of Golden Arches appear (cleverly!) as part of the reindeer's antlers, and the "McDonald's" name appears in small gold letters near the bottom of the mug. $10.00 – 20.00.

Row 2.

1. Season's Greetings, a 3⁵/₈" green ceramic mug with gold decoration showing the head of a reindeer. The Golden Arches are incorporated into the reindeer's antlers, and "Season's Greetings" appears just below the reindeer's nose. "McDonald's" is located below the word "Greeting" in very small gold letters. This mug was made in China by "HG." It has the same graphics as the red mug listed above but is heavier and slightly larger. $10.00 – 20.00.

2. Season's Greetings, a 3³/₄" green ceramic mug with white decoration showing Hamburglar, Ronald, Grimace, and Birdie dressed for cold weather and caroling. No date, but the bottom says "Made in China." $10.00 – 20.00.

3. 3³/₄" dark green mug showing Ronald McDonald sitting in a red chair in front of a fireplace and Christmas tree reading a book to three children. "Made in China" appears in white on the bottom. This mug is recent (2000 or 2001) and was most likely available through a McDonald's Christmas catalog available to owners, managers, and employees. $10.00 – 20.00.

4. 5¹/₄" tumbler with green panel showing Ronald McDonald sitting in a red chair in front of a fireplace and Christmas tree reading a book to three children (same graphic that appears on mug listed above and shown to left). The tumbler is recent (2000 or 2001) and was probably available through a McDonald's Christmas catalog available to owners, managers, and employees. $10.00 – 20.00.

A CHRISTMAS CAROL (THREE UNDATED PROTOTYPES, BUT PROBABLY 1989 – 1990)

The three glasses I list here were to be part of a set of McDonald's Christmas Carol glasses, but this set was never produced. They are so similar in design to the 1990 Nutcracker set that it seems almost certain that the Christmas Carol was passed over in favor of the Nutcracker promotion. It is not known how many prototype Christmas Carol glasses were made or how many there were to be in the set. I show three of them here. Each shows a scene from Charles Dickens's *A Christmas Carol* which was published in 1843, and each has a quotation from Dickens's story on the reverse. Each has a McDonald's logo on the back and a sticker on its bottom saying: "This item was made under sampling conditions. The production item may differ slightly." The design and graphics on these glasses are beautiful, and it's a loss for collectors that they weren't produced. There's a story here, and I wish I knew what it was! These three glasses were found in Illinois. $350.00 – 500.00 each.

Views of characters on three Christmas Carol prototypes.

1. Jacob Marley's ghost addresses Scrooge.
2. The Cratchit family gathered in front of the fireplace.
3. A rehabilitated Scrooge walking down the street extending Christmas greetings.

REVERSE VIEWS OF CHRISTMAS CAROL PROTOTYPES FEATURING CHARACTERS' QUOTATIONS.

1. Marley's ghost's warning: "I am here tonight to warn you that you have a chance and hope of escaping my fate."
2. Tiny Tim's words: "'God bless us every one!' said Tiny Tim, the last of all."
3. Scrooge's Christmas greeting: "Merry Christmas to you, young lady. And you, too, lad, A Merry Christmas to you all."

NUTCRACKER SET OF FOUR TUMBLERS

This set of four tumblers came out for Christmas 1989, but they bear a 1990 copyright date. They were distributed primarily in South Carolina, more specifically in the Charleston area. Store managers that I talked to at the time of the promotion confessed that this was a not an altogether successful promotion because McDonald patrons were more interested in Christmas tree ornaments than glasses. These glasses are very colorful with nice graphics. $10.00 – 15.00 each.

1. Marie and the Prince glided across the dance floor in Toyland.
2. The Nutcracker led the toys to battle against the Army of Mice.
3. "The Sugar Plum Fairy lives here in the Land of Sweets," said the Nutcracker.
4. Marie cried out with delight, "A Nutcracker, Godfather, he is so beautiful."

CLASSIC FIFTIES MILKSHAKE GLASSES

Row 1: Set of four 1993 Classic Fifties milkshake glasses.

This set of four glasses was distributed in central Ohio south of Canton by a franchise group of fifteen or so stores in late summer 1993. The idea of the promotion was to capture 1950s nostalgia by showing Speedee and early McDonald's restaurants and signs on old fashioned milkshake glasses. For some reason, the first glass to be issued during the promotion (showing Speedee on top of a McDonald's sign with Golden Arch) was difficult to find, and it still is, though one might well wonder why since presumably an equal number of each glass was produced. The date 1993 appears in very small print in blue beneath the graphics.

1. Speedee with 15¢ sign on top of McDonald's sign which says: "McDonald's Speedee Service System/Hamburgers/We have sold over 20 Million." Golden Arch in background. Red, yellow, and blue decoration. $10.00 – 15.00.

2. Speedee running with sign which says "I'm 'Speedee,'" "McDonald's" above Speedee. Red and blue decoration. $5.00 – 10.00.

3. "McDonald's Restaurant Circa 1957," showing a typical McDonald's restaurant from the late 1950s and the 1960s. Red, blue, and yellow decoration. $5.00 – 10.00.

4. "The Original Shake, Burger & Fries," showing those products in red, yellow, and blue. $5.00 – 10.00.

Row 2: Classic fifties milkshake glasses, set of four (redesigned) 1995, and a curious error glass.
Two years after the original issue of this very regional set, a new promotion was launched, a testament to its appeal. In most respects this set of four glasses greatly resembles its predecessors, but a close look at the two sets side by side will reveal noticeable design differences. The first glass (Speedee on the arches with 15¢ sign) has been changed to include a red 1958 automobile (instead of shrubbery beneath the McDonald's sign); "McDonald's" is now in solid red letters; and "5 Million" instead of "20 Million." The second ("I'm 'Speedee'") glass is unchanged. The third glass has a few changes: "Circa 1957" is now in blue instead of red, and "McDonald's" above the restaurant window is in solid red letters instead of red outlined letters. In addition, the blue screening on the restaurant is quite different. The fourth glasses are essentially the same, but on the 1995 version the fries are larger, and the cheese on the burger is yellow, not clear as on the 1993 version. In general, the lettering on the 1995 set is heavier. My overall impression is that the 1995 set is a design refinement and improvement, but the glasses are much more available than the 1993 glasses. $4.00 – 9.00 each.

1. Speedee with 15¢ sign on top of McDonald's sign with arch, red (General Motors 1957 – 1958) two-door hardtop below sign.

2. Speedee running with "I'm 'Speedee'" sign, red and blue decoration.

3. "McDonald's Restaurant Circa 1957" showing early McDonald's restaurant.

4. "The Original Shake, Burger & Fries" with yellow cheese on the burger and larger fries.

5. Error glass: "The Original Shake, Burger & Fries" with missing yellow paint decoration. $15.00 – 20.00.

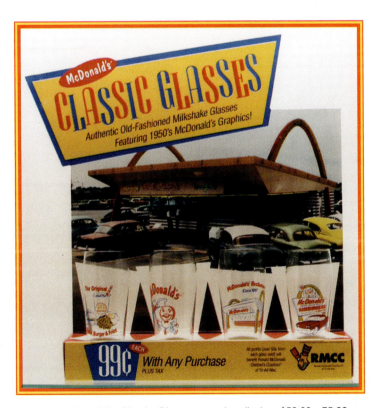

1995 McDonald's Classic Glasses counter display. $50.00 – 75.00.

THREE PLASTIC COMMUTER MUGS

1. 3³/₄" thick-walled, wide-based, narrow-necked commuter mug with a big handle, "McDonald's" in white script on red. This mug has an anti-skid rubberized base to prevent it from sliding off the dashboard. $4.00 – 7.00.

2. ©1993 McDonald's Premium Blend Coffee, a thick plastic 6" coffee tumbler with red sipping lid. On the reverse, written in black over a large Golden Arch: "McDonald's Premium Blend Coffee is a gourmet blend of 100% Arabica beans from Columbia, Brazil, and Central America. The roasted beans are freshly ground just before brewing for a rich, delicious flavor." $5.00 – 10.00.

3. 3⁷/₈" thick-walled, wide-based, narrow-necked light beige commuter mug with handle and anti-skid rubberized base to prevent it from slipping around. It has a black and yellow McDonald's logo along with "540 N. Trimble Rd., Mansfield, Ohio." $7.00 – 10.00.

MISCELLANEOUS CONVENTION PIECES

Row 1.

1. McDonald's 1976 Store Managers Convention July 14 – 16 Dearborn, Michigan, a 5¹/₂" clear glass mug with red and yellow decoration. $20.00 – 35.00.

2. 1976 Store Managers Convention July 25 – 27, New Orleans, Louisiana, a 5¹/₂" mug with red and yellow decoration. $20.00 – 35.00.

3. McDonald's Operators Convention 1976, a 4¹/₈" bowl-shaped glass with brown decoration featuring a fish. $40.00 – 60.00.

4. McDonald's 1977 Store Managers Convention July 10 – 12, San Diego, California, a 5¹/₂" clear glass mug with red and yellow decoration. $20.00 – 35.00.

Row 2.

1. 1977 Store Managers Convention July 27 – 29 Washington, D. C., a 5¹/₂" pedestal style mug with red and yellow decoration. $20.00 – 35.00.

2. Albany (New York) Region Bounty Hunters 1979 Managers Convention, a 5¹/₈" mug with black decoration. $15.00 – 25.00.

3. New York Region Managers Convention 1979, a 5¹/₂" mug with red and yellow decoration. The round graphic in the center of the mug shows a pugilistic rooster wearing boxing gloves, "new york street fighters" and two McDonald's logos form a circle around the roosters. $20.00 – 35.00.

4. 1979 Oklahoma Market Assistant Managers' Convention, Tulsa, Oklahoma, a 5" mug with red decoration. $15.00 – 25.00.

MISCELLANEOUS CONVENTION AND MEETINGS PIECES

Row 1.

1. Store Managers Convention Houston, Texas July 22 – 24, 1979, a 5^{1}/$_{2}$" clear glass mug with red and yellow decoration showing a handshake. $15.00 – 25.00.

2. McDonald's Operators Meeting San Diego 1979, a 5^{3}/$_{8}$" clear thick plastic mug with yellow and red decoration. On the reverse: "Be a Pepper 79er." $10.00 – 20.00.

3. 1981 National Accounting & Tax Meeting (Chicago), "We Are Family," a 5^{3}/$_{4}$" white milk glass pedestal mug with blue-gray decoration showing outline of North America and vector lines pointing to Chicago. $15.00 – 25.00.

4. McDonald's Albany (NY) Region Assistants Day 1981, a 5^{1}/$_{2}$" mug with blue decoration. $20.00 – 35.00.

Row 2.

1. 1982 Manager's Convention, Dearborn, Michigan, a very heavy mug with recessed base and fancy handle on its left-hand side, 6^{1}/$_{2}$", black decoration. $15.00 – 20.00.

2. San Francisco 1982, a 5^{3}/$_{4}$" large-based mug with frosted decoration. This beautiful mug was given to attendees of the 1982 worldwide owner/operator convention which was hosted by San Francisco in 1982. $30.00 – 50.00.

3. Florida Operator's Association Orlando 1983, a 5^{1}/$_{2}$" mug with red, yellow, and white decoration. $15.00 – 20.00.

4. "Hands On Hot 'n Hustle McDonald's Manager's Convention 1984," a 5^{1}/$_{4}$" yellow plastic mug with red decoration. On the bottom: "Harmony" with the number 4989 near the center of the bottom. This modest convention premium reflects the company's dedication to employee dedication, good food, and customer satisfaction. $15.00 – 25.00.

MISCELLANEOUS CONVENTION PIECES

Row 1.

1. 1986 Store Managers' Convention Columbus Region, "The Heat Is On," a thick 6½" plastic mug with red lid and red, black, and yellow decoration. $5.00 – 10.00.

2. Columbus Region 1986 Assistants & Swing Managers' Convention, a 3½" clear glass Libbey mug with red decoration. $7.00 – 12.00.

3. Priority One, a heavy 5¼" clear glass mug with an applied pewter-colored metal badge which has the McDonald's arches directly above the words "Priority One." This mug was presented as an incentive to store managers at the 1987 Chicago McDonald's convention, one mug per store. American version. $20.00 – 30.00.

4. Priority One, Canadian version. This mug is exactly like the American version to its left, except for one big difference: there's a small Canadian mapleleaf in the center of the metal badge right under the arches. The Canadian version seems to be much rarer than its American counterpart. $25.00 – 40.00.

Row 2.

1. 1989 Co-Op Presidents/Advertising Agency Convention shot glass with graphic focusing on "Performance Concepts," blue and yellow decoration. $10.00 – 15.00.

2. "Maintaining Your Free Enterprise," a 5½" clear glass mug with red decoration. Made by Libbey. This mug with a message was a premium given to convention attendees, probably to assure them that their relationship with headquarters would continue without any major changes and that owners and operators were "free" to be innovative with promotions and marketing. This mug probably dates from the early to mid 1980s. $30.00 – 45.00.

3. "McDonald's Corporation, Washington, D.C. Region, 703 – 698 – 4000" in red along with yellow arches on a white 4⅞" ceramic tankard. This item was probably given as a special gift to attendees at a Washington, D.C. regional convention in the mid 1980s. "China" is embossed on the bottom. $25.00 – 40.00.

4. PERSECO, McDonald's 1996 Worldwide Convention, New Orleans, Louisiana, USA, April 22 – 25, 1996, a 6¾" double-walled insulated mug with blue sipping lid, decorated insert in red, yellow, blue, and white, and co-sponsored by Coca-Cola. $5.00 – 10.00.

5. "gsf" on one side, "Proud Supplier & Distributor to McDonald's" on the other, a 5¾" double-walled insulated mug made by Whirley in Warren, Pennsylvania. GSF stands for Golden State Foods, an early supplier of hamburger to California drive-ins before it became one of McDonald's major suppliers. Golden State Foods still supplies McDonald's and is considered a "giant" in the food processing industry (Love, *Behind the Arches*, 129, 133). $6.00 – 12.00.

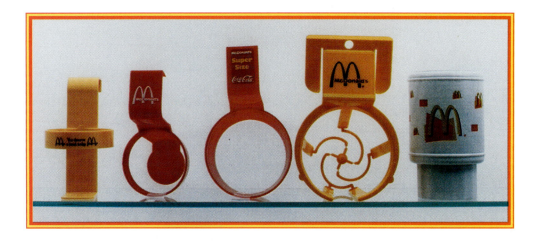

FIVE DIFFERENT DRINK HOLDERS

Many McDonald's plastic cups came with plastic holders which could be attached to various locations in cars and boats. A few of them are shown here. These simple accessories were commonly discarded or broken, and they haven't survived in great quantities.

1. 5$\frac{1}{4}$" yellow cup holder with black decoration: "You deserve a break today" with two McDonald's logos. Bottom says "Road Buddy Auto Beverage Holder Hook In Door Teraco USA." This advertising campaign slogan was introduced in 1971 and resurrected in 1980. $4.00 – 7.00.

2. 5$\frac{1}{4}$" red cup holder with white McDonald's logo on horizontal surface, made by Allied Plastics in Gastonia, North Carolina. $4.00 – 7.00.

3. 4$\frac{7}{8}$" yellow jumbo-sized cup holder with black McDonald's logo on horizontal surface. Made by Whirley in Warren, Pennsylvania. $5.00 – 8.00.

4. 3$\frac{3}{4}$" red "McDonald's Super Size Coca-Cola" stamped on face of holder with sticker on horizontal surface saying "McDonald's Super Size Coca-Cola." $5.00 – 8.00.

5. 5$\frac{3}{8}$" plastic can holder/cooler, gray with McDonald's logos. "Patent Pending" on bottom, no other information. $2.00 – 5.00.

DISNEY

MISCELLANEOUS DISNEY ISSUES

1. 1987 Disney "Classic Movie Cinderella," a 5¼" plastic mug. $7.00 – 10.00.

2. Early 1990s black Euro Disney Resort mug with "McDonald's" in yellow script underlined on reverse. This mug is from France — and made in France as the bottom indicates, and supposedly the mugs were available only to those people who participated in a play or skit at the Euro Disney resort. $10.00 – 15.00.

3. 1997 Disney's Hercules sport bottle. This 4⁷⁄₈" blue plastic sport bottle #3, shaped like an Ionic column, was part of the Disney *Hercules* movie promotion. There's a straw hole in the center of the scrolled Ionic cap and an oval decal showing the Disney Hercules character. The "bottle" is undated, and the Golden Arches do not appear on it. Writing on the bottom of the base is as follows: "Mfg. for McD Corp. © Disney China/Chine SV 22 wash before use." The plastic bag that the bottle came in has the date (1997) and the usual warnings about small parts and the dangers of plastic bags in three languages: English, Spanish, and Portuguese. $8.00 – 12.00.

4. Late 1990s white ceramic mug made in France promoting the Disney Channel movie *Doug*. Near the McDonald's logo near the bottom of the mug we see "©Disney/Jumbo Pictures," and vertically closer to the top we see "CE Simon Marketing 75002 Paris." $10.00 – 15.00.

TWO DISNEY TUMBLER SETS

Row 1: Disney Animated Film Classics set of four (ca. 1985 – 1988, Canada), co-sponsored by Coca-Cola.

This set of four undated Canadian tumblers pays tribute to four of Disney's most successful animated films. The Coca-Cola wave logo has both English and French text, and two of the movie titles are rendered in both French and English. Great graphics and wraparound action but since lots of these were produced, they are not particularly rare. $8.00 – 12.00 each.

1. Cinderella/Cendrillon
2. Fantasia
3. Peter Pan
4. Snow White and the Seven Dwarfs/Blanche Neige Et Les Sept Nains

Row 2: Disneyland set of four (1989).

This set of four tumblers was issued by Midwest McDonald's franchises in the Missouri and Arkansas areas during the early summer of 1989. Joplin, Missouri, is thought to have been the center of this promotion. $10.00 – 15.00 each.

1. Mickey Mouse in Tomorrowland with an account of Walt Disney's "vision of Tomorrowland" on the reverse.
2. Minnie Mouse in Fantasyland with a brief history of the development of Fantasyland on the reverse.
3. Donald Duck in Critter Country with interesting facts about "Splash Mountain" and connections with Disney's *Song of the South* on which this attraction was based.
4. Goofy in Adventureland with a description of the evolution of this entertainment concept on the reverse.

WALT DISNEY WORLD 25TH ANNIVERSARY SET OF FOUR

Row 1: Walt Disney World 25th Anniversary "Remember the Magic" set of four (1996).

This set of four double Old Fashioned tumblers was distributed from August 30 through September 26 by McDonald's although this sponsorship takes the form of a small adhesive sticker on each glass saying "McDonald's celebrates the magic of Walt Disney World." This sticker in lieu of the usual McDonald's logo was a disappointment to many McDonald's collectors. "Walt Disney World Remember the Magic" is embossed on the bottom around the base, and a Walt Disney World 25 logo appears on the center of the bottom. $3.00 – 5.00 each.

1. Goofy with boogie board at Typhoon Lagoon and Blizzard Beach.
2. Donald Duck and Disney Castle.
3. Lumiere the Candlestick and Hollywood Tower, Disney Studios.
4. Mickey Mouse dressed as a magician a la Fantasia.

Row 2: Walt Disney World Millennium Celebration set of four (1999).

These heavy $4^5/_8$" tumblers (made in France) were available in October 1999 for $1.49 each with the purchase of a large sandwich or meal combination. There's one glass for each park: Epcot, Animal Kingdom, Disney Studios, and Magic Kingdom. The front panel of each of these square tumblers has a multicolored graphic featuring Mickey Mouse in costume appropriate to each park. The other three panels have pressed glass decoration (the TV ads describe it as "sculpted") relating to the particular park and to the year 2000. In the center of the bottom the McDonald's logo is inscribed. If you look at the base from the outside you'll see these words hidden in the thick base: "Walt Disney World 2000 Walt Disney World Celebration." Nice glasses, but eBay will be clogged with them for years! $2.00 – 4.00 each.

1. Mickey a la Fantasia, Epcot.
2. Mickey on Safari, Animal Kingdom.
3. Mickey as Director, Disney Studios.
4. Mickey at the Magic Kingdom.

HOME VIDEO SET OF THREE, JAPAN

This set of three 4¼" glasses was issued by Japanese McDonald's restaurants in the mid to late 1980s to promote the release of various Disney videos. These glasses came in decorated cardboard packages which showed and promoted the other two glasses in the set. Add $10.00 to the value of each glass if you have the original package it came in.

1. Alice in Wonderland, Tea Party scene, red McDonald's logo. $40.00 – 60.00.
2. Donald Duck with magnifying glass examining hologram, orange McDonald's logo. $60.00 – 80.00.
3. Mickey Mouse in Fantasia, pink McDonald's logo. $40.00 – 60.00.
4. Mickey Mouse in Fantasia cardboard package.

DISNEY "HATCH-MATCH" PAPER AND PLASTIC GAME CUPS

These cups, co-sponsored by Coca-Cola, promoted Walt Disney's summer 2000 Dinosaur film. Each cup tempted players with two Dinosaur game pieces. I was able to find six different cups. The promotion ran from May 18 to June 12. $2.00 – 4.00 each (add $1.00 for intact game pieces).

1. "Play to Win a Rock Solid Winnebago Adventurer," a large 7⅛" wax-coated paper cup with large dino eye and hatching egg motif.
2. "Play to Win a Rock Solid Winnebago Adventurer," a super-sized 7⅛" wax-coated paper cup with large dino eye and hatching egg motif.
3. "Play to Win a Million Big Ones," a large 7⅛" wax-coated paper cup with large dino eye and hatching egg motif.
4. "Play to Win a Million Big Ones," a super-sized 7⅛" wax-coated paper cup with large dino eye and hatching egg motif.
5. "Play to Win a Million Big Ones," a large 7" plastic cup with blue paper money motif, made by Sweetheart, 32 oz.
6. "Play to Win a Million Big Ones," a super-sized 7" plastic cup with blue paper money motif (no information on bottom).

WALT DISNEY WORLD RESORT IN FLORIDA SET OF FOUR
Row 1.

 This very unusual "set" features four Disney characters, Mickey, Minnie, Donald, and Goofy, at Disney's Animal Kingdom. A white McDonald's logo approximately ³/₄" square appears on the back of each glass. There's no Japanese writing or date on the glass, but the boxes that the glasses come in have only Japanese writing on them. I should add that each glass has a dominant color scheme which matches the box that it comes in. $30.00 – 50.00 each; add $5.00 each for box.
1. Minnie with camera, female gorilla with baby, red lettering and title bar, 6³/₄" beer glass.
2. Donald in explorer's garb with flashlight, dragon-like creature in water, lavender lettering and title bar, 5³/₄" goblet.
3. Goofy with shovel and large bone, dinosaur fossil skeleton against rock background, blue lettering and title bar, 7³/₈" wine or toasting glass.
4. Mickey with binoculars, female elephant with baby, green lettering and title bar, 6" highball tumbler.

Row 2.
1. Boxes beneath corresponding glasses in Disney Florida set.

WALT DISNEY WORLD "100 YEARS OF MAGIC" SET OF FOUR

2002 "100 Years of Magic, Walt Disney World," a set of four heavy 5⅛" tumblers issued in March of 2002. This glassware set, according to the paper cup which preceded it and the paper bag that each was wrapped in as it went over the counter, was intended to be a "celebration of Walt Disney's life and imagination (taking) place at all four Walt Disney world parks." Furthermore, "Each glass is a McDonald's exclusive that features Disney trivia and lots of your favorite characters. Collect all 4!" "Bring home a reminder of the celebration!" Walt Disney was born in 1901, so the 100 years referred to on the glasses and in the overall promotion was to that time span as well as the combined years of his many entertaining creations. There is too much detail on each glass to describe here: lots of colors and lots of Disney characters and interesting facts. Each glass has a predominent character, however, and a quotation by Walt Disney at the bottom. The McDonald's "information" is embossed in the bottom and readable when you hold the glass up to the light and look at the bottom where the following information is inscribed: "Share a Dream Come True, 100 Years of Magic, Walt Disney World." The inside bottom of the base is ringed with small embossed McDonald's arches which are also visible if you look at the base as the glass is sitting on a flat surface. In most areas, the glasses sold for $1.99 each plus tax. This set will probably never be rare, but they are good looking and a major event for McDonald's and Disney. $2.00 – 4.00 each.

1. Mickey Mouse "debuted in 1928's 'Steamboat Willie'": "...it was all started by a mouse."
2. "Tinker Bell starts the fireworks nightly in the Magic Kingdom Park": "Fantasy...lies beyond the reach of time."
3. Goofy "first known as 'Dippy Dawg,' stars in 'Mickey's Jammin' Jungle Parade.'" Animal Kingdom: "...nature herself writes the most interesting stories."
4. Buzz Lightyear and EPCOT, "Experimental Prototype Community of Tomorrow." "Today we are shapers of the world of tomorrow."

DUKES of HAZZARD

SET OF SIX DUKES OF HAZZARD PLASTIC CUPS

The Dukes of Hazzard set of six TM & ©Warner Bros. Inc. 1982. This set features the main characters from the legendary *Dukes of Hazzard* television series. "The show, which critics loved to hate, aired from 1979 to 1985 on CBS, ranking No. 1 for its time slot each season" (AP, 8-1-04). The same image appears on both sides of the cup with McDonald's logos separating them on both sides. "Tri-Plas" with an Arabic numeral is the only decipherable information that appears on the bottom, so good luck trying to figure out who made these cups. They seem to be more available in Ohio and Illinois than in other places, though I am informed that their geographic distribution was focused on the St. Louis, Missouri, area. Some things to keep in mind are that the Dukes followers are serious, this was a fairly limited promotion, and as a result these cups are aggressively priced. Luke and Uncle Jesse consistently command premium prices. Bo, Boss Hogg, and Daisy seem to be a little easier to get. Sherrif Rosco is in the middle price range. $8.00 – 20.00.

Row 1.

1. Bo
2. Boss Hogg
3. Daisy

Row 2.

1. Luke
2. Sheriff Rosco
3. Uncle Jesse

TWO FRENCH SETS

Row 1: 1998 breakfast set.

This set includes a tumbler, mug, and bowl. These three pieces came packaged in a box labeled "Verrerie Cristallerie D'Arques J. G. Durand & Cie 62510 Argues France, Made in France 1922/98." The three pieces in this set show Ronald in a big wheel pulling a mini-trailer full of Christmas presents and Grimace with a laptop computer (taking orders) in a futuristic landscape. The color on these pieces is wonderful. Value: $15.00 – 25.00 each; $75.00 – 100.00 for the set of three.

1. Tumbler showing Ronald McDonald in big wheel with trailer full of presents and Grimace in party hat taking orders on laptop computer.
2. Mug showing Ronald McDonald in big wheel with trailer full of presents, Grimace with laptop, dinosaur drinking milkshake, fish floating in the sky background, Fry Guys, Birdie flying air bike.
3. Bowl, 6½", showing Ronald in big wheel with trailer full of presents, Grimace with laptop computer, fish swimming in sky, futuristic background.

Row 2: Pure Collection, set of four.

These 5¼" straight-sided tumblers issued in the late 1990s feature swinging young almond-eyed girls enjoying themselves, dancing, surfing, and just generally being alluring. Each glass has a colored band with round holes at the bottom. A small McDonald's logo appears inside the "p" of the "pure," and a slightly larger logo appears on the back of the band. There's no date or other helpful information. The main idea of the graphic on each glass is that $x + y = z$. Hard to get if you live on this side of the pond. Pure is a design house and distributor of various popular consumer products. $10.00 – 20.00 each.

1. Green base: girl in sunglasses + platform shoe = girl dancing.
2. Blue base: crescent moon + girl dancing = guy with tongue hanging out.
3. Orange base: girl + scuba fins = dolphin.
4. Yellow base: surfboard + waves = three girls.

GARFIELD GLASS TUMBLERS

SET OF FOUR GARFIELD GLASS TUMBLERS

This set of undated glasses was never promoted and sold through the restaurants to the best of my knowledge. They have a 1978 United Feature Syndicate Inc. copyright which coincides with Garfield's debut in 41 newspapers on June 19, 1978, but the 1978 date should not be regarded as the actual distribution date. These glasses do have the McDonald's logo and were available briefly through various outlet stores. (I recall buying ten unopened cases at a flea market in western Pennsylvania in 1989 for 75¢ per glass.) It is my guess that these glasses may have been rejected in favor of the Garfield mug promotion. I assume that these tumblers became available at about the same time as the Garfield mugs in 1987 – 1988. $9.00 – 12.00.

1. Are we having fun yet? Garfield towing Odie on waterskis, shark in pursuit.
2. Home, James: Garfield on rear seat of bicycle built for two, Odie as chauffeur in front.
3. Just me and the road: Garfield driving Porsche speedster and towing Odie on skateboard.
4. Poetry in motion: Garfield on skateboard with eyes closed headed for collision with Odie on skateboard.

FOUR PIECES FROM GERMANY

Row 1.

1. 5¹/₂" ceramic tankard/stein, light blue and white diamond pattern decoration, pewter lid with McDonald's arches and "Munchen" engraved on it. At the top of the mug on the light blue background we have the following in darker blue lettering: "Munchen Ubertrifft Viele Furstliche Stadte Durch Seine Lage Und Sauberkeit. An Bewohnern Zahlt Man 18000, Die Aber Nicht Alle Wohnen Konnten, Wenn Sich Nicht Etliche Mit Scheunen Und Winkeln Behelfen. Noch Volkreicher Macht Diese Stadt, Dass Aus Vielen Nationen Umher Adel Und Kunstler, Die Die Leutselickeit Des Bayernfursten Anlockt, Dahin Kommen." On the bottom: "Der Text Zu Diesem Krug Ist Dem Zwischen 1572 Und 1618 Enstandenen Stadte-Buch 'Civitates Orbis Terrarum' Von Georg Braun Und Franz Hogenberg Entnommen." Text near rim translated: "Munich surpasses many grand cities because of its location and cleanliness. One hundred eighty thousand citizens live in the city...all these people couldn't live there without barns...some live outside the city...the city becomes more crowded...many people from many nations, nobility, aristocrats, artists are coming there...the city is attracting educated people." The text on the bottom is a commentary on the rim text and is roughly translated as follows: "The text is from a city book written by Georg Braun and Franz Hogenberg between 1572 and 1618." I'm not sure what all of this has to do with McDonald's, but I suspect the tankard was made to commemorate the 6000th store opening in Munich. This very special tankard exudes fine workmanship and was undoubtedly quite limited in production. It was probably available only to higher level management and organization people. $250.00 – 500.00+.

2. McDonald's Deutschland, a 5" gray ceramic tankard/stein with black and yellow decoration. $30.00 – 50.00.

Row 2.

1. "Keys to Quality," a 5" gray ceramic tankard/stein with red and gold decoration. Gold lettering in red oval says: "Quality Assurance**Equipment Purchasing**Purchasing**International Purchasing," and below the oval: "with Compliments Pfungstadter Brewery West Germany." $30.00 – 50.00.

2. "Einfach gut fruhstucken!," a 3⁷/₁₆" cobalt blue ceramic mug with gold decoration. Small Golden Arches encircle the base of the mug. English translation: "It's just great to have breakfast!" Same design on both sides. $20.00 – 30.00.

GRAND OPENING AND GROUNDBREAKING ISSUES

Row 1.

1. McDonald's 4,000 "To commemorate the opening of the 4000th McDonald's store September 9th (1976) Montreal, Canada," a 5¹/₂" French-English goblet with red decoration. $20.00 – 35.00.

2. McDonald's "Store 6000 Munchen (Munich, Germany), 29. November 1980," a 5" stoneware tankard with blue decoration. $75.00 – 150.00.

3. "Toledo, Ohio's Newest City" on one side of a 5¹/₂" goblet style glass with small pedestal base, and "World's Newest McDonald's, 1560 E. Alexis Road, December, 1982" on the other. Black and yellow decoration, gold rim. $8.00 – 15.00.

4. McDonald's, 4946 No. Milwaukee Ave., Grand Opening August, 1982, a 3⁷/₈" yellow ceramic mug with red decoration. "Made in England" appears on the bottom. $15.00 – 25.00.

Row 2.

1. McDonald's of Freeport, Maine, Groundbreaking Ceremony, July 13, 1984, a 3³/₄" white ceramic mug with slate-blue decoration. Groundbreaking drinkware is quite rare, so this mug is especially interesting and desirable. $30.00 – 50.00.

2. McDonald's Grand Opening 3701 Pleasanton Road, September, 1985, a 5¹/₂" clear glass mug with red and yellow decoration. $15.00 – 25.00.

3. "In Commemoration of McDonald's Ground Breaking Ceremony Philadelphia Naval Base December 6, 1985," a 3⁵/₄" white ceramic mug with blue decoration. The reverse has a blue anchor and chain on it. "China" appears on the bottom. $25.00 – 45.00.

4. McDonald's Grand Opening September 1987 Texas Children's Hospital, a 3³/₄" white ceramic mug with red and gold decoration. "China" on bottom. $15.00 – 25.00.

MISCELLANEOUS GRAND OPENING PIECES

Row 1.

1. McDonald's Grand Opening 1988, Mercy Hospital (Springfield, Mass.), a 3³/₄" white ceramic mug with green decoration. $10.00 – 18.00.

2. McDonald's Pennfield Grand Opening May 24, 1990, a 5⁵/₈" mug with red and yellow decoration. Pennfield is a township with a prominant high school which shares the same name just north of Battle Creek, Michigan. My guess is that this mug comes from that area. This mug has a recessed starburst bottom and a thumb rest handle. $20.00 – 30.00.

3. McDonald's of Richmond (Virginia), June 1990 Grand Opening, a 3⁵/₈" blue ceramic mug with mustard colored decoration. $10.00 – 15.00.

4. McDonald's of West Town Corners Grand Opening Celebration November 13, 1991, a 3⁵/₈" white ceramic mug with green decoration on both sides. $15.00 – 20.00.

5. "Celebrating the 12,665th McDonald's July 1993 Well Road West Monroe," a clear glass 6³/₈" cowboy boot mug with yellow decoration on the front facing of the boot. This uncommon figural item was made in Canada (embossed on bottom) and celebrates the opening of the West Monroe, Louisiana, store. $25.00 – 50.00.

Row 2.

1. McDonald's Deltona (Florida) Grand Opening December 1993, a 3⁵/₈" mug with blue-green decoration. $10.00 – 15.00.

2. "McDonald's of Forest Lakes Grand Opening May 1994," a 3³/₈" old fashioned glass with yellow decoration and dimpled base. The graphic shows a road with three trees leading to the Golden Arches and a rising sun with two large birds flying just above the sun. There are lots of housing developments called Forest Lakes which makes identification difficult. I believe this glass is probably from Forest Lakes, Arizona, and it is obviously a very limited production piece. $25.00 – 45.00.

3. Grand Opening, McDonald's of Winter Springs (Florida) October 1994, a 3³/₄" white ceramic mug with maroon decoration. $15.00 – 20.00.

4. Grand Opening, McDonald's of Woodsville, New Hampshire, November 8, 1994, a 3³/₄" cobalt blue mug with gold decoration on one side. Botton says "HG Made In China." $15.00 – 25.00.

5. McDonald's (Houston) Texas Children's Hospital Grand Reopening September 1995, a 3⁵/₈" green ceramic mug with white decoration. $10.00 – 15.00.

Hamburger University opened in 1961 in the basement of the Elk Grove Village, Illinois, restaurant and that same year graduated students with bachelor of hamburgerology degrees. The university is an ongoing operation which generates much memorabilia including quite a variety of mugs and glasses.

MISCELLANEOUS HAMBURGER UNIVERSITY ISSUES

Row 1.

1. "Hamburger U. 10,000th Student," a 6$\frac{1}{8}$" square-footed goblet with a green panel and gold Hamburger University logos and a rectangular window through which the viewer sees a drawing of Hamburger University with a U.S. flag in red, white, and blue flying in front of it. Below the picture: "Class #209, November 6, 1975." The base is 2$\frac{1}{4}$" square. Early Hamburger University glasses like this one are quite desirable. $50.00 – 80.00.

2. Hamburger U. 10,000th Student, a 6$\frac{1}{2}$" round-footed goblet with a green background panel and gold Hamburger University logos. This glass is quite similar to the one listed above and shown to its left. It has a clear rectangular window through which the viewer sees the same drawing of Hamburger University with the same caption: "Class #209, November 6, 1975." Another rare early glass. $50.00 – 80.00.

3. McDonald's Hamburger University Time Capsule Dedication April 15, 1985, a 5$\frac{3}{8}$" white ceramic mug with black and gold decoration and gold rim. $25.00 – 35.00.

Row 2.

1. McDonald's Hamburger University "Class 200," a 4$\frac{5}{8}$" white ceramic tankard with gold rim and black and yellow decoration. Date uncertain, probably from the 1970s, since class 390 graduated in 1987 (see next mug). $30.00 – 50.00.

2. McDonald's Hamburger University 30,000 Student, a 5$\frac{1}{4}$" ceramic tankard with black, yellow, and gold decoration. On the reverse: "Class 390, January 12 – 22, 1987." $30.00 – 45.00.

3. "Congratulations McDonald's Seniors," a 5$\frac{1}{2}$" amber tankard style mug with white decoration depicting a graduation cap and diploma. This unusual mug was given to its former owner in 1983 for outstanding achievement in a McDonald's training program. $25.00 – 40.00.

Row 3.

1. "Congratulations McDonald's Seniors," a 5$\frac{1}{2}$" clear glass mug with sunburst bottom and red decoration depicting a graduation cap and diploma. The style of this mug is quite different from the mug listed above in row 2, but I assume that its issue date is also 1983. $25.00 – 40.00.

2. McDonald's Congratulations 1989 Graduate, a 5$\frac{1}{2}$" mug with red and yellow decoration. $15.00 – 25.00.

3. Hamburger University, One Ronald Lane, Oak Brook, Illinois 60521, a 5$\frac{1}{2}$" clear glass mug with red and yellow decoration. $15.00 – 25.00.

MISCELLANEOUS HAMBURGER UNIVERSITY ISSUES

Row 1.

1. "Canadian Institute of Hamburgerology" and a small Canadian McDonald's logo inside a red circle on one side and a picture of the institute in black on the other side of a 7^1/$_8$" beer glass. An unusual glass! $30.00 – 50.00.

2. McDonald's Training Consultant, Hamburger University, a 5^1/$_4$" cream-colored ceramic mug with black and gold decoration and gold rim. $25.00 – 35.00.

3. McDonald's Hamburger University, a 4^5/$_8$" white ceramic tankard mug with gold rim and black and yellow decoration. This particular mug has a nicely crazed surface and the initials (JHB) of its former owner on the reverse. $25.00 – 35.00.

Row 2.

1. McDonald's Hamburger University, a 5^1/$_8$" cream-colored ceramic tankard with black and gold decoration and gold rim. $20.00 – 30.00.

2. McDonald's Hamburger University logo in green on one side of a 3^3/$_4$" cream-colored ceramic mug. "Made in China" appears on the bottom in small black lettering. $7.00 – 12.00.

3. McDonald's Hamburger University, a 3^7/$_8$" white ceramic commuter mug with yellow and black decoration and black rubber skid pad on bottom. From the late 1990s. $8.00 – 12.00.

Row 3.

1. Hamburger University HU, a 3^3/$_4$" white ceramic mug with the identical green decoration on both sides and a green rubber detachable coaster base. "HG Made In China" appears on the bottom. This appears to be a late 1990s mug. $5.00 – 10.00.

2. "Center of Excellence," a 4" high Hamburger University clear glass mug with gold decoration showing the McDonald's arches above the HU of Hamburger University. "USA" is imprinted on the bottom. $20.00 – 35.00.

3. Hamburger University, Oak Brook, Illinois, a 5^1/$_2$" clear glass mug with green and yellow decoration. $10.00 – 15.00.

SIX ACHIEVEMENT AWARD PIECES

Row 1.

1. "Profiles In Leadership 1979," a 4³/₄ gray tankard mug with red line around rim and black decoration elsewhere. $25.00 – 45.00.

2. "Indianapolis Region/1981/Liz Petry/The Leader In The/Mideast Zone," a 4³/₈" clear glass mug with etched decoration. This mug has a large McDonald's logo etched on the reverse. This kind of personalized mug was a one-of item awarded for exceptional achievement, so it's hard to price. $50.00 – 100.00.

3. "Indianapolis Region/1981/Kim DePoy/The Leader In The/Mideast Zone," a 4³/₈" clear glass mug with etched decoration, identical to the mug to its left except for the employee's name. This mug has a large McDonald's logo etched on the reverse. This kind of mug was a personalized one-of item awarded for exceptional achievement, so it's hard to "price." $50.00 – 100.00.

Row 2.

"QSC Contest 1980" and "QSC Contest 1981" with McDonald's arches in black inside a triangular design on a 4³/₄" cast aluminum tankard. "Carson-Freeport, Pennsylvania" is stamped on the handle, indicating that this is a western Pennsylvania item given to exceptional employees. According to John Love in his book *Behind the Arches* (p.114), the acronym (quality, service, and cleanliness) "originated with Kroc, and he used QSC to distinguish McDonald's from all other competitors in an industry that was otherwise rife with duplication." The two tankards I show here were awarded to an employee in Butler, Pennsylvania. $30.00 – 45.00.

1. "QSC Contest 1980."

2. "QSC Contest 1981."

3. "Outstanding Achievement, McDonald's Pittsburgh Region," a 4³/₄" cast aluminum mug with inscribed black deco-lettering. The manufacturer's name is stamped on one side of the handle: "Carson-Freeport, Pennsylvania." This tankard dates from the early 1980s. $30.00 – 45.00.

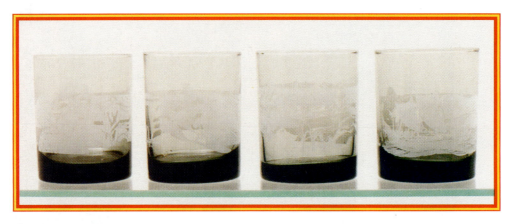

HAWAIIAN SEA GLASSWARE SET OF FOUR

This set of four 3⁷/₈" old fashioned tumblers came in a sturdy gift box suitable for shipping. They probably date from the last half of the 1980s; they were still available in the late 1980s from various McDonald's in Hawaii. With a little detective work, collectors could still locate them for quite some time after the promotion ended. The box is labeled "Hawaiians and their Sea Glassware, A Souvenir from Hawaii," so it seems to have been aimed at tourists, and indeed, quite a few of these glasses have found their way to the mainland. The tumblers were made by Libbey and are smoke-colored with frosted decoration which celebrates Hawaii's culture, occupations, leisure activities, and attractions. Glasses: $4.00 – 7.00 each; souvenir box: $5.00

1. Fishermen bringing in their nets at sunset.
2. Three surfers surfing, sun in background.
3. Outrigger races: two boats with five paddlers in each boat.
4. Sunset with large catamaran in foreground, island background, small outrigger, people on hill by shore waving.

HONG KONG CHRISTMAS SET OF FOUR TUMBLERS AND COCA-COLA CANS

This is a very interesting set of four heavy 5" tumblers (made in France according to a sticker on the bottom) each of which features one of the four major McDonaldland characters and the Coca-Cola contour bottle with Christmas decorations in a wheeled vehicle. Each glass was packaged in a distinctively colored box with an accompanying 250 mL can of Coke with the same design as the glass. This is a nice set, a collaboration between Hong Kong McDonald's and Hong Kong Coca-Cola, available on eBay but expensive when you add the shipping. $15.00 – 20.00 for each tumbler; $5.00 – 10.00 for each unopened can; $80.00 – 140.00 for complete set of four tumblers and cans in original boxes.

Row 1.
1. Birdie
2. Grimace
3. Hamburglar
4. Ronald

Row 2.
1. Birdie the Early Bird with Christmas ornaments and round contour bottle graphic.
2. Grimace with Christmas packages, tree, and contour bottle.
3. Hamburglar with large candle and Coca-Cola bottlecap.
4. Ronald McDonald driving truck with wreath, candle, and gifts.

HUNCHBACK OF NOTRE DAME MUG SET

These four embossed mugs with multicolored panels were made in Indonesia and distributed in Australia in September of 1996 by McDonald's to promote Disney's *Hunchback of Notre Dame* movie, even though McDonald's name and logo do not appear anywhere on them. Evidently there was a rights problem or sponsorship conflict of some kind which may have involved Disney and other fast-food restaurants in Australia. Burger King had the rights to Hunchback promotions in the U.S. but did not do a glass promotion. Characters' names are embossed on the bottom of each mug. If you put these mugs side by side with the *Flintstones* and *Batman Forever* mugs (page 100), you can see enough obvious design similarities to make the case for McDonald's sponsorship. $5.00 – 10.00 each.

1. Esmeralda
2. Gargoyles
3. Phoebus
4. Quasimodo

IN-HOUSE EMPLOYEE PREMIUMS and CATALOG ORDER ITEMS

IN-HOUSE EMPLOYEE PREMIUMS AND CATALOG ORDER ITEMS

These items served as awards, rewards, or incentives for employees or were given out by management on special occasions to inspire performance or to encourage employee commitment. They tend to feature marketing slogans; therefore, many of them may have been given out at conventions and meetings. In addition, drinkware such as these could be ordered by owners, managers, and assistant managers from in-house catalogs. They were not generally available to the public.

Row 1.

1. History of McDonald's to 1984 (1984 or 1985). This interesting $4^{5}/_{8}$" ceramic mug graphically illustrates and commemorates McDonald's milestone achievements from the introduction of McDonald's Playlands in 1971 to 1984 McDonald's sponsorship of the Los Angeles Summer Olympics. It effectively continues the historical review initiated by the earlier, smaller 1974 mug. If you have questions about McDonald's, this mug can provide answers to many of them. $25.00 – 45.00.

2. History of McDonald's to 1974 (1974 or 1975). This 4" ceramic mug graphically illustrates significant milestones in McDonald's history from the first store opening in Des Plaines, Illinois, in 1955 to the 3,000th store opening in 1974. McDonald's trivia buffs will love this very busy mug! $35.00 – 50.00.

3. "It's People...1979," a $5^{5}/_{8}$" heavy clear glass mug with yellow and red decoration. Very nice recessed bottom and twenty optically pleasing vertical panels encircle the mug. $15.00 – 25.00.

4. ©1980 Los Angeles Olympic Committee white stoneware tankard with 1984 Los Angeles Summer Olympics logo and McDonald's logo. On the bottom: "Designed & Decorated in Los Angeles by Papel Official Licensee ©1980 L. A. Olympic Committee." $20.00 – 30.00.

Row 2.

1. 1984 Crew Decathlon tankard, $5^{1}/_{2}$" tall with the 1984 Los Angeles Olympics logo on one side. No markings on bottom. $25.00 – 40.00.

2. "It's A Good Time For The Great Taste," a $5^{1}/_{2}$" mug with McDonald's logo, frosted decoration. This advertising slogan was introduced in 1984. $8.00 – 12.00.

3. "Be Daring, First & Different," an unusual $5^{1}/_{2}$" clear glass mug with blue decoration on a white panel. The McDonald's logo is incorporated into a cowboy hat, and there's a bandanna near the bottom. This mug probably dates from the 1970s and was intended to encourage operator innovation. $20.00 – 40.00.

4. "Be Daring, First & Different," a $3^{7}/_{16}$" white ceramic mug with blue decoration. This mug, like its promotional partner to the left, was an in-house employee incentive premium. No date or origin markings. $20.00 – 40.00.

MISCELLANEOUS IN-HOUSE MUGS

Row 1.

1. McDonald's Atlanta Region, a 5¹/₂" amber glass tankard with white decoration. "YOU" appears on the back, suggesting that this tankard is associated with the "We do it all for you" tagline which McDonald's used from 1975 to 1979 to increase employee sensitivity towards customers. $10.00 – 20.00.

2. "McDonald's All Star 1985," with Canadian Maple Leaf logo, a 3⁹/₁₆" mug with gold on the rim and red and yellow and white decoration. This unusual white mug has a slightly raised field of "McDonald's" in white all over its surface which is very subtle and very beautiful. This mug was probably given to outstanding employees in various Canadian stores and was not available to the public. "Made in China" appears on the bottom. $30.00 – 50.00.

3. "Top Gun Competition," a 3³/₄" black ceramic mug with bright gold decoration showing the McDonald's arches with wings and a jet fighter headed upwards over the arches. This mug was a gift to top-performing employees, probably on a very limited distribution basis in the mid 1980s when *Top Gun* the movie (1986) was released. Made in Japan. $35.00 – 50.00.

4. "1 In A Million," a 5¹/₂" mug with red decoration showing a huge Arabic numeral "1" and a small McDonald's logo just beneath it. This boldly designed mug was available only to management. $25.00 – 40.00.

Row 2.

1. McDonald's All American Team, a 5" white ceramic tankard with McDonald's logo at the top of a red, white, and blue shield. This mug is also available with a 1983 date below the shield. Tankard without date: $15.00 – 25.00; tankard with date. $25.00 – 45.00.

2. Taking Charge of Number One, a 6¹/₄" black ceramic tankard with red, gray, and yellow decoration. This mug is from the Springfield, Massachusetts, Hartford, Connecticut, area. Dated versions from other regions of the country exist. I have seen one mug dated 1985 with Assistant Manager Dallas Region on it. $25.00 – 40.00.

3. "Delivering The Difference," a 5" cobalt blue mug with gold decoration. $15.00 – 20.00.

4. "Delivering The Difference," a 5" cobalt blue mug with gold decoration and Jim Decaturs's name in gold near the rim. $20.00 – 30.00.

MISCELLANEOUS IN-HOUSE PIECES

Row 1.

1. "Good Time Great Taste Because It's Your Place" in gold decoration on 3³/₄" cobalt blue mug, "China" on bottom. The "Good Time Great Taste" slogan dates from 1984, which helps to date this mug. $15.00 – 25.00.

2. "The Customer Counts," a 5⁵/₈" clear glass mug with red decoration. Inside the "O" in "Counts" there are some hard to describe people symbols. The mug's intention is to remind McDonald's employees how important customers are. Overall style of mug suggests a 1980s date. $15.00 – 25.00.

3. Frosted Canadian McDonald's logo on 5¹/₂" goblet. This goblet type was packaged and sold in sets of four. $8.00 – $12.00.

4. "McDonald's" in purple, green, red, and blue script under a thin yellow Golden Arches on the front and "McDonald's" in the same colors but even smaller script within the right Golden Arch on the reverse. This 3³/₄" mug was made in China by Linyi and has a silver phoenix registration mark on the bottom. $10.00 – 15.00.

Row 2.

1. McDonald's "First Team" mug with Linda Rauen's name in black near the bottom. This 3¹/₄" ceramic mug, which was made in the USA, has a gold band just below the rim. There is no decoration on the reverse. Mugs of this type are very special and available only to employees, and not too many of them are seen in the after market. This one goes back at least 15 years. $25.00 – 40.00.

2. "Servin' Up Smiles 1990," a 5⁵/₈" clear glass mug with gray frosted decoration and fancy recessed starburst base. (Difficult to capture decorative details in a photograph!) $15.00 – 25.00.

3. "Williamston January 1992," a 3¹/₂" clear glass mug with gray (fake frosted) decoration showing a rocking chair with a pillow with a McDonald's logo on it. Identical decoration both sides. Williamston is near East Lansing, Michigan. This limited production mug was probably given to retiring employees. (Another difficult to photograph piece.) $15.00 – 25.00.

4. Grimace holding year 2000 flag, a 6¹/₈" double walled white insulated plastic mug given to employees of the "Harrell Management Company" group of McDonald's stores in west central Michigan. This mug was an employee incentive premium, a special gift. Along with the mug, each employee got an 8¹/₂" x 11" magnetized "Putting People First" schedule on which the employee could write down his or her work hours. Nine stores from the Harrell Management Company are listed on the schedule. $15.00 – 25.00.

THREE INSULATED PLASTIC MUG AND TUMBLER SETS

Row 1.

©1974 Insulated plastic mug and tumbler featuring McDonaldland characters. This mug and tumbler set features early versions of Ronald, Captain Crook, Grimace, Hamburglar, Big Mac, Gobblins, and the Professor waving a white-gloved hand. Made by Thermo-Serv. These early pieces are hard to find and quite desirable. $15.00 – 25.00 each.

1. Mug, 4", "Thermo-Serv" on bottom, characters posing as group.

2. Tumbler, 6³/₈", "Made in USA, Thermo-Serv, a division of Westbend" on bottom.

1978 mug and tumbler set. These two pieces share the same design and were marketed as a set. Both have double insulated walls and show the McDonaldland characters posing under a tree. Mug and tumbler: $6.00 – 10.00 each.

3. Mug with characters under a tree.

4. Tumbler with characters under a tree.

Row 2.

McDonald's slogans and tag-lines. This mug and tumbler set shows McDonald's slogans, facts, and advertising lines and promotional jingles and references to products spiralling around the cup and tumbler in a variety of colors at a 45 degree angle. $5.00 – 8.00 each.

1. Mug with multicolored taglines and slogans.

2. Tumbler with multi colored taglines and slogans.

INSULATED BEVERAGE MUGS WITH SIPPING LIDS

Row 1.

1. 1990 – 1991, 6¼" pink and black with "reuse" icon and "Enjoy Coca-Cola Classic." Next to the handle appearing vertically are these words: "Refill this cup at participating McDonald's for only 49¢ (plus tax). Good thru 12/31/91." This is a hot-cold "Thermo" mug made by Whirley Industries in Warren, Pennsylvania. $5.00 – 10.00.

2. 1991 St. Louis Cardinals, a white 6¼" mug with red handle and cap, co-sponsored by Coca-Cola Classic and KMOX Radio, "The Voice of St. Louis." Large McDonald's red and yellow block logo on one side and Cardinal logo on the other. Next to the handle appearing vertically in black letters; "Refill this cup at participating McDonald's for only 49¢ (plus tax). Good thru 12/31/91." On the bottom: "Thermo Hot!/Cold! Whirley Industries, Inc. Warren, Pennsylvania, U.S.A." $5.00 – 10.00.

Row 2.

1. 1991 – 1992, a 6¼" black mug with pink handle and cap, co-sponsored by Coca-Cola Classic. Pink decoration on one side features Speedy holding a "Real Value" sign; on the other there's a similar round graphic with "McDonald's" above and below "Mickey D's." Vertically in pink lettering near the handle: "Refill this cup at participating McDonald's for only 49¢ (plus tax). Good thru 4/30/92." On the bottom: "Thermo Hot!/Cold! Whirley Industries, Inc. Warren, Pennsylvania, U.S.A." $5.00 – 10.00.

2. 1991 – 1992, 6½" black, white, and magenta promoting KSN and KIX 94 FM Country. There's a refill offer that goes like this: "Refill Offer Good At Participating McDonald's Through 6/1/92. Prices May Vary. 49¢ Plus Tax." $4.00 – 8.00.

3. 1992, 6" insulated mug with red handle and sipping lid featuring "McDonald's" in red 45 degree script and three representations (each) of French Fries and Cheeseburgers. On the bottom: "Made in USA" along with recycling code #5. $4.00 – 8.00.

1992 AND 1993 TEXAS HIGH SCHOOL COACHES ASSOCIATION MUGS

Row 1.

1992, "High School Coaches Association Inc., Proud Sponsor of the 1992 McDonald's All Star Games." These 6¼" gray insulated "Thermo" hot-cold mugs with gray lids are co-sponsored by Coca-Cola Classic and made by Whirley Industries in Warren, Pennsylvania. Near the handle the following appears vertically: "Refill this mug at participating McDonald's for only 49¢ plus tax. Not valid with any other offer. Good through 12/31/92." There are three mugs with hip graphics and color variations in this set; these mugs are regional and quite difficult to find. $8.00 – 15.00 each.

1. "McDonald's" in pink, blue, and green grid below, icon of state of Texas in pink with gray McDonald's logo, green Coca-Cola Classic Texas state flag logo, blue Texas High School Coaches logo.

2. "McDonald's" in blue, pink, and purple grid below, icon of state of Texas in blue with gray McDonald's logo, pink Coca-Cola Classic Texas state flag logo, purple Texas High School Coaches logo.

3. "McDonald's" in emerald green, pink, and purple grid below, icon of state of Texas in emerald green with gray McDonald's logo, pink Coca-Cola Classic Texas state flag logo, blue Texas High School Coaches logo.

Row 2.

1993 "Texas High School Coaches Association Inc., Proud Sponsor of the 1993 McDonald's All Star Games." This set of three 6¼" gray insulated "Thermo" hot-cold mugs with gray lids, splashy graphics, and color variations is co-sponsored by Coca-Cola Classic and made by Whirley Industries in Warren, Pennsylvania. Near the handle the following appears in vertical black letters: "Refill this mug at participating McDonald's for only 49¢ plus tax. Not valid with any other offer. Good through 12/31/93." Icon of state of Texas with gray McDonald's logo, Coca-Cola Classic Texas state flag logo, and Texas High School Coaches Association logo all appear in black. These are tough to find regional mugs. $8.00 – 15.00 each.

1. "McDonald's" in black with blue underline and arch of progressively larger pink, blue, and yellow balls.

2. "McDonald's" in black with green underline and arch of progressively larger pink balls.

3. "McDonald's" in black with pink underline and arch of progressively larger blue balls.

INSULATED PLASTIC BEVERAGE MUGS WITH SIPPING LIDS

Row 1.

1. 1993 "Hot & Fresh Coffee 10¢ Refill," a 5⅝" mug with black handle and cap (cap not shown), made by Whirley in Warren, Pennsylvania. Same graphics both sides. There's a ton of information in small print inside the handle which boils down to this: the offer was good until 8/31/94 in these Texas locations: Abilene, Brady, Breckenridge, Brownwood, Eastland, San Angelo, Snyder, and Sweetwater. "Offer expires 8/31/94. Please limit one refill per customer per visit. Prices may vary." $5.00 – 10.00.

2. 1993 "What do you want with your coffee?," a 5⅝" oatmeal colored mug with red handle and sipping lid and virtually every item on McDonald's breakfast menu listed in various colors and type styles. Near the bottom of the mug near the handle there's a "Reuse" recycling icon and "©1993 McDonald's Corporation." Made by Whirley Industries in Warren, Pennsylvania. $8.00 – 12.00.

Row 2.

1994 "Texas High School Coaches Association Inc., Proud Sponsor of the McDonald's All Star Games." This set of three 6¼" wildly decorated "Thermo" hot-cold mugs also carries the "What You Want Is What You Get" slogan in addition to being co-sponsored by Coca-Cola Classic. Near the handle in vertical white lettering: "Refill mug at participating McDonald's for only 49¢ plus tax. Not valid with any other offer. Good through 12/31/94." Each mug has a state of Texas icon in white with red McDonald's logo, a red and white Coca-Cola Classic Texas state flag logo, and a Texas High School Coaches Association logo. Made by Whirley Industries in Warren, Pennsylvania. Hard to find regional issues. $7.00 – 13.00.

1. McDonald's sign in purple and white, multicolored lightning bolt and triangle designs in background, purple lid.
2. McDonald's sign in blue and white, multicolored background with lightning bolts and triangle designs, blue lid.
3. McDonald's sign in red and yellow, multicolored background with lightning bolts and triangle designs, red lid.

INSULATED PLASTIC BEVERAGE MUGS WITH SIPPING LIDS

Row 1.

1. 1993 McDonald's Racing Team, a 5⅝" mug with red cap showing Hut Stricklin and Junior Johnson and car #27. Made by Whirley Industries, Warren, Pennsylvania. $4.00 – 8.00.

2. 1994 McDonald's Racing Team double-walled insulated hot-cold plastic mug with sipping lid featuring Junior Johnson and Jimmy Spencer and their Thunderbird, co-sponsored by FM 98 WCOS Back-to-Back Country Favorites. Appearing vertically under the handle: "©1994 McDonald's Corporation. Refill this mug at participating McDonald's for only 25¢ plus tax. Not valid with any other offer. Prices may vary. Good through 12/31/94." Made by Whirley in Warren, Pennsylvania. $4.00 – 8.00.

Row 2.

1995 "Texas High School Coaches Association Inc., Proud Sponsor of The McDonald's All Star Games." This set of three 6¼" boldly decorated "Thermo" hot-cold mugs features a zoom close-up of the Golden Arches with a multicolored background. Each mug has a Texas state icon with McDonald's arch, a Texas state flag Coca-Cola Classic logo, and a Texas High School Coaches Association logo. Near the handle in vertical white letters we see: "Refill mug at participating McDonald's for only 49¢ plus tax. Not valid with any other offer. Good through 12/31/95. ©1995 McDonald's Corporation." Regional distribution makes these mugs hard to find. Made by Whirley Industries, Warren, Pennsylvania. $7.00 – 13.00 each.

1. "McDonald's" in large letters at bottom, yellow and white arch, purple and green background, green handle and cap, sponsors' logos in purple and white.

2. "McDonald's" in large letters at bottom, yellow and white arch, red and blue background, red handle and cap, sponsors' logos in blue and white.

3. "McDonald's" in large letters at bottom, yellow and white arch, blue and green background, blue handle and cap, sponsors' logos in green and white.

INSULATED PLASTIC BEVERAGE MUGS WITH SIPPING LIDS

Row 1.

1. 1995 Thermo Hot Cold 6¼" mug made by Whirley in Warren, Pennsylvania. This mug is identical in general design to the 1995 Texas High School Coaches Association mug shown on page 56 row 2, no. 2 (red and blue background), but it doesn't have the Texas All Star Games sponsorship information on it. It has the "Always Coca-Cola" logo on it. Red cap and handle. $4.00 – 7.00.

2. 1995, "20th Anniversary April 1, 1995, First Drive-Thru Booth, Oklahoma City, Oklahoma." Co-sponsored by Coca-Cola and showing a 1957 Chevrolet beneath the Golden Arches and a 1975 – 1995 sign. This is a 6¼" "Thermo" hot-cold mug made by Whirley in Warren, Pennsylvania. $6.00 – 12.00.

1995, 49¢ refill mugs set of two (or more?) with large McDonald's arches in front of three colored stripes (blue, pink, and purple), McDonald's in purple script underlined near the bottom, and matching lid and handle colors. Same design both sides with a Coca-Cola Classic logo between the panels. Printed on the side of the mugs under the handle is this message: "Refill this mug at participating McDonald's for only 49¢ plus tax. Not valid with any other offer. Prices may vary. Good through 7/31/95." These pearl-colored "Thermo Hot-Cold" mugs were made by Whirley Industries in Warren, Pennsylvania. I show two mugs here, but there is probably a third one as well. $6.00 – 10.00 each.

3. Mug with blue cap and handle.

4. Mug with pink cap and handle.

Row 2.

1996 "Texas High School Coaches Association Inc." set of three 6¼" "Thermo" hot-cold mugs made by Whirley Industries in Warren, Pennsylvania. This set of three mugs shares most of the characteristics of its predecessors but offers a few departures. Each mug features a McDonald's sign with cowboy boot, hot pepper, cowboy hat, Texas star, and bucking bronco as graphical motifs. At the bottom of each mug we have: "One FREE Extra Value Meal for head coach & bus driver with team of 10 or more." Vertically, near the handle, we have: "Refill mug at participating McDonald's for only 49¢ plus tax. Not valid with any other offer. Good through 12/31/96. ©1996 McDonald's Corporation." Finally, these mugs have an "Always Coca-Cola" logo. These are hard to find regional issues. $7.00 – 12.00 each.

1. Green and white McDonald's sign on red background, red cap and handle.

2. Yellow and white McDonald's sign on black background, black handle and cap.

3. Red and yellow McDonald's sign on purple background, purple handle and cap.

INSULATED PLASTIC MUGS WITH SIPPING LIDS

Row 1.

1. ©1997 6³/₄" mug with large yellow and white arches on background of blue with red oval dots. This mug has a red cap with a rotating cover which exposes the sipping hole and vent hole. The 1997 copyright date appears next to the red handle, but actually I found this cup being sold in a McDonald's store in early February of 2001, a new cup with an earlier copyright date! On the bottom: "Whirley, Warren, Pennsylvania, USA." $2.00 – 4.00.

2. ©1998 McDonald's logo in red block, on a metallic gray 6¹/₄" mug with black handle and black sipping lid. Co-sponsored by Coca-Cola. Made by Whirley in Warren, Pennsylvania, U.S.A. $2.00 – 4.00.

3. ©1999 McDonald's Corporation, an 8¹/₄" white insulated mug with red handle and red sipping cap from Stuart, Iowa. The sipping lid has a movable cover which swivels and exposes and covers the access holes. McDonald's arch logo on both sides in red and yellow. Made by Whirley in Warren, Pennsylvania. $5.00 – 8.00.

Row 2.

1. ©2000 Bill Elliott Silver Anniversary 1976 – 2000 mug with Bill and his car pictured along with the logos of numerous sponsors. Black sipping lid and handle. This 6¹/₄" mug is made by Whirley in Warren, Pennsylvania. A summer 2000 issue. $3.00 – 5.00.

2. "Coffee Club," a 5³/₄" gray mug with pink handle and sipping lid depicting a multicolored steaming cup of coffee. Same design on both sides with "What you want is what you get" near the bottom. Made by Whirley in Warren, Pennsylvania. $2.00 – 4.00.

3. "McDonald's Earth Effort," a gray 5⁷/₈" mug with blue cap promoting McDonald's efforts to protect the environment. The central graphic on both sides of the mug is a flower comprised of four sets of arches. The bottom says: "Super Thermo, Betras USA, 14 oz. Insulated Beverage Mug." Recycling logo on side in blue. $3.00 – 6.00.

INSULATED MUGS WITH SIPPING LIDS

Row 1.

1. McDonald's yellow and black arch logo, co-sponsored by Coca-Cola, a 6¹/₈" hot-cold "Thermo" mug made by Whirley in Warren, Pennsylvania. Orange, yellow, red, and black decoration. Vertical "Enjoy Coca-Cola" script has wave type design. Orange handle and sipping lid. $2.00 – 4.00.

2. "McDonald's," co-sponsored by Coca-Cola, a 6¹/₈" mug with red handle and red sipping lid. Vertical "Enjoy Coca-Cola" script has spear end under the "a" of "Coca" and extension of "C" in "Cola" going through the loop in the "l" of "Cola." McDonald's logo on both sides, red and yellow band around bottom. Bottom says: "22 oz. ThermoHot!/Cold! Whirley Industries, Inc. Warren, Pennsylvania. U.S.A." $2.00 – 4.00.

3. "McDonald's Potosi," a 6¹/₄" gray mug with purple cap and handle, made by Whirley in Warren, Pennsylvania. "McDonald's" appears in yellow script above a purple heart and the word "Potosi." Same design both sides. Potosi is just southwest of St. Louis, Missouri. They didn't make a lot of these mugs. $8.00 – 12.00.

Row 2.

1. McDonald's Racing Team, "Taking It To Go," a 5¹/₂" gray mug with black collar and sipping lid. Same graphics on both sides. "Made in U.S.A." on bottom. The indented base is designed to fit into those little cup holders so common in today's cars. $3.00 – 6.00.

2. McDonald's Nanaimo – Parksville (British Columbia, Canada) "Bypass for life Nanaimo And District Hospital Foundation," a 6³/₄" insulated plastic mug with green handle and sipping lid with swivel stopper. This gray mug is sponsored by Parksville Qualicum Beach CKCI 1350 Great Music Great Memories, WAVE The Island's Own Life Rock, and Nanaimo's Country CKEG AM 1570." Made by Whirley in Warren, Pennsylvania. The locations listed on this mug are on Vancouver Island, British Columbia. $10.00 – 15.00.

TWO INSULATED PLASTIC BEVERAGE TUMBLERS

Row 1.

1. "McDonald's" in script at 45 degrees underlined with rectangular McDonald logos repeated three times around the tumbler. This 6³/₄" tumbler was made by Whirley in Warren, Pennsylvania. A rotating white plastic stopper makes it possible to plug the sipping hole when the tumbler is not in use. $5.00 – 10.00.

2. "Conoco, Hottest Brand Going, The Best Place To Fill Up In Roland!", a 6³/₄" white plastic tumbler with red decoration and cap with white rotating plastic stopper. Roland is a small town in Oklahoma. The tumbler was made by Whirley Industries in Warren, Pennsylvania. $5.00 – 10.00.

MISCELLANEOUS JAPANESE ISSUES AND FOOD MENU SET OF THREE

Row 1.

1. "McDonald's 100th store opening celebration 1976, monumental year for McDonald's Japan," a 5¼" stoneware tankard made in Germany featuring Ronald McDonald posing beside the tankard's circular 100th store graphic. Mugs like this were available only to management and store operators and are therefore not easy to obtain. $100.00 – 150.00.

2. ©1988 Touchstone Pictures and Amblin Entertainment Inc. *Who Framed Roger Rabbit* mug. This white ceramic mug shows Roger in a blue frame on one side and in a red frame on the other. He looks perplexed, and well he might be for there is indecipherable Japanese writing coming into his left ear on the handle side with the McDonald's logo. $15.00 – 25.00.

Japanese Christmas season glass in orange and red gift box (1996 or 1997). This small 4³⁄₈" glass, which has a small graphic showing a Golden Arch below a hand flipping hamburgers, was given to employees at a number of stores during the Christmas season in 1996 or 1997. I do not know the scope of this distribution. I suspect it was fairly limited. $40.00 – 60.00 for the glass; add $5.00 for the box.

3. Hand with spatula flipping stack of hamburgers in red square background, "McDonald's" name under spatula and Golden Arch below.

4. Gift box that hamburger flipping glass came in.

5. Big Mac billboard on highway with rear view of yellow Porsche Speedster, a 6³⁄₈" Japanese tumbler which was not distributed. This glass is probably a sample glass or prototype. $50.00 – 80.00.

FOOD MENU SET OF THREE

Row 2.

This set of three 4¼" glasses was issued by selected Japanese McDonald stores in the mid 1990s (the boxes bear a ©1995 copyright date, but there is no date on the glasses). Two of the glasses promote and depict McDonald's menu items, and the third one shows a pair of red shoes belonging to Japan's "Donald McDonald." There is no Japanese writing on the glasses, but there is some Japanese writing on the bottom of each box next to the date. $35.00 – 55.00 each, add $5.00 for the box.

1. Fries, shake, and burger in blue circle, smaller variations of same food items occupying the remaining areas of the glass.

2. Fries, shakes, and burgers in slightly reduced size and the following text in blue encircling the glass: "The McDonald's Happy Meal Guys, the Hamburger, Cheeseburger, or Fries and Chicken McNuggets. Soft drink in a McDonald's Happy Meal."

3. Donald McDonald's red shoes, "McDonald's" in white and yellow in script on back with line drawings of Donald's head in pink and red.

4, 5, 6. Three boxes arranged to show the entire McDonald's marketing message.

MIDDLE EAST SET OF NINE COMMEMORATIVE STORE OPENING TUMBLERS

This is a set of nine 5¹/₂" tumblers issued in the spring of 2000 in Kuwait. Each glass has beautiful multicolored graphics which promote the attractions of each of the nine Middle East countries in the set. Each glass has a Coca-Cola logo, several McDonald's logos, and very noticeable Arabic script. The date of the opening of the first store in each of the countries appears on each glass, making the set an interesting and important historical glass record. These glasses are extremely difficult to obtain. Sets are especially difficult to assemble. Distribution in Kuwait was limited and erratic. Expect to pay premium prices for them. $35.00 – 75.00 each.

Row 1.

1. Bahrain. First Store Opened on 15th December 1994.
2. Egypt. First Store Opened on 20th October 1994.
3. Jordan. First Store Opened on 7th November 1996.
4. Kuwait. First Store Opened on 15th June 1994.

Row 2.

1. Lebanon. First Store Opened on September 1996.
2. Oman. First Store Opened on 3rd March 1994.
3. Qatar. First Store Opened on 13th December 1995.
4. Saudi Arabia. 1st Store Opened in Western Region on 19th January 1996.
5. U.A.E. First Store Opened on 21 December 1994.

MAC TONIGHT

MISCELLANEOUS MAC TONIGHT ISSUES

Row 1.

1. Make it Mac Tonight, a 3⅝" dark blue coffee mug featuring crescent moon (Ray Charles) character. No McDonald's logo on mug, but "©1988 McDonald's Corp." and "Button-Up" appear near the bottom in small white print. There's a "Made in Korea" sticker on the bottom. $8.00 – 12.00.

2. Mac Tonight, a 3⅝" dark blue coffee mug featuring crescent moon (Ray Charles) character and piano keyboard. No McDonald's logo on mug but "©1988 McDonald's Corp." and "Button-Up" appear near the bottom in small white print. Made in Korea sticker on bottom. $8.00 – 12.00.

3. Mac Tonight, a 3⅝" dark blue coffee mug featuring crescent moon (Ray Charles) character holding microphone. No McDonald's logo on mug but "©1988 McDonald's Corp." and "Button-Up" appear near the bottom in small white print. "Made in Korea" sticker on bottom. $8.00 – 12.00.

4. "Make it Mac Tonight," a 3¾" black ceramic mug featuring crescent moon (Ray Charles) character and city skyline. This mug has a small McDonald's logo just below the word "Tonight." $8.00 – 12.00.

Row 2.

1. Mac Tonight, 4⅛" old fashioned glass. $8.00 – 12.00.

2. Mac Tonight, 5⅜" highball tumbler. $8.00 – 12.00.

3. Mac Tonight, 6¼" tumbler. $8.00 – 12.00.

4. Mac Tonight, 6⅞" 28 oz. tumbler. $10.00 – 14.00.

5. Mac Tonight, 6½" straw holder/jar with plastic cover. $10.00 – 14.00.

MISCELLANEOUS MAC TONIGHT AND BLAST BACK WITH MAC ISSUES

Row 1.

1. Mac Tonight, $3^5/8$" plastic travel mug with receptacle base and sipping lid made by Mini Max. $4.00 – 8.00.

2. Make it Mac Tonight, a $6^1/8$" insulated blue and white plastic coffee mug with crescent moon (Ray Charles) character. $4.00 – 6.00.

3. Mac Tonight, a $5^1/8$" Canadian plastic cup showing Mac at the wheel of a red 1957 Chevy convertible, city skyline in background. Canadian McDonald's logo and "Enjoy diet Coke" logo are featured near the top of the cup just above the hood of the Chevy. No date on cup, but it has to be 1988 or 1989 when this promotion was in full swing. On bottom of cup: "The Collectibles, Canada Cup Inc. Toronto, Made in Canada, Fabrique au Canada." $5.00 – 10.00.

4. Mac Tonight, 32 oz. plastic cup, McDonald's logo, city skyline, and Coca-Cola Classic logo on each side. $2.00 – 4.00.

Row 2.

1989 "Play McDonald's Blast Back with Mac," a 5" wax-coated paper cup with attached game piece on side, co-sponsored by Coke. $5.00 – 10.00; subtract $2.00 for missing game piece.

1. Front view of "Blast Back with Mac" cup.

2. Game piece view of "Blast Back with Mac" cup.

3. 1989 "Play McDonald's Blast Back with Mac," a $6^5/8$" wax-covered paper cup with game piece on side, co-sponsored by Coke. $5.00 – 10.00; deduct $2.00 for missing game piece.

4. 1989 "Play McDonald's Blast Back with Mac," a 7" wax-coated paper cup with game piece on side, co-sponsored by Coke. The McDonald's block logo on this cup is $1^1/8$" square, noticeably larger than the cup listed below and shown to its right. The blue color on this cup is very dark. This cup appears to be the same size as the cup to its right, but in fact it is larger; it will not nest snugly in its companion to the right. $5.00 – 10.00; deduct $2.00 for missing game piece.

5. 1989 "Play McDonald's Blast Back with Mac," a 7" wax-coated paper cup with game piece on side, co-sponsored by Coke. The McDonald's block logo on this cup is 1" square, noticeably smaller than the cup to its left. The blue color on this cup is brighter than the almost black-blue on the larger cup listed above. This cup easily fits into the cup to its left with room to spare, and when this cup is filled with liquid and poured into the larger cup, the liquid stops about $1/2$" below the rim. This may be a small distinction, but collectors should know that these two 7" cups are different in some important respects. $5.00 – 10.00; deduct $2.00 for missing game piece.

EARLY 1970s SET OF SIX CLEAR GLASS FIGURAL PROTOTYPE McDONALD'S CHARACTER GLASSES

These unusual and truly rare figural tumblers resulted from McDonald's first attempt to create a set of character glass-es for marketing and promotional purposes. According to people with knowledge of this promotion, the McDonald's business affairs and marketing department rejected the manufacturer's prototypes because technology was not then available to produce this type of tumbler in color. Supposedly, the manufacturer spent over seventy thousand dollars producing the molds for these glasses which McDonald's ultimately rejected. I do not know how many of these glasses were produced, but I have handled personally and taken the picture of the set of six pictured here, and I have seen another "short" set of four which as far as I know is still in the hands of a prominent collector. In addi-tion, I recently received an inquiry from a collector in Hawaii who has two of these tumblers. My feeling is that a small number of these figurals survived. It is possible but not likely that you will be able to find any of these tumblers. The Ronald tumbler is a little taller than the other five. Each tumbler with the exception of Ronald has the character's name embossed on the reverse. My impression when handling these tumblers was that the characters' likenesses were crude and grotesque compared to the versions we are now familiar with. In fact, the tumblers are puzzling and would have meant absolutely nothing to McDonald's hamburger buyers in the early days of the franchise. It's easy to see why they didn't make it beyond the prototype stage. They are not attractive. Still, they are historically significant and valuable, so much so that I will not presume to suggest a value. (Photos courtesy of David and Kathy Clark, Gal-latin, Tennessee.)

1. Captain Crook
2. Ronald McDonald
3. Mayor McCheese

REVERSE VIEWS OF CAPTAIN CROOK, RONALD, AND MAYOR McCHEESE FIGURAL PROTOTYPES

1. Captain Crook
2. Ronald McDonald
3. Mayor McCheese

FRONTAL VIEWS OF THE BIG MAC, GRIMACE, AND HAMBURGLAR FIGURAL PROTOTYPES

1. Big Mac
2. Grimace
3. Hamburglar

REVERSE VIEWS OF THE BIG MAC, GRIMACE, AND HAMBURGLAR FIGURAL PROTOTYPES
1. Big Mac
2. Grimace
3. Hamburglar

THE SIX FIGURAL PROTOYPES IN A ROW (PHOTO BY THE AUTHOR WITH PERMISSION OF DAVID AND KATHY CLARK.)
1. Ronald
2. Hamburglar
3. Mayor McCheese
4. Captain Crook
5. Grimace
6. Big Mac

SET OF SIX EARLY 70s PROTOTYPE CHARACTER TUMBLERS

The glasses shown here represent a second attempt by McDonald's to produce and market a cast of official specification character glasses. Only one complete set is known to exist, but three glasses from the set were pictured in *Tomart's Guide to Character & Promotional Glasses, 2nd Edition*, 1993 (page 87), so it is possible that individual glasses can be found. Evidently, production problems and registration complications led to the demise of this set. Markowski reports that the three glasses she shows in her book had "rejected" written on them with red crayon. The cast of characters here is slightly different from the lineup most McDonald's patrons have come to know. In this set we have the Gobblins instead of Hamburglar and Evil Grimace instead of Grimace, and there are some small differences in the appearance of the characters. Obviously, these glasses occupy a key position in the evolution of the McDonald's characters sets, if only we knew more about them! (Photographs courtesy of Robert Wilson, River Island Collectors' Museum, Springville, California.)

1. Big Mac
2. Gobblins
3. Evil Grimace

RONALD McDONALD, CAPTAIN CROOK, AND MAYOR McCHEESE FROM THE EARLY 70s PROTOTYPE TUMBLER SET

1. Ronald McDonald
2. Captain Crook
3. Mayor McCheese

1975 – 1976, 12 OZ. SET OF SIX McDONALDLAND CHARACTERS

This is a set of six 12 oz. 5¹/₈" Brockway tumblers featuring the six major McDonaldland characters. Front and back of each glass are the same: a single character with its name near the bottom of the glass. There is no other writing, no Golden Arches, not even the name "McDonald's." This is the earliest set of character glasses actually issued by McDonald's, and they pre-date the more common and better known Collector Series. It is thought by some collectors that this set was distributed in New England (possibly the greater Boston area) as a test promotion, but their widespread availability seems to belie this assumption. In any case, at the time of this promotion there was some concern that the paint on the images might have contained some lead. This may account for their relatively short-lived presence and the subsequent issuing of the second Collector Series. Close examination of these glasses will reveal color and design variations, suggesting that there may be two different sets, one set with ® or ™ both after the character's name and right next to the character's feet; and another set with ® or ™ after the character's name only. These registration, trademark, and decoration variations in addition to the often encountered Brockway sample glass stickers frequently found on the glasses' bottoms are a bit confusing and perhaps best left for advanced collectors to pursue. Most collectors will be content with a basic set of six glasses.

Row 1.
® and ™ after character's name only. Glasses with these characteristics and variations are much rarer than the glasses in Row 2. Glasses 2 and 4 are probably sample or test glasses. $10.00 – 15.00 for numbers 1 (without Brockway sample sticker), 3, 5, and 6; $25.00 – 50.00 for numbers 1 (with Brockway sample glass sticker), 2, and 4.
1. Ronald McDonald ® (Brockway glass sticker on bottom identifies this glass as "It. No./Deco 541, Desc. N – 75 – 6.")
2. Captain Crook ™ (red coat, patterned vest, patterned sword variation).
3. Big Mac ®
4. Mayor McCheese ® (plain pink coat)
5. Grimace ®
6. Hamburglar ® with Brockway sticker on bottom: "It. No./Deco 541 Desc.408" (shown here in place of single ® version).

Row 2.
® and ™ both after character's name and near character's feet. These glasses are the ones most frequently found (with the exception of #2 which is probably a sample or test glass). $8.00 – 12.00 each for numbers 1, 3, 4, 5, 6, and 7; $50.00 – 100.00 for #2.
1. Ronald McDonald ® (standard red and yellow decoration).
2. Ronald McDonald ® (ocher and dark red less common variation).
3. Captain Crook ™ (peach colored sword and vest; this version most frequently found, lavender jacket with dot pattern)
4. Big Mac ®
5. Mayor McCheese ® (lavender coat with small-dotted pattern)
6. Grimace ®
7. Hamburglar ®

COLLECTOR SERIES SET OF SIX FROM 1976 – 1977 AND SOME VARIATIONS

This set of six undated 16 oz. Libbey glasses is the second of McDonald's widely distributed sets. It features the major McDonaldland characters front and back in the same static poses that are on the earlier 12 oz. set. Characters' names appear in black lettering. Curiously, McDonald's name does not appear on these glasses, nor do the Golden Arches. These glasses were made in great quantities and probably distributed in 1976 – 1977. The store display containing these glasses says "Collect All 6/(McDonald's logo) Glasses To Go/Get a different glass every week." These glasses are plentiful on eBay. $2.00 – 3.00 each.

Row 1.

1. Ronald McDonald
2. Captain Crook
3. Big Mac
4. Mayor McCheese
5. Grimace
6. Hamburglar

Row 2.

1. Ronald McDonald with red lettering and smaller Ronald McDonald image.
This glass is a variation of the more usual Ronald McDonald Collector Series glass. Ronald's image on this glass is only 3^1/$_8$" high compared to his 3^3/$_4$" image on the black-lettered more common version. $7.00 – 10.00.
2. Big Mac lacking blue paint on hat and uniform.
This is an error glass; technically, it should not have made its way to a McDonald's restaurant for distribution. But the reality is that production errors occur with some frequency. Glasses with errors like this one are of interest to some collectors because they are oddities and much rarer than the normal examples most people collect. It is difficult to assign a definite value to examples like this, but some collectors prize them for their uniqueness. After all, not many of them made it past quality control to the distribution stage. $15.00 – 25.00.
3. Grimace with dark blue, rough matte finish, white mouth, and stumpy feet.
This is a color and design variation of the more common purple Grimace in the Collector Series. This variation, as well as the red-lettered Ronald, probably occurred because of the heavy demand for the Collector Series glasses. Since they were not all produced at one location, variations were unavoidable. $7.00 – 10.00.

THE TWO 1977 SETS OF McDONALDLAND ACTION SERIES TUMBLERS

This set is the successor to the Collector Series, and it's quite an advance because for the first time we have the McDonald's name on a character glass; we have characters in action; we have the Golden Arches on the Big Mac, Hamburglar, and Mayor McCheese glasses; and we have a set that comes in two sizes/styles: a $5^5/_8$" version with a small pad base and a $6^1/_8$" version with a creased base. The taller glasses were distributed regionally and seem to command slightly higher prices than the shorter ones which were widely distributed. Both designs are plentiful on eBay. This issue signaled that McDonald's was beginning to take glassware promotions very seriously. $4.00 – 6.00 each for the $5^5/_8$" series; $6.00 – 10.00 each for the $6^1/_8$" series.

Row 1: The $5^5/_8$" Action Series set of six.

1. Ronald McDonald leapfrogging over Gobblins near Filet O' Fish Lake
2. Captain Crook in sinking boat
3. Big Mac as traffic cop on roller skates chasing Gobblins and kids
4. Mayor McCheese taking picture of kids
5. Grimace and Gobblins on pogo sticks
6. Hamburglar on railroad car reaching for hamburgers coming out of engine's smokestack

Row 2: The $6^1/_8$" Action Series set of six.

1. Ronald McDonald leapfrogging over Gobblins near Filet O' Fish Lake.
2. Captain Crook in sinking boat.
3. Big Mac as traffic cop on roller skates chasing Gobblins and kids.
4. Mayor McCheese taking picture of kids.
5. Grimace and Gobblins on pogo sticks.
6. Hamburglar on railroad car reaching for hamburgers coming out of engine's smokestack.

THE 1980 McDONALDLAND ADVENTURE SERIES GLASS TUMBLERS AND PLASTIC CUPS

This very attractive set of six glasses featuring McDonaldland characters in action is, in my opinion, the apex of design sophistication for McDonald's. The graphics are wonderful, witty, complex, and engaging, and the 6$\frac{1}{8}$" creased bottom glass shell (used for the 1977 Action Series) is just right. Distribution of these glasses was irregular, so they can be rather hard to find. $12.00 – 18.00 each.

Row 1.

1. Ronald McDonald Saves The Falling Stars, Grimace and Gobblins loading stars into cart
2. Captain Crook Sails The Bounding Main, Mayor McCheese and Gobblins on desert island.
3. Big Mac Nets The Hamburglar, Big Mac throwing net over Hamburglar.
4. Mayor McCheese Rides A Runaway Train, Hamburglar and Grimace in forward cars.
5. Grimace Climbs A Mountain, Grimace planting McDonald's flag on top of mountain, Gobblins and Mayor McCheese looking on.
6. Hamburglar Hooks The Hamburgers, Hamburglar in helicopter with mechanical claw trying to get hamburgers from Big Mac who is on an island with hamburgers.

Row 2.

These 4$\frac{3}{4}$" yellow plastic cups, like their glass counterparts above, show the McDonaldland characters involved in various adventures. These cups are very difficult to find in good condition. They are much rarer than the glasses (the author has been able to find only four of them!) and will cost you for excellent copies. $10.00 – 20.00 each.

1. Ronald McDonald Saves the Falling Stars.
2. Hamburglar Hooks the Hamburgers.
3. Grimace Climbs a Mountain.
4. Captain Crook Sails the Bounding Main.

Not shown: Big Mac Nets the Hamburglar and Mayor McCheese Rides a Runaway Train.

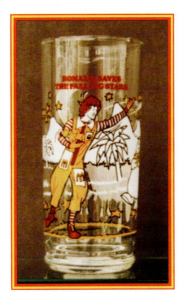

1980 RONALD McDONALD ADVENTURE SERIES PROTOTYPE

Ronald who? Ronald's last name (McDonald) does not appear in the title on this glass, and that makes this glass unusual and rare, even though the other graphics are identical to the production version. This glass has a manufacturer's production label on the bottom dated 3-19-1980 which is interesting since I have another example of this glass with Ronald's first and last names which has a production label dated 3-6-1980. Both glasses were approved by an inspector. Something happened, and the glass approved last lost out to an earlier design with both of Ronald's names. Perhaps "Ronald" alone sounded too casual or too familiar? The point for collectors is this: test and sample glasses are out there to be found, so you have to learn to look at glasses carefully for differences and variations. It could be well worth your while. $100.00 – 200.00+.

HAMBURGLAR, ONE TUMBLER FROM A LARGER SET

These 5¹/₂" tumblers were, according to my sources, issued in Japan although they look very "western." These glasses are not very well known in the U.S. and there is no agreement about their origin; they are just now beginning to trickle in. For now they are quite rare and expensive. $50.00 – 100.00 each.

1. Hamburglar with cape holding on to steering wheel of flying roadster, Eiffel Tower and Arc de Triomphe in the background.

Not shown: Ronald McDonald in hang glider.

EMBOSSED BOTTOM ACTION SERIES SET OF FOUR TUMBLERS
This set of four glasses was a very limited California promotion, and they are rather difficult to obtain. The graphics on these glasses are identical to those on the 1977 McDonaldland Action Series, but the whole conception is redeemed by an unusual inset base with embossed McDonald's arches encircling it and the McDonald's logo boldly embossed on the bottom. $40.00 – 75.00 each.

1. Ronald McDonald leapfrogging over Gobblins near Filet O' Fish Lake.
2. Big Mac as traffic cop on roller skates chasing Gobblins and kids.
3. Grimace and Gobblins on pogo sticks.
4. Hamburglar on railroad car reaching for hamburgers coming out of engine's smokestack.

McVOTE '86 THREE-GLASS SET PLUS TWO COLOR VARIATIONS

These three colorful glasses promote McDonald's three big sandwiches, the Big Mac, the McD.L.T., and the Quarter Pounder in the context of a mock election with anthropomorphic hamburgers campaigning for our votes. The idea was to get customers to "vote" for their favorite sandwiches by buying and eating them. $8.00 – 12.00 each.

Row 1.

1. Big Mac coming down the steps of a jumbo jet, crowds of supporters holding signs which say "Big Mac, No One Else Stacks Up" and "Vote for Mac."

2. Quarter Pounder campaigning from caboose of train with sign saying "He's the Big Cheese in Burgers," crowds holding signs saying "Quarter Pounder with Cheese in '86" and "Count on Him."

3. McD.L.T. riding in open car with sign saying "All the Makings of a Winner" and crowds with signs saying "Vote for Me McD.L.T." and "McD.L.T. for Burger of the Year."

Row 2.

1. Big Mac with dark brownish red and dark olive green colors instead of bright red and bright yellow-orange. This glass is strikingly different from the regular issue. It is probably a test/sample glass. $30.00 – 50.00 (?).

2. Quarter Pounder with Cheese in mauve and gray instead of bright red and bright yellow-orange, quite different from the regular issue and probably a test/sample glass. $30.00 – 50.00 (?).

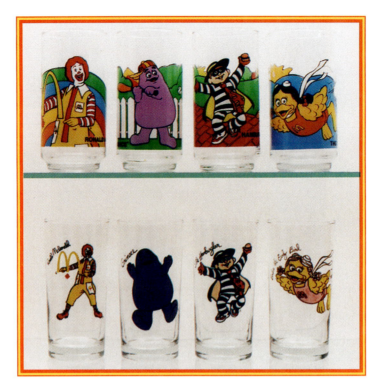

TWO CANADIAN CHARACTER SETS

Row 1.

This set of four undated glasses was distributed in late 1988 in Canada. It features three familiar characters and a new one, and each glass sports the McDonald's logo in black with a little maple leaf below the arches and an English/French "Enjoy Coca-Cola" trademark. It appears that the artwork was meant to appeal to children. There isn't much detail, but the colors are bright, and the characters are very happy and quite youthful looking. $9.00 – 14.00 each.

1. Ronald McDonald posing with Golden Arches in front of a rainbow.
2. Grimace playing baseball in front of picket fence and house and trees.
3. Hamburglar walking down a red brick road holding a hamburger in his left hand, sun coming up from behind distant hills and farm.
4. Birdie the Early Bird flying through the sky, clouds and happy smile face sun in background.

Row 2.

This undated set of four highball tumblers was first noticed by collectors in 1996, but it could have been issued a year or two earlier. The characters are the same ones that appear on the 1988 Canadian set, and at least three of the poses are strikingly similar, but these glasses have no background scenes, and Grimace is not playing baseball. Characters' names appear in black script, and there's no other writing on the glasses. These glasses are probably in-house glasses which had to be ordered through a catalog. They also come in a 5", 11-ounce round-bottom version, so there are really two sets of these to collect. $8.00 – 12.00 each.

1. Ronald McDonald
2. Grimace
3. Hamburglar
4. Birdie the Early Bird

McDonaldland Characters from Asian Mug Sets

Row 1.

Not much is known about this mug set, but I do know that these 2⅞" mugs feature the early McDonaldland characters and are quite rare in the U.S. Each mug has a large McDonald's logo on it and a continuous band of Golden Arches around the base. I presume they were issued in the early 1980s since McDonald's first restaurant in the Philippines was opened in 1981. The bottom of each mug has black McDonald's arches with "Philippines" beneath them. A collector I know has five of these mugs. I list three of those in addition to the two I own and show here. $50.00 – 100.00 each.

1. Hamburglar driving a car on one side of the McDonald's logo and his head with neck scarf flying in the wind on the other.
2. Mayor McCheese holding McDonald's flag in one hand and spectacles in the other on one side of the McDonald's logo and Mayor McCheese's head on the other.
Not shown: Ronald McDonald
Not shown: Big Mac
Not shown: Hamburglar and Mayor McCheese
Unconfirmed 6th mug not shown: (?)

These 4⅝" mugs are undated and apparently not often encountered. I have been told by knowledgeable sources that they were either a limited regional promotion in the midwest or Rocky Mountain states or a Philippines issue. The latter conjecture is probably more likely. The "Good Time…Great Taste" advertising campaign and slogan date from 1984, so I'm assuming that these mugs date from that time period. The "Good Time. Great Taste" slogan appears on the bottom of each mug along with a block McDonald's logo in red and yellow. The flat handles on these mugs are unusual in that they feature a graphic of the character and are contoured to mimic the shape of the character. The reverse side of these rare mugs is sparsely decorated with only a small red and yellow McDonald's block logo. $15.00 – 30.00 each.

3. Grimace riding multicolored musical notes on front of mug, Grimace's name off to the side with McDonald's block logo, Grimace playing the trombone on the flat handle.
4. Hamburglar surfing with large orange and yellow sun in background, McDonald's block logo off to the side, Hamburglar's name below, and Hamburglar again on the flat handle wearing baseball glove and catching baseball.
Not shown: Birdie the Early Bird
Not shown: Ronald McDonald

Row 2.

These 3¾" undated mugs came out in the fall of 2000. Each character's name appears in script on the reverse of the mug. The Ronald McDonald and Hamburglar mugs have "Thailand" embossed on their bottoms; there is no information on the bottom of the Birdie and Grimace mugs. The graphics and overall quality of these mugs are impressive. $15.00 – 25.00 each.

1. Birdy
2. Grimace
3. Hamburglar
4. Ronald McDonald

MISCELLANEOUS MCDONALDLAND CHARACTER ISSUES

1. Ronald McDonald in sitting position on 3⅝" mug made in Staffordshire, England, by Kiln Craft. This version of Ronald resembles the 1976 – 1977 Collector Series representation except that here Ronald's hands are much closer to his face. A large McDonald's logo appears on the back of this mug. $15.00 – 25.00.

2. "Master Pizza," a 3¾" white mug showing Hamburglar, Birdie, and Grimace in black and white decoration looking at a large colorful picture of a McDonald's pizza. Presumably, the characters are in an art gallery or museum; Hamburglar is holding a program, and Grimace is holding a magnifying glass. This mug, which was found in Canada and has no markings on it which would help to identify it, would date from the early 1990s when McDonald's was introducing pizza to their menu. $15.00 – 25.00.

3. Ronald McDonald riding carousal horse, a 3¾" white ceramic mug with same decoration on both sides. This mug is said to have a Las Vegas provenience. On the bottom: "CCA China." From the late 1990s. $5.00 – 10.00.

4. Ronald McDonald's face on a red 3½" ceramic mug, white interior. There are inscriptions on the bottom, but they are not readable. $12.00 – 18.00.

5. Ronald McDonald in red script below a picture of Ronald on one side of a 3¹¹⁄₁₆" white ceramic mug and "It's A Good Time For The Great Taste" advertising slogan and McDonald's block logo on the other. Variously sized yellow stars fill up the space between the panels. "Clayton Genuine Stoneware" appears on the bottom. The previous owner of this mug, a prominent McDonald's collector, had written "Malaysia" on a piece of tape on the bottom. I do not know if this means that the mug was made in Malaysia or distributed in Malaysia. The mug probably dates from 1984 when the "It's A Good Time For The Great Taste of McDonald's" national advertising campaign was introduced. $20.00 – 30.00.

MISCELLANEOUS DRINKWARE

THREE PROMOTIONAL CANNISTERS

1. 7¾" cannister goblet with lid, black decoration featuring large arches with a bar of people's profiles just below it, then "Profiles in Leadership 1979, Compliments Lidejo Sales Promotion Agency." (Without the lid, this piece would find its way into the stemware classification!) $25.00 – 40.00.

2. 5½" cannister jar, clear glass with red decoration, "McDonald's" on one side and "We Couldn't Do It Without You" on the other. $8.00 – 12.00.

3. 5½" cannister jar, clear glass with black decoration on both sides: "McDonald's Corporation, Washington, D.C. Region, 703-698-4000." $10.00 – 15.00.

MISCELLANEOUS COFFEE MUGS

Row 1.

1. McBlimp, Airship McDonald's, a gray 3¹/₂" coffee mug with yellow, blue, and red decoration and "What A Sight!" just below the rim and the inside of the mug. This mug dates from 1985 when McDonald's put an advertising blimp into the sky above New York City. $12.00 – 18.00.

2. McDonald's Collectors Club, a 3³/₄" coffee mug showing fries, shake, and burger, not an official McDonald's issue, rather a mug made exclusively for members of The McDonald's Collectors Club which was established in 1990. $8.00 – 12.00.

3. "McMoms," a colorful 3³/₄" ceramic mug showing a mom being pulled, I presume, towards a McDonald's restaurant by her small daughter. There's nothing on the mug to identify it as an official McDonald's mug, but it was produced by the McMom's organization which sells various McDonald's related products. Made in China. $10.00 – $15.00.

4. "McMug" on one side of 3³/₄" glass mug and McDonald's logo on the other. Red decoration. Made by Anchor Hocking. $7.00 – 10.00.

Row 2.

1. 3³/₄" white ceramic mug with Ronald's red shoes all over it, made in China. The red shoes have a connection with various in-store programs to speed up the service. One crew pin, for example, pictures the shoes and has the slogan "steppin it up" on it. $5.00 – 10.00.

2. McDonald's "Worldwide" 3³/₄" ceramic mug with the colorful flags of 24 nations on it. Presumably these are countries with McDonald's franchises in them in the early 1980s. "Wan feng Made in China" appears on the bottom. $15.00 – 25.00.

3. "McDonald's International Classic," a gray 3³/₄" mug with pastel pink, purple, and silver decoration consisting of a ring with "International Classic" in it centered over a triangle. "McDonald's" appears horizontally in silver right through the middle of the triangle and the circle. $10.00 – 20.00.

4. 3¹/₂" white ceramic mug with red decoration showing a McDonald's logo between the words "Hotter" and "Faster" no fewer than fourteen times around the cup. Made by Kiln Craft in Staffordshire, England. $15.00 – 25.00.

MISCELLANEOUS COFFEE MUGS

Row 1.

1. 4¹/₂" Pyrex Ware mug by Corning with "Made Exclusively For McDonalds ©1982" on the bottom. Unless you look at this mug closely, you will not know that this is a McDonald's issue and you will not see the Golden Arch border encircling the bottom of the plastic base. $7.00 – 10.00.

2. Canadian Headquarter's Building and McDonald's logo on 3¹/₂" Luminarc glass mug. $12.00 – 16.00.

3. 3⁷/₁₆" clear glass mug with black decoration showing "Larry" in a tuxedo on one side and "Larry Says…'Get Back The Gap!'" on the other along with a McDonald's logo. Made by Anchor Hocking. $8.00 – 15.00.

4. 3³/₄" clear glass mug with Canadian McDonald's logo in red and yellow, dating from the mid to late 1990s. This heavy, rather large mug has on its reverse side in red: "the Simon Difference." Simon, a marketing group which originated and arranged many promotions for McDonald's over the years, has an office in Toronto, Canada. $5.00 – 10.00.

Row 2.

1. 3³/₄" orange coffee mug with red Canadian McDonald's logo on front and "You, You're The One, Midland" on the reverse. This advertising campaign slogan was introduced in 1976. "Made in England" is inscribed on the mug's bottom. $15.00 – 20.00.

2. McDonald's, "We're here when you need us, 1-800-421-4332," a 3⁵/₈" white ceramic mug with red and gold decoration, "Made in England" on bottom. $10.00 – 15.00.

3. "You deserve a break today," a 4¹¹/₁₆" clear glass mug with red decoration which includes a large McDonald's arch logo. The "You deserve a break today" slogan was introduced in 1971 and used again in 1980. $10.00 – 20.00.

4. "We've got everything under the sun," a 3³/₄" white ceramic mug with red and yellow decoration. Just above the message there's a smiling sun in yellow. Below the message there's a yellow McDonald's logo. $10.00 – 15.00.

MISCELLANEOUS COFFEE MUGS

Row 1.

1. "WMAC" on both sides of a 3⁵/₈" white ceramic mug with the "M" in the form of yellow Golden Arches and the other three letters in black. This is probably a radio station mug. The station in question is probably 940 News Talk AM Radio in Macon, Georgia. (I discovered this information too late to include it in the radio station category.) $5.00 – 10.00.

2. "My Chicken's McChicken," a 3³/₈" bone-colored coffee cup with black and yellow decoration and 3³/₈" mouth diameter. McChicken mugs were given to employees for this new product rollout in northeast Ohio in late 1979 or early 1980. The Cleveland market had to decide between McChicken and McSteak which was being test marketed in California, and it chose McChicken. Unfortunately, the McChicken sandwich tanked in Cleveland, and it was dropped for a few years, then brought back again using all white meat instead of a mix of white and dark meat. $8.00 – 12.00.

3. "My Chicken's McChicken," a 3³/₄" bone-colored coffee cup with black and yellow decoration and 3" mouth diameter, a slightly smaller cup than the one shown to its left, listed above. $8.00 – 12.00.

4. "Chicken McNuggets Fiesta," a 3⁵/₈" yellow ceramic mug with orange and brown decoration with "Japan" on bottom. There is no date on this mug, but Chicken McNuggets were introduced in 1982. $10.00 – 20.00.

Row 2.

1. "Scouting Fever 1981, Chattahoochee Council, B.S.A.," a 3³/₈" white ceramic mug with red and yellow decoration. The Chattahoochee Council is in Georgia. Decoration on one side only. This is a very limited distribution item. $20.00 – 35.00.

2. "Excellence Through Growth 1990, Fall Round-Up B.S.A.," a 3⁷/₁₆" ceramic mug with red and blue decoration on the front and a large black McDonald's logo on the reverse. This Boy Scout mug is a very limited distribution item. $20.00 – 30.00.

3. "Choccolocco Council 1...The Closer You Get To Scouting...The Better It Looks," a 3¹/₂" white ceramic mug with blue, yellow, black, and red decoration. The front graphic shows a Boy Scout jogging towards a pile of scouting paraphernalia, a large McDonald's logo appears on the reverse. This council is in Alabama. $20.00 – 30.00.

4. "Happy Halloween," a 3⁵/₈" white ceramic mug with black and orange decoration showing the McDonald's logo, a haunted house, full moon, bats, and witch on a broomstick. Design on one side only. No date and no place or origin on bottom. $8.00 – 14.00.

COFFEE MUGS AND TWO CUP AND SAUCER SETS

Row 1.

1. "Scrabble Game" mug showing a stick figure Scrabble character with a #1 on it indicating with its left hand that McDonald's is number 1. Red McDonald's arches appear just above the left hand. This 3⁵/₈" mug has "Banawe Canada" on its bottom. I assume this was a Canadian promotion. $15.00 – 25.00.

2. "Rock 'N Roll Chicago…Keep On Rollin'," a 3¹¹/₁₆" white ceramic mug with black decoration featuring a late 1950s Chevrolet Corvette on both sides of the mug, a cross-collectible if ever there was one: antique cars, rock 'n roll, and McDonald's! "Made In China/Headwind" on the bottom. $15.00 – 30.00.

3. Roc Donald's (sign with tusks forming the Golden Arches)/Summer 1994 A.D. (tusk logo crudely stitched on animal hide), a 3³/₄" bone-colored mug with black, red, and yellow decoration. This mug was available only to McDonald's owners and operators during the summer of 1994, one year after the Flintstones Bedrock mug promotion. $15.00 – 25.00.

4. McDonald's Arches and Ronald's shoe in gold on both sides of a 3¹³/₁₆" gray ceramic mug with "HG Made In China" on bottom. No date but probably issued in the mid to late 1990s. $5.00 – 9.00.

Row 2.

1. "I (red heart) McDonald's (logo)" in red on a 3¹/₂" white ceramic heart-shaped mug. $10.00 – 15.00.

2. McDonald's espresso cup and saucer from Sao Paulo, Brazil. This tiny cup and saucer stands only 2¹/₄" tall and looks like it may have been made for children. It's probably an espresso set. On the bottom of each piece: "Nicolas Lanas Barrios Decolor Tel 2802200 Sao Paulo." $25.00 – 35.00.

3. McDonald's coffee cup and saucer, caffe Ottolina, Italy. The 5⁵/₈" saucer has "caffe Ottolina" in black near its inside rim; the "o" in Ottolina is a heart. The cup has a McDonald's logo in black and yellow with "Italia" below it in green. These pieces were made in Italy. $20.00 – 30.00.

4. "McDonald's Restaurant, U.S. 220 North, U.S. 220 South, Martinsville, Virginia," a 3¹/₄" yellow plastic mug with red decoration. This mug has a fragile square handle right at the top rim on the side opposite the graphic. This handle and the relative thinness of the mug indicate to me that it is fairly early, i.e., before the evolution of the travel mug. $10.00 – 20.00.

THREE BEVERAGE MUGS

1. "McSpresso," a black heavy plastic 6¹/₄" mug with sipping lid with identical red and yellow decoration on both sides. Bottom says "Royal Crest Inc. Made in U.S.A." Distributed in the Centralia-Olympia Washington area. $5.00 – 10.00.

2. "McDonald's" in black lettering on both sides of a 6⁷/₈" stainless steel coffee tumbler with black plastic bottom and cap. Sticker on bottom says: "18/8 Stainless Steel China." $10.00 – 15.00.

3. Insulated coffee mug with paper insert showing the sun rising over an ideal country village in a pastoral setting with homes, a car driving down a road, a church, fields, trees, birds, etc., and (you guessed it!) a McDonald's restaurant with the arches on a tall pole. Here's a case of the medium being the message. $5.00 – 8.00.

MISCELLANEOUS MUGS WITH LOGO OR McDONALD'S NAME ALONE

Row 1.

1. McDonald's, a $5^{1}/_{2}$" clear glass mug with red and yellow logo. $10.00 – 15.00.

2. McDonald's, a $5^{1}/_{8}$" clear glass mug with paneled base and black decoration. $10.00 – 15.00.

3. McDonald's logo above a tri-colored bar on a white $4^{7}/_{8}$" ceramic tankard mug dated 1978 on bottom of mug. $8.00 – 15.00.

4. McDonald's logo in white on front, 1981 in white on reverse of a heavy dark $5^{1}/_{2}$" tankard mug. $15.00 – 25.00.

Row 2.

1. McDonald's logo etched on $5^{1}/_{2}$" black glass mug. $15.00 – 25.00.

2. McDonald's, a $3^{3}/_{4}$" yellow ceramic coffee mug with red decoration, made in China. $5.00 – 8.00.

3. Red McDonald's arches logo on one side of a $3^{3}/_{4}$" yellow ceramic mug. "Made in China" on the bottom. $10.00 – 20.00.

4. McDonald's, a $3^{5}/_{8}$" yellow ceramic coffee mug with black decoration. $5.00 – 8.00.

MISCELLANEOUS DRINKWARE WITH LOGO OR McDONALD'S NAME ALONE

Row 1.

1. McDonald's, a 3⁷/₈" red ceramic mug with black decoration, made in Japan. $5.00 – 8.00.

2. McDonald's, a 3¹¹/₁₆" dark gray ceramic mug with light gray decoration. $5.00 – 8.00.

3. McDonald's, a 3⁷/₈" light gray ceramic mug with black decoration. "China" on bottom. $5.00 – 8.00.

4. McDonald's, a 3³/₄" purple ceramic mug with light gray decoration. $5.00 – 8.00.

Row 2.

1. McDonald's, a 3³/₄" cobalt blue mug with gold decoration, made in China. $5.00 – 8.00.

2. McDonald's, a 3¼" high 12 oz. cobalt blue coffee cup with the Canadian maple leaf logo in a subdued blue which is barely visible against the darker cobalt blue background. "McDonald's" appears in white with white dots below it. This big cup probably came with a saucer and was a premium for employees. $15.00 – 25.00.

3. McDonald's, a 4³/₈" cobalt blue tankard with gold decoration. $6.00 – 9.00.

4. McDonald's, a 4⁵/₈" blue tankard with gold decoration. $6.00 – 9.00.

MISCELLANEOUS MUGS WITH LOGO OR McDONALD'S NAME ALONE

Row 1.

1. McDonald's, a 3³/₄" black ceramic mug with gold McDonald's script decoration. $5.00 – 8.00.

2. McDonald's logo in platinum on both sides of 3³/₄" black ceramic mug with white marbling. $5.00 – 10.00.

3. Black 3³/₄" mug with seven gold McDonald's logos encircling the bottom. No markings on mug to indicate date or manufacturer. $5.00 – 10.00.

4. Cobalt blue 3³/₄" mug with seven gold McDonald's logos encircling the bottom. "China" on bottom in white. $5.00 – 10.00.

Row 2.

1. White 3³/₄" ceramic mug with seven red McDonald's logos encircling the bottom of the mug. $8.00 – 12.00.

2. McDonald's logo in red (one side only) on 3" white ceramic mug which has "Made in England" on the bottom. An English issue? $10.00 – 15.00.

3. White ceramic mug 3⁷/₁₆" high with a gold McDonald's logo inside a country schoolhouse inside a large red apple, no other decoration or writing except on the bottom which says "Linyi China." The graphic reflects McDonald's support for schools, students, and teachers and may be part of a larger promotional package. $5.00 – 10.00.

MISCELLANEOUS MUGS WITH LOGO OR McDONALD'S NAME ALONE

Row 1.

1. McDonald's "Coast to Coast" coffee cup featuring Speedee with sign saying "Est. 1955 Oak Brook, Illinois USA." On the reverse: "McDonald's ®." Red and blue decoraton on white ceramic. This retro-designed mug is not dated, but the box it came in tells us that it was marketed by Super Planning Co. Ltd. and that it was made in Japan, ©1999. It was not distributed in the United States. $25.00 – 35.00.

2. "I'm Speedee, Touch of Service," a 3³/₄" white ceramic mug with blue, red, and yellow decoration showing Speedee with his sign above small yellow McDonald's arches. This is a modern mug, and my instincts tell me it is Japanese in origin and that it is contemporaneous with the "Coast to Coast" mug to its left. $20.00 – 30.00.

3. Treasure Craft McDonald's Diner sculpted mug with handle on reverse. This 4¹/₄" ceramic mug made in China comes from the late 1990s and is in the shape of a late 1950s McDonald's hamburger stand, unusual and cute, to say the least! $10.00 – 20.00.

4. "McDonald's" in green script on 5¹/₈" canning jar. The jar warns us on the bottom that it is "Not For Hot Products" and "Not For Home Canning." This particular jar came with a white plastic cap with coin slot. $2.00 – 4.00.

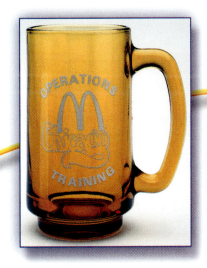

MISCELLANEOUS DRINKWARE PIECES

Row 1.

1. Juice glass, 3³/₈" with daisy design and McDonald's arches around bottom, yellow, white, and orange decoration. $5.00 – 10.00.

2. Juice glass, 3³/₄" with frosted panel and clear McDonald's logo. $5.00 – 10.00.

3. Frosted 6³/₈" cooler or iced tea tumbler with "McDonald's" in underlined yellow script and yellow and white bands at top and bottom. This is a Canadian glass, a radio station giveaway in 1989 – 1990. It came in boxed sets of four in both tall and medium sizes. $5.00 – 8.00.

4. Water glass with white decoration, 3³/₄" made by Anchor Hocking. Decoration shows Speedee with sign saying "I'm 'Speedee'" and there's also this: "15¢, Coast to Coast Reg. U.S. Trademark 1957." Issue date of glass is uncertain; while it appears to be an early McDonald's glass, it is extremely likely a modern fabrication produced by someone who thought it was a neat idea. Maybe it is, and maybe it isn't. In any case, treat this glass as a modern curiosity and not as a McDonald's issue. For what it's worth: most of these glasses seem to be coming out of California; it's likely that they are a California inspiration. $15.00 – 25.00.

Row 2.

1. Big Mac Multi-Language, a 5" glass promoting the Big Mac Sandwich which was introduced in 1969 as follows: "McDonald's introduces Big Mac. A meal disguised as a sandwich." The Big Mac's ingredients ("Twoallbeefpattiesspecialsaucelettucecheesepicklesonionsonasesameseedbun") appear in five languages (English, German, Italian, Spanish, and Greek) in colored bands encircling the glass in yellow, red, and black. The glass dates to the mid 1970s when McDonald's advertising began to focus on their products' ingredients. $8.00 – 12.00.

2. 1982 Knoxville World's Fair, a 5¹/₂" flare promoting the fair, co-sponsored by Coca-Cola and McDonald's. $5.00 – 8.00.

3. McDonald's Hamburgers, a 4¹/₂" ceramic fountain mug designed in a retro mode to look old, co-sponsored by Coca-Cola ("Always Coca-Cola" on reverse) and featuring the old McDonald's sign with Speedee and the 15¢ sign and "McDonald's Speedee Service System Hamburgers we have sold over 100 Million." $10.00 – 15.00.

4. McDonald's Collectors Club 2000, a 5⁵/₈" tumbler showing shake, fries, and hamburger on a rocket ship heading for the stars. This tumbler was given to registered attendees of the McDonald's Collector's Club which met in Chicago from June 28 to July 1, 2000. There were fewer than 200 registered convention attendees, so this glass can be considered pretty rare even though it's not an official McDonald's issue. $10.00 – 20.00.

MISCELLANEOUS TUMBLERS INCLUDING A TIFFANY DESIGN PROTOTYPE

Row 1.

1. Pizza, a 5⅞" Canadian glass with Golden Arches substituting for the z's in the word *pizza*, red, white, and gold decoration. $15.00 – 20.00.

2. The Denim Collection from McDonald's, a 6⅛" tumbler co-sponsored by Coca-Cola, probably dating from the late 1970s. (A shorter sample version of this glass recently appeared on eBay with a starting bid of $25.00.) $8.00 – 12.00.

3. Ronald's shoe in red and yellow decoration on both sides of 6¼" tumbler. These tumblers, sold in boxed sets of four, date from the 1990s. $3.00 – 5.00.

4. Ronald's shoe with "McDonald's" just beneath it in frosted decoration on a a 6½" tumbler. $4.00 – 8.00.

Row 2.

1. Tiffany style leaded glass window design with McDonald's logo, yellow, black, and orange decoration. This glass is a test glass which anticipates later similar designs but was never put into production. It has a manufacturer's sticker on its bottom dated 10/15/80. $100.00 – 300.00+.

2. Tiffany style leaded glass window design tumbler with Canadian McDonald's logo on one side and Drink Coca-Cola on the other. $6.00 – 9.00.

3. Tiffany style leaded glass window design tumbler with Canadian McDonald's logo on one side and Buvez Coca-Cola on the other. There's also an Australian version of this glass and the one to its left. $7.00 – 10.00.

FOUR MONOPOLY TUMBLERS AND A PLASTIC MUG

1. Rich Uncle Pennybags, a 5$\frac{1}{8}$" double old fashioned glass with black, white, and frosted decoration. This glass has a 1996 Hasbro copyright and a 1997 McDonald's copyright and was one of the prizes that McDonald's customers could win by playing the Monopoly game. Large gray McDonald's arches appear on the reverse. The glass was not easy to "win" but it quickly became available on the aftermarket, and it is seen frequently on eBay. $10.00 – 15.00.

2. Rich Uncle Pennybags, a 5$\frac{1}{8}$" double old fashioned glass with multicolored decoration. This glass is identical in design to the widely available black and white version, and it has the same dates, 1996 Hasbro, Inc., and 1997 McDonald's Corp. It has large yellow McDonald's arches on the reverse. The rationale for this glass is not clear. It is rarer than the black and white version, but it is available. Did McDonald's have a design team shakeup in the middle of the promotion? $15.00 – 20.00.

3. Monopoly red plastic mug with white decoration showing Rich Uncle Pennybags and his cane inside a Christmas wreath with the McDonald's logo. White snowflakes appear on front and reverse. McDonald's in script underlined is on the reverse. There are no dates on this mug, but it was probably available at the same time the old fashioned glasses were available in 1996 – 1997. This mug does not appear to have been widely distributed, and consequently it is not well known. $5.00 – 10.00.

4. Compagnie De Distribution D'Electricite, ©1998 Hasbro, Inc., a 5$\frac{1}{4}$" tumbler with green, black, yellow, and white decoration from France. Gray McDonald's logo on the reverse. This is one of two tumblers that McDonald's customers in France might win by playing the Monopoly game. Players report that these glasses were extremely difficult to win. $20.00 – 35.00.

5. Compagnie De Distribution Des Eaux, ©1998 Hasbro, Inc., a 5$\frac{1}{4}$" tumbler with black, white, and green decoration from France. Gray McDonald's logo on the reverse. This is one of two tumblers that McDonald's customers in France might win by playing the Monopoly game. This glass and its "partner" (listed above) are difficult to obtain. $20.00 – 35.00.

1995 MONOPOLY PAPER CUPS

Left.

1. ©1995 "Play Now! Win $1,000,000, Pull To Play," a 7" wax-coated paper cup showing Rich Uncle Pennybags displaying paper money in outstretched arms within the Monopoly gameboard with two purplish-blue game pieces. Coca-Cola logo just under his left arm. The back panel shows three prizes: (1) Dream Home, (2) Dodge Viper, and (3) paper money, coins, and a deed. Four prizes are listed: $200,000 cash toward a dream home, (2) Dodge Viper, (3) $25,000 cash toward mortgage or rent, and (4) Great McDonald's Food." Printed right below Rich Uncle Pennybags: "Prizes and Odds Established As Of 4/28/95." $5.00 – 8.00. (Deduct $1.00 – 2.00 for missing game pieces.)

2. ©1995 "Monopoly Play for 50,000,000 Prizes…Play Now! Win A Dodge Viper, Pull To Play," a 7" wax-coated paper cup showing Rich Uncle Pennybags driving a Dodge Viper surrounded by the Monopoly game board, co-sponsored by Coca-Cola, and with two purplish-blue game pieces still intact. "Prizes And Odds Established As Of 4/28/95." Four prizes are described on the back panel of this cup: (1) a one million dollar cash annuity, (2) $200,000 towards a dream home, (3) $25,000 cash towards a mortgage or rent, and (4) "Great McDonald's Food." Three prize images are shown: (1) a treasure chest full of money, (2) a home, and (3) coins and bills along with a deed. $5.00 – 8.00. (Cups without game pieces: subtract $1.00 – 2.00.)

3. ©1995 "Monopoly Play for 50,000,000 Prizes…Play Now! Win A Dodge Viper, Pull To Play," a 7" wax-coated paper cup showing Rich Uncle Pennybags driving a Dodge Viper surrounded by the Monopoly game board, co-sponsored by Coca-Cola, and with two purplish-blue game pieces still intact. "Prizes And Odds Established As Of 4/28/95." So far this cup is identical to the one described above and shown to its left, but if you look closely at this one you will see that the reverse is quite different. On this cup, only three prizes are described: (1) the one million dollar annuity, (2) $200,000 cash toward a dream home, and (3) "Great McDonald's Food." Only two prize images are pictured: the treasure chest and the dream home. At the bottom of this cup we find the "Questions? Comments? See the Manager or Call 1-800-244-6227" logo/icon. $5.00 – 8.00. (Cups without game pieces: subtract $1.00 – 2.00.)

Right.

1. ©1995 "Monopoly Play for Over 100 Million Prizes…Play Now! Win A Dodge Viper, Pull To Play," a 7" wax-coated paper cup showing Rich Uncle Pennybags wearing a Santa Claus hat and driving a Dodge Viper with a Christmas wreath on the grill inside a Monopoly game board with two green game pieces still intact. "Prizes and Odds Established As Of 11/23/95." Co-sponsored by Coca-Cola. Panel on reverse lists and pictures two prizes: a treasure chest ($1,000,000 cash) and a log cabin "vacation home" ("$200,000 cash toward a vacation home"). Below the prize listings there is a "Questions? Comments? See the Manager" logo/icon. $5.00 – 8.00. (Subtract $1.00 – 2.00 for missing game pieces.)

2. ©1995 "Play Now! Win $1,000,000, Pull To Play," a 7" wax-coated paper cup showing a Santa-hatted Rich Uncle Pennybags riding in a sleigh and throwing money up into the air within a Monopoly gameboard frame with two green game pieces. Co-sponsored by Coca-Cola. "Prices And Odds Established As Of 11/23/95." The reverse panel on this cup shows and lists two prizes: a Dodge Viper and "$200,000 cash toward a vacation home." Beneath these images the "Questions? Comments? See the Manager" logo/icon appears. $5.00 – 8.00. (Deduct $1.00 – 2.00 for missing game pieces.)

3. ©1995 "Play Now! Win $1,000,000, Pull To Play," a 7" wax-coated paper cup showing a Santa-hatted Rich Uncle Pennybags riding in a sleigh and throwing money up into the air within a Monopoly gameboard frame with two green game pieces. Co-sponsored by Coca-Cola. "Prices And Odds Established As Of 11/23/95." So far this cup is identical to the one described above and shown to its left, but if you look closely, you will notice that two prizes are pictured: a Dodge Viper and a log cabin vacation home, while four prizes are described: (1) Dodge Viper, (2) $200,000 cash toward a vacation home, (3) Trip for 2 to the 1996 Olympic Summer Games, and (4) Great McDonald's food. Finally, near the bottom we see the "Proud Sponsor" USA Olympic logo. $5.00 – 8.00 (Deduct $1.00 – 2.00 for missing game pieces.)

1995 MONOPOLY PAPER CUPS

Row 1.

1. ©1995 "Play Now! Win A Dodge Viper, Pull To Play...50,000,000 Prizes, Prizes and Odds Established As Of 4/28/95," a 6³/₈" wax-coated paper cup showing Rich Uncle Pennybags driving a Dodge Viper on a Monopoly game board featuring Marvin Gardens, Coca-Cola co-sponsorship, and two purplish-blue game pieces. Near the top of the cup just to the right of the seam there are a McDonald's Monopoly logo and a Questions? Comments? logo. At the bottom of the cup, just to the right of the seam is a McDonald's block logo, and to the left a Coca-Cola logo. $5.00 – 8.00. (Deduct $1.00 – 2.00 for missing game pieces.)

2. ©1995 "Play Now! Win A Dodge Viper, Pull To Play...50,000,000 Prizes, Prizes and Odds Established As Of 4/28/95," a 6³/₈" wax-coated paper cup showing Rich Uncle Pennybags driving a Dodge Viper on a Monopoly game board featuring Marvin Gardens, Coca-Cola co-sponsorship, and two purplish-blue game pieces. This cup appears to be identical to the cup described above and pictured to its left, but if you observe closely you will see that there are important differences. On this cup, instead of the three logos described on the cup above and to the left, there is a vertical column of eight yellow Golden Arches just to the right of the cup's seam resting on a Monopoly logo near the base of the cup. $5.00 – 8.00. (Deduct $1.00 – 2.00 for missing game pieces.)

3. ©1995 "Play Now! win $1,000,000, Pull To Play...50,000,000 Prizes, Prizes And Odds Established As Of 4/28/95", a 6 ³/₈" wax-coated paper cup with two purplish-blue game pieces showing Rich Uncle Pennybags running on the Monopoly game board with a bag of money and featuring Boardwalk in the background. Near the top of the cup just to the right of the seam there are a McDonald's Monopoly logo and a Questions? Comments? logo. At the bottom of the cup, just to the right of the seam is a McDonald's block logo. There's a Coca-Cola logo just to the left of the seam at the bottom of the cup. $5.00 – 8.00 (Deduct $1.00 – 2.00 for missing game pieces.)

4. ©1995 "Play Now! win $1,000,000, Pull To Play...50,000,000 Prizes, Prizes And Odds Established As Of 4/28/95," a 6³/₈" wax-coated paper cup with two purplish-blue game pieces showing Rich Uncle Pennybags running on the Monopoly game board with a bag of money and featuring Boardwalk in the background. This cup appears to be identical to the cup described above and pictured to its left, but if you observe closely you will see that there are important differences. On this cup, instead of the three logos described on the cup above and to the left, there is a vertical column of eight yellow Golden Arches just to the right of the cup's seam resting on a Monopoly logo near the base of the cup. $5.00 – 8.00. (Deduct $1.00 – 2.00 for missing game pieces.)

Row 2.

1. ©1995 "Play Now! Win A Jeep Cherokee With A Sea-Doo Watercraft, Pull To Play…Over 100 Million Prizes, Prizes And Odds Established As Of 11/23/95," a 6³/₈" wax-coated paper cup featuring Rich Uncle Pennybags driving a Jeep Cherokee on the Monopoly game board with the Short Line Railroad property prominently displayed. Coca-Cola co-sponsorship, two green game pieces. Near the base of this cup just to the right of the seam is a McDonald's block logo. $5.00 – 8.00 (Deduct $1.00 – 2.00 for missing game pieces.)

2. ©1995 "Play Now! Win A Jeep Cherokee With A Sea-Doo Watercraft, Pull To Play…Over 100 Million Prizes, Prizes And Odds Established As Of 11/23/95," a 6³/₈" wax-coated paper cup featuring Rich Uncle Pennybags driving a Jeep Cherokee on the Monopoly game board with the Short Line Railroad property prominently displayed, Coca-Cola co-sponsorship, two green game pieces. This cup appears to be identical to the cup described above and pictured to its left, but if you examine this cup closely you will notice that it has a "Questions? Comments? See the Manager" logo just to the right of the seam near the bottom of the cup instead of the McDonald's block logo. $5.00 – 8.00 (Deduct $1.00 – 2.00 for missing game pieces.)

3. ©1995 "Play Now! Win $200,000 Cash Toward A Vacation Home, Pull To Play…Over 100 Million Prizes, Prizes and Odds Established As Of 11/23/95," a 6³/₈" wax-coated paper cup showing Rich Uncle Pennybags in Santa Claus hat in front of a Pacific Avenue snow-covered log cabin property. Near the top of the cup, just to the right of its seam, is a McDonald's Monopoly logo and near the base just to the right of the seam is a McDonald's block logo. This cup has two green game pieces and is co-sponsored by Coca-Cola. $5.00 – 8.00. (Deduct $1.00 – 2.00 for missing game pieces.)

4. ©1995 "Play Now! Win $200,000 Cash Toward A Vacation Home, Pull To Play…Over 100 Million Prizes, Prizes and Odds Established As Of 11/23/95," a 6³/₈" wax-coated paper cup showing Rich Uncle Pennybags in Santa Claus hat in front of a Pacific Avenue snow-covered log cabin property. This cup has two green game pieces and is co-sponsored by Coca-Cola. This cups appears to be identical to the one described above and pictured to its left, but careful examination shows important differences. There's a McDonald's Monopoly logo near the top of the cup just to the right of its seam, but instead of having the McDonald's block logo near the base just to the right of the seam we have a "Questions? Comments? See the Manager" logo. $5.00 – 8.00. (Deduct $1.00 – 2.00 for missing game pieces.)

93

1996 MONOPOLY PAPER CUPS

Left.

1. ©1996 "Pull Here To See If You've Won!" "Deluxe Monopoly," a 6³/₈" wax-coated paper cup showing Rich Uncle Pennybags, the Monopoly game board, and many prizes including a 1996 Saleen Mustang Speedster, Apple Macintosh Performa Computers, and Citibank Gold Visa Shopping Sprees," Coca-Cola co-sponsorship, and two red game pieces. Red band around top of cup says "Win a Cannondale Mountain Bike!/Win A Hyatt Vacations Hawaiian Trip For 4!" $5.00 – 8.00. (Deduct $1.00 – 2.00 for missing game pieces.)

2. ©1996 "Pull Here To See If You've Won!...Deluxe Monopoly," a 6³/₈" wax-coated paper cup showing Rich Uncle Pennybags, the Monopoly game board, and many prizes including a 1996 Saleen Mustang Speedster, Apple Macintosh Performa Computers, and Citibank Gold Visa Shopping Sprees." Coca-Cola co-sponsorship but missing the red game pieces which were never attached. Red band around top of cup says "Win a Cannondale Mountain Bike!/Win A Hyatt Vacations Hawaiian Trip For 4!" I don't know if the missing game pieces make this cup more valuable or less valuable than the cups with game pieces. $4.00 – 6.00 (?).

3. ©1996 "Pull Here To See If You've Won!...Deluxe Monopoly," a 6³/₈" wax-coated paper cup showing Rich Uncle Pennybags, the Monopoly game board, and many prizes including a trip to the Monopoly World Championship in Monte Carlo 1996 and Sony Handycam Vision Camcorders. Coca-Cola logo appears near the top of the cup just to the right of the seam. Red band at top of cup says: "Win a $5,000 Citibank Gold Visa Shopping Spree!/Win a 1996 Saleen Mustang Speedster!" $5.00 – 8.00. (Deduct $1.00 – 2.00 for missing game pieces.)

Right.

1. ©1996 "Deluxe Monopoly Win $1,000,000 Instantly," a 7" wax-coated paper cup showing Rich Uncle Pennybags with cane and top hat just above two red game pieces and surrounded by Monopoly board properties and prize icons. Cup has a predominantly dark blue background. Co-sponsored by Coca-Cola. Some of the prizes: Sea-Doo Jet Boats, McDonald's New Arch Deluxe Sandwiches, Trips to the Monopoly World Championship in Monte Carlo 1996, and $15.00 Prizes. $5.00 – 8.00. Deduct $1.00 for missing game pieces.

2. ©1996 "Deluxe Monopoly Win $1,000,000 Instantly," a 7" wax-coated paper cup showing Rich Uncle Pennybags with cane and top hat just above the yellow area where the game pieces are supposed to be. This cup is identical to the cup just to its left and listed above, but the game pieces were never applied to it. I'm not sure if the cup is more or less valuable than the "normal" version, but it is definitely a "different" cup. $4.00 – 9.00 (?).

3. ©1996 "Deluxe Monopoly Win A 1996 Saleen Mustang Speedster," a 7" wax-coated paper cup showing Rich Uncle Pennybags with cane and top hat just above two red game pieces and surrounded by Monopoly board properties and prize icons. The cup has a predominantly red background. Co-sponsored by Coca-Cola. Some of the prizes: Hyatt Hotels and Resorts Weekend Trips, Sony Discman CD Players, Brine Tournament Volleyball Sets, and $1,000 Cash Prizes. $5.00 – 8.00. (Deduct $1.00 for missing game pieces.)

4. ©1996 "Deluxe Monopoly Win A 1996 Saleen Mustang Speedster," a 7" wax-coated paper cup showing Rich Uncle Pennybags with cane and top hat just above the yellow area where the game pieces are supposed to be. This cup is identical to the cup just to its left and listed above, but the game pieces were never applied to it. I'm not sure if the cup is more or less valuable than the "normal" version, but it is definitely a "different" cup. $4.00 – 9.00 (?).

MISCELLANEOUS MONOPOLY CUPS FROM 1997, 1999, AND 2000

Row 1.

1. Monopoly "You Can Win Right Now!" 6³/₈" paper cup ©1996 Hasbro, ©1997 McDonald's, ©1997 Westin Hotels, ©1997 Jaguar Cars. Co-sponsored by Coca-Cola. This cup was used during the 1997 McDonald's Monopoly game contest for shakes and medium soft drinks, and it did not have an attached game piece, though two-thirds of the cup's area picture the prize-winning game pieces. The front panel advises the customer to "Find game stamps on large fries, super size fries, large soft drinks, and hash browns." $5.00 – 8.00.

2. ©1997 Monopoly "Play Now! Win A '97 Jaguar XK8!", a 7" paper cup co-sponsored by Coca-Cola with two blue game pieces and showing Rich Uncle Pennybags driving a Jaguar convertible. This very colorful cup promoted the 1997 McDonald's Monopoly game and shows all the properties on the Monopoly game board. One panel shows the prizes: "$200,000 Better Homes and Gardens Dream Home Cash; RCA Home Theatre 60" Projection TV." $3.00 – 7.00. (Deduct $1.00 for missing game pieces.)

3. ©1997 Monopoly "Play Now! Win $1,000,000," a 7" wax-coated paper cup featuring Rich Uncle Pennybags pushing a wheelbarrow full of cash in the center of the Monopoly gameboard, two blue game pieces, and Coca-Cola co-sponsorship. Instant winner prizes shown: "$5,000 Citibank Gold Visa Shopping Spree and Westin Resort Vacation for Two." $3.00 – 7.00. (Deduct $1.00 for missing game pieces.)

Row 2.

1. Monopoly "Play To Win Corvette Convertible!," a 7" paper cup co-sponsored by Coca-Cola with attached game-pieces in the middle of a white starburst. This colorful cup promoted the spring 1999 Monopoly game and shows a red Corvette as well as most of the Monopoly game board. $2.00 – 5.00. (Deduct $1.00 for missing game pieces.)
©2000 "Monopoly, the Winning Starts March 23rd at McDonald's"/"Monopoly 2000, Play To Win $1,000,000 and more," a medium-sized 6³/₈" paper cup co-sponsored by Coca-Cola and promoting McDonald's annual Monopoly game which ended April 20, 2000. $0.50 – 1.00.

2. "The Winning Starts March 23rd at McDonald's" panel.

3. "Play to Win $1,000,000 and more" panel.

4. ©2000 "Monopoly 2000 Start Playing! Start Winning!", a 5¹/₄" medium-sized Styrofoam coffee cup promoting the annual Monopoly game. Graphics include the Monopoly 2000 logo with Rich Uncle Pennybags and paper money and dollar signs floating around the cup. $1.00 – 3.00.

MONOPOLY PAPER CUPS

Row 1.

©2000 "Monopoly 2000, Play to Win Zenith 56" HDTV & DVD Player," or "Monopoly 2000, Play to Win Chrysler PT Cruiser," large paper cups with busy brightly colored decoration showing the Monopoly game board and "Win Instantly" prizes such as Zenith TV's and DVD players, cash, and Whirlpool appliances. The Monopoly game returns for spring 2000 with at least two different cups. Each cup has two peel-off game pieces which players attach to the "matching game board property." $1.00 – 2.00. (Deduct $0.50 – 1.00 for missing game pieces.)

1. Large cup showing 56" Zenith HDTV.
2. Super size cup showing 56" Zenith HDTV.
3. Large cup showing Chrysler PT Cruiser.
 (Not shown: super size cup showing Chrysler PT Cruiser)
4. ©2001 "Pick Your Prize!" Monopoly "Play to win! Win and Choose!," a large 7¹/₈" paper cup promoting McDonald's yearly Monopoly game and asking the question "So...How do YOU want your $1,000,000?, Cash? Gold? or Diamonds?" This large cup has the Coca-Cola logo and the Smile logo and shows a young African American male and has two blue game pieces. It also shows other "Prize Choices": trucks, cars, vacations, and recreational vehicles. "We love to see you smile" slogan vertically on seam, also the information that "Game is scheduled to end 8/9/01." $1.00 – 2.00.

Row 2.

1. ©2001 "Pick Your Prize!" Monopoly game McFlurry cup. This 3¹³/₁₆" regular-sized McFlurry cup has two game pieces and promotes the summer 2001 Monopoly promotion. The cup asks the consumer "So...What's YOUR thing?" and shows prizes such as the Razor Scooter, Samsung Digital Audio Player, and Nintendo Game Boy Advance. Various sponsors are listed on the seam and inside the bottom rim; also along the seam: "Game is scheduled to end 8/9/01." As far as I know, this cup and the cup in position 4 in row #1 above were the only two paper cups in this promotion. $1.00 – 2.00.

©2003 "Monopoly Best Chance Game...Don't Lose Out!," a pair of two cups promoting McDonald's new Monopoly game, in design very unlike previous years before the 2001 game piece scandal. Rich Uncle Pennybags appears on a red Monopoly background and there are two black game pieces per cup good for food at McDonald's, Best Buy Bucks good for discounts on electronics at Best Buy stores, instant winner game pieces for Samsung Portable DVD Players (large blue cup), and instant winner game pieces for Canon Elph Digital Camera and Photo Printer (super size pink cup). The promotion began 10/14/03 and ended 11/10/03. The electronic prizes are pictured, and there is Coca-Cola script, "how are we doin'?" graphic, modern arch logo, pitch in icon, and of course the Best Buy logo. $1.00 – 2.00. (Deduct $0.50 for missing game pieces.)

2. Large 7" blue Monopoly "Don't Lose Out!" cup.
3. Super size 7" pink Monopoly "Don't Lose Out!" cup.

TWO PLASTIC MONOPOLY CUPS

2001 "Pick Your Prize! Monopoly Play to Win!" plastic cups with "smile" and Coca-Cola logos. The Monopoly game board graphics are gone for this year, but the idea is still the same: fabulous prizes including an MR2 Spyder, a Sequoia, a Tundra, cash, gold, and diamonds. A very small Rich Uncle Pennybags is shown emerging from the middle "O" in "Monopoly." The main graphic features the top two-thirds of a blond woman's head on the large cup and a black-haired young man on the Super Size cup, and the emphasis is on choosing your own prize. There are two game pieces on each cup. "We love to see you smile" slogan appears in a blue vertical strip, and contest information including game expiration date (8/9/01) appear vertically in white print on the orange background. Some of the large cups have "Whirley Sandusky, Ohio USA" on their bottoms and some do not; the super size cups I have seen do not list a maker. $0.50 – 1.00 with game pieces.

1. Large 7" cup with blond-haired woman, "So...How do You want your $1,000,000?" showing cash, gold, and diamonds.

2. Super Size 7³/₈" cup showing black-haired young man, "So...What Drives You Wild?" showing an MR2 Spyder, a Sequoia, and a Tundra.

97

1977 SMOKED GLASS SPORTS MUGS SET OF FOUR AND 1984 OLYMPIC SUMMER GAMES SET OF FOUR MUGS

Row 1.

This is a set of four embossed mugs with McDonaldland characters engaged in four different sports. These mugs are undated but were probably distributed in 1977. Each character's name is embossed near the bottom of the mug under the character. The front and back designs are identical, and a large embossed McDonald's logo appears on the bottom of each mug. Restaurant advertising urged customers to "Collect all four McDonaldland SportsMugs" (no space between "Sports" and "Mugs"). Distribution of these mugs was limited and regional, but they are available. $8.00 – 12.00 each.

1. Ronald McDonald throwing a football
2. Hamburglar as a hockey goalie
3. Grimace shooting a basketball
4. Captain Crook hitting a baseball

Row 2.

These mugs commemorate the 1984 Los Angeles Summer Olympic Games. With the handle on the right, the mugs are identical from the front, showing the 1984 games logo. The reverse sides shown here feature four cubes outlined in white, yellow, red, or blue. Each of the cubes contains an icon of an Olympic sport in white, yellow, red, and blue. These mugs, normally referred to by the color of the cube outlining on each mug, are fairly plentiful. $1.00 – 2.00 each.

1. White: baseball, volleyball, basketball, soccer
2. Yellow: weightlifting, wrestling, track, archery
3. Red: steeplechase, fencing, ice skating, cycling
4. Blue: sailing, kayaking, sculling, swimming

GARFIELD GLASS AND PLASTIC MUG SETS OF FOUR

Row 1.

These undated mugs feature Jim Davis's famous cat character. Garfield is depicted on each mug in an action scene with one or more other characters (Odie, Jon, Pooky), and there is a white bubble containing one of his philosophical sayings. Copyright dates on the glasses say "1978 United Feature Syndicate Inc." Garfield made his newspaper debut on June 19, 1978, in forty-one newspapers, but the mugs were actually distributed nationally in 1987. These mugs are plentiful and inexpensive. $1.00 – 2.00 each.

1. I'm not one who rises to the occasion.
2. Use your friends wisely.
3. It's not a pretty life but somebody has to live it.
4. I'm easy to get along with when things go my way.

Row 2.

These 4¼" mugs, which have the same graphics as the glass mugs above, were distributed in the New England states instead of the glass mugs because, I am told, glass mugs could not be distributed in those states at that time. In any case, these mugs are much rarer than their glass counterparts. It is very difficult to find these mugs in excellent condition. An embossed Canadian maple leaf on the bottom of each mug suggests that they were made in Canada. $7.00 – 12.00 each.

1. I'm not one who rises to the occasion.
2. Use your friends wisely.
3. It's not a pretty life but somebody has to live it.
4. I'm easy to get along with when things go my way.

Row 3.

These undated mugs, referred to as the "checkerboard" mugs because of their colored grid backgrounds (yellow, blue, green, and red), had a much smaller distribution than the other set of Garfield mugs (above). They bear a 1978 United Feature Syndicate Inc. copyright date but were distributed at the same time the other set was distributed. They are definitely more regional and uncommon than the other Garfield mug set. Each mug has two related humorous sayings by Garfield. $5.00 – 8.00 each.

1. Yellow: The early cat gets the hotcake/This is the only alarm clock I need to set.
2. Blue: Whoever invented evenings probably invented teddy bears too/I'd like mornings better if they started later.
3. Green: I never met a dinner I didn't like/And what will you fellas have for breakfast?
4. Red: I've never seen a sunrise…I'm waiting for the movie/Such a beautiful sunset…and me without a horse.

TOLEDO ZOO PANDA SET OF THREE MUGS (1988)
These three Libbey mugs were available at McDonald's restaurants in the greater Toledo, Ohio, area for a limited time. Interesting scientific information about pandas appears on the back of each mug. $7.00 – 10.00 each.
1. Pandas
2. Nan : Nan
3. Le : Le

FLINTSTONES BEDROCK AND BATMAN FOREVER MUG SETS OF FOUR
Left.
These textured and embossed glass mugs were issued nationally in the summer of 1993 to coincide with the appearance of the Flintstones movie. Their "crude" design was controversial amongst collectors who were disappointed by the relative obscurity of the mugs' design. The theme of each mug isn't immediately clear until one examines hard-to-read embossing on the bottom for the mug's name. (Note: The bottom embossing also tells us that the two taller mugs were made in France, and the two shorter ones were made in the USA.) $3.00 – 5.00 each.
1. Mammoth Mug
2. Rocky Road Mug
3. Pre-Dawn Mug
4. TreeMendous Mug

Right.
Actually, McDonald's official name for these mugs and this promotion was "Gotham City Glassware Mugs" or "Gotham Glasses," and it was touted as a "Dynamic Deal." These four textured and embossed glass mugs were issued nationally during the summer of 1995 at about the same time the movie *Batman Forever* was released. Actually, restaurant displays asked the customer to "Look what's coming up in June." The mugs could be obtained for 99¢ each "with any Extra Value Meal or other food purchase." Once again, collectors were disappointed that a major promotion resulted in mugs and not colorful tumblers, but large numbers of these mugs traveled over the counter and out of store doors! Characters' names are embossed on the bottom of each mug. (Note: The first two mugs listed here were made in the USA, and the second two were made in France; this set of mugs was issued in Canada also, and the mugs that were issued in French-English speaking cities have both French and English writing on their bottoms which makes them slightly different and quite a bit rarer than their US counterparts.) US mugs: $3.00 - $5.00 each; Canadian bi-lingual mugs: $5.00 - $7.00 each.
1. Batman
2. The Riddler
3. Two-Face
4. Robin

COFFEE MUG HISTORIC LOGO SET OF FOUR AND ENGLISH IRONSTONE SET OF FOUR
Row 1: Coffee mug historic logo set of four (late 1990s).
This neat set of four $4^5/_8$" mugs features the major designs and logo themes of McDonald's from the early days of the franchise to the 1990s. The set comes in a white box with Golden Arches all over it. The bottom of each cup has on it: "Made exclusively for Group II Communications, INC, Hales Corners, Wisconsin 53130 in Thailand." $8.00 – 11.00 each.
1. Slashed arch logo from the 1950s and early 1960s (no graphics on reverse).
2. Speedy with "Custom Built Hamburgers" sign. On the reverse: "Do you folks know…you have consumed over 15 million Custom Built McDonald's Hamburgers!"
3. 1980s coffee mug with bands of yellow, orange, and brown arches.
4. 1990s Caution Hot! mug.

Row 2: "Coffee Time Foursome in English Ironstone" made by Kiln Craft Tableware, Staffordshire Potteries Ltd Stoke-on-Trent England (early 1990s).
This is a set of four $3^5/_8$" ironstone mugs with McDonald's Arch logo and brown plastic caps which also serve as coasters. The mugs come in four different colors and are housed in a brown plastic tray when not in use. "Made in England" appears on the bottom of each mug. Not dated but probably from the early to mid 1990s. Not shown here are the cardboard packaging and tray. The name of the set is printed on the packaging. Individual mugs with caps $5.00 – 8.00 each; complete set of four mugs with caps and tray, $30.00 – 40.00.
1. Beige mug with brown logo
2. Brown mug with white logo
3. Navy blue mug with white logo
4. Yellow mug with brown logo

THE GREAT MUPPET CAPER, SET OF FOUR US AND CANADIAN TUMBLERS (1981)

The Great Muppet Caper movie provided the inspiration for this set of four Libbey glasses featuring Jim Henson's lovable Muppet characters. Significantly, this was the first McDonald's promotion to feature non-McDonald's characters, and it turned out to be one of their most successful promotions. It was also a first for Libbey because they had to show the characters' true colors, making it necessary for them to use a five-color silkscreen process to show more than five colors. The artwork was designed by Daryl Cagle who designed over 2,000 licensed Muppet products from 1979 to 1989 (*Collector Glass News*, #43, July/August 1997, p. 16). There are colorful wrap-around action scenes on each glass, and most of the best-known characters seem to be represented. These glasses are plentiful since they were distributed heavily nationwide as well as in Canada and to some extent in Europe. The Canadian version has a small yellow maple leaf under the Golden Arches but otherwise the American and Canadian versions are identical. But since they are "foreign," Canadian Muppet Caper glasses tend to bring higher prices than their American counterparts. I picture here the Canadian set below the US set showing different panels.

Be advised that there's also an owner-operator's version of this glass which is quite rare and desirable. Many collectors believe that prior to the promotion, the owners or operators of McDonald's franchises in the US were sent a glass that reminded them to commit to the promotion before a certain date. Supposedly there was only one of these glasses sent to each U.S. McDonald's owner/operator in 1981, so there can't be more than the number of store owner/operators there were in the US at that time. I have talked to many knowledgeable McDonald's collectors about the number of glasses that might have been sent to operators, and they simply don't know. It's not likely that each store manager got one of there glasses. Most franchise owners may have received one; certainly big franchise owners with large numbers of stores received one of these glasses. Confusion, speculation, and uncertainty reign when this topic comes up. A prominent collector told me that the number of glasses sent out was "around a thousand." This may very well be the case. In any case, it's very unlikely that a thousand of these glasses have survived. Unless you look very carefully at every Muppet Caper glass you come across, you may miss this one. It looks very similar to the regular issue!

Special Note: There are at least two known sets (and possibly a third) of Muppet Caper glasses which have a gold finish on the outside and a silver finish on the inside. According to the owner of one of these sets, they originally came in a two-foot wide display case, but the glasses were separated from the case when the case was damaged. These glasses were never intended for distribution and are obviously extremely rare. Value: unknown.

US Muppet Caper issue: $2.00 – 4.00 each; Canadian Mupper Caper issue: $4.00 – 6.00 each.

Row 1.
1. Happiness Hotel with Muppet characters on doubledecker bus
2. Kermit the Frog and other characters riding bicycles
3. Kermit the Frog, Fozzie Bear, and the Great Gonzo in hot air balloon
4. Miss Piggy on motorcycle

Row 2.
1. Happiness Hotel bus
2. Characters riding bicycles
3. Fozzie in hot air balloon
4. Miss Piggy from the back showing Arches logo with maple leaf

The Great Muppet Caper owner-operator's glass, ©1980 Henson Associates, Inc.
This glass features Miss Piggy on a motorcycle busting through the front page of a McDonald's "Extra!" newspaper with the headline "The Muppets Are Coming!" Another third of the glass shows the Great Gonzo as a reporter taking a "Flash!" picture with the words "Commitment date: February 2, 1981," and another third with Fozzie and Kermit reading a newspaper which says: "Muppet Glasses Big Winner At McDonald's! Symptoms of Muppet Mania are Everywhere, *Washington Post*, The Muppets have as many adult fans as children followers!, *United Press*, Most Popular Entertainment on Earth, *Time Magazine*." $350.00 – 600.00 +.

Muppet Caper owner/operator's glass with view of Miss Piggy on motorcycle.

Muppet Caper owner/operator's glass with view of Fozzie and Kermit reading newspaper.

NETHERLANDS ISSUES

SET OF SIX MUGS WITH HUMOROUS DUTCH ANECDOTES AND THREE OTHER DUTCH MUGS

Row 1.

Each mug has a red and yellow McDonald's logo near the bottom with "Lekker gezellig" beneath it. The text on these mugs at first glance appears to be uniform, but closer examination will show that each mug has its own unique typographical characteristics. "IMI Promotions Utrecht-Brussels-Paris" is printed on the bottom of each mug. $10.00 – 15.00 each, $75.00 – 100.00 for the set of six.

1. In de jungle gaat een/luiaard van boom tot boom./Plotseling wordt hij/overvallen door een bende/slakken. Later vraagt/de politie: "Zou u de daders/herkennen?"/"Nee," zegt de luiaard,/"Het ging allemaal zo snel."

English Translation: In the jungle a sloth goes from tree to tree. Suddenly it is mugged by a bunch of snails. Later the police asked: "Could you identify who did it?" "No," replied the sloth, "it all happened so fast."

2. Twee aardappelen komen/elkaar tegen. Zegt/de een tegen de ander:/"Hoe is het met je broer?"/Antwoordt de ander:/"Slecht, hiz zit in de puree."

English Translation: Two potatoes meet each other. The one asks the other: "How is your brother?" "Bad," says the other, "he is a mashed potato."

3. Er zitten twee mannen te/vissen. Vraagt de een/aan de ander:/"Kan ik een dobber van/je lenen?"/"Ja", zegt de ander, "maar/waarom?" De een: "Die/van mij gaat steeds onder."

English Translation: Two men are fishing. One asks the other: "Can I borrow a bobber from you?" "Yes," replies the other, "but why?" "Because mine keeps going under."

Row 2.

1. Een bedelaar belt aan bij/een villa en vraagt/aan de dame die opendoet/om een plakje cake./"Waarom niet een/boterham?" Vraagt de/dame. Bedelaar: "Omdat/ik vandaag jarig ben."

English Translation: A beggar rings the doorbell at a villa and asks the lady who opens the door for a piece of cake. "Why not a sandwich?" asks the lady. "Because it is my birthday," answers the beggar.

2. "In dit restaurant wordt/Frans, Duits, Engels, Spaans,/Iers, Italiaans, Grieks en/Zweeds gesproken", staat op/de deur. "Niet te geloven",/reageert een verbaasde/bezoeker tegen de ober./"Wie spreekt al die talen?"/"De gasten, meneer."

Posted on the door of a restaurant is a sign which reads: "French, German, English, Spanish, Irish, Italian, Greek, and Swedish spoken here." "Unbelievable!" reacts the surprised customer to the waiter. "Who speaks all these languages?" "The guests, sir."

3. Een arts krijgt een/paniekerig telefoontje:/"Dokter, hij heeft 't/weer! Hij zegt dat-ie/een Big Mac is!"/Dokter: "Oke, breng 'm/maar hier."/"Ja, maar dan heb ik/niets meer te eten!"

English Translation: A doctor receives a panicky phone call: "Doctor, he's at it again! He says he is a Big Mac." "OK," replies the doctor, "Bring him to my office." "Yes, but then I won't have anything else to eat."

Row 3.

A pair of two breakfast coffee mugs co-sponsored by Douwe Egberts Coffee. One of the 3¹/₂" mugs features a city skyline with stars, moon, buildings, and McDonald's logos; the other features the same skyline with a blazing sun. In vertical lettering on each side of the handle: "McDonald's schenkt: Douwe Egberts koffie...lekkere koffie...1996 25 jaar McDonald's in Nederland." $15.00 – 25.00 each.

1. Morning mug with rising sun, yellow sky
2. Night mug with stars and moon and blue sky
3. "Verkeerd 'N Koffie," a 3¹/₂" white ceramic mug with black decoration (the same on both sides). This mug comes from Amsterdam; Verkkeerd is a hot milk and coffee drink. The bottom of the mug tells us that it was made by Kiln Craft in Staffordshire, England. $10.00 - 20.00.

PAPER CUPS AND WAX-COATED PAPER CUPS

SET OF FOUR PAPER CHRISTMAS CUPS

1988 "Happy Holidays" in red below red McDonald's logo in red-lined box, "Please Put Litter In Its Place" on top of logo, with green snowflake designs composed of kids in winter clothes, same decoration both sides. The cup is dated on the inside rim of its base. The cup comes in four different sizes. $2.00 – 4.00.

1. 4⁵/₈" Christmas cup
2. 5" Christmas cup
3. 6⁵/₈" Christmas cup
4. 7" Christmas cup

TWO DISNEY PAPER CUPS SETS

Row 1: 1995 "Walt Disney Home Video Masterpiece Collection Trivia Challenge" set of four.

These are large 7" cups with pull-off game pieces on the front of each cup and Coca-Cola co-sponsorship. They promote a Trivia Challenge game with "Over 300 Million Prizes." Each cup features a picture of a famous Disney video with a "Did You Know?" trivia question below it. To win, players had to "answer the Disney trivia question by rubbing off the box directly above the correct answer. Rub off ONLY ONE box. Your prize will be revealed in the rubbed-off box." The prizes listed and shown vary from cup to cup, so the prize panel on each cup is different from the other cups. The bottom of each cup informs us that "Prizes and odds established as of 3/29/96." $3.00 – 5.00 each; deduct $1.00 for missing game piece.

1. *Alice in Wonderland*, prizes listed: $1,000,000, Sony Discman, Disney Video, Free Food and More!
2. Front side of Alice cup with game piece (same design on each cup).
3. *Dumbo*, prizes listed: $1,000,000, IBM Aptiva, Disney Video, Free Food and More!
4. *The Little Mermaid*, prizes listed: $1,000,000, Sony Maximum Television Home Entertainment System, Disney Video, Disney Book from Mouse Works Classics Collection!
5. *Mary Poppins*, prizes listed: $1,000,000, Animation Fantasy Walt Disney World Family Vacation, Disney Video, Free Food and More!

Row 2: Two views of the 1995 "Disney's Masterpiece Collection Tivia Challenge" set of three.

These are 6¼" wax-coated paper cups with pull-off game pieces on the front and Coca-Cola co-sponsorship. These medium-sized cups have a slightly different design and are waxier than the 7" cups listed above. The pull-tab game piece and the Trivia Challenge rules are the same as on the larger cups, but the prizes shown are fewer and different, and the bottom border of each cup features a graphic of a specific Disney video. The "How to Play" panel informs us that "prizes and odds established 3/29/96." $3.00 – 5.00 each; deduct $1.00 for missing game piece.

1. Disney's *Pete's Dragon* featured on base, prizes shown: $1,000,000, Disney Video! (*Pete's Dragon* video shown)
2. Disney's Pocahontas featured on base; prizes shown: "A Disney book from Mouse Works Classics Collection!" (*Pocahontas* and *Lady and the Tramp* videos shown).
3. Disney's *The Many Adventures of Winnie The Pooh* featured on base, prizes shown: "A Walt Disney World Family Vacation for 4 to Florida!" and "A Disney Video!" (*Winnle the Pooh* video shown).
4. *Pete's Dragon* gamepiece panel.
5. *Pocahontas* prize panel.
6. *Winnie the Pooh* rules panel.

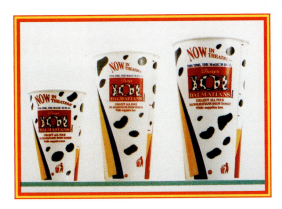

DISNEY *101 DALMATIANS* AND "25 YEARS OF MAGIC" PAPER CUPS

Left: 1996 "Disney's *101 Dalmatians*...Now in Theatres! This Time, The Magic Is Real," set of three.

These paper cups have large McDonald's Arches promoting the Disney film and they urge the customer to "Collect All Four 101 Dalmatians Snow Domes! While supplies last." Black Dalmatian spots all over these cups drive home the point. $2.00 – 4.00 each.

1. 4¹/₂" 101 Dalmatians cup
2. 6³/₈" 101 Dalmatians cup
3. 7" 101 Dalmatians cup

Right: 1996 "McDonald's celebrates 25 years of magic at the Walt Disney World Resort," a set of two 7" cups.

These cups promote Disney World and ask the customer to "Come Remember the Magic!" Each cup is busy with images, facts, and dates about Disney World and McDonald's. Both cups have Coca-Cola logos on them. I provide details from each cup below. $2.00 – 5.00 each.

1. Yellow Arches on blue at top, blue mouse ears on red at bottom; "Action" in large yellow letters.

1971: "Everyone was digging McDonald's new ad theme, 'You Deserve a Break Today — So Get Up and Get Away to McDonald's.'"

1989: "The opening of Disney-MGM Studios made Mickey the biggest mouse on the planet. The landmark 'Earffel Tower' wears a hat size of 342³/₈"!"

1991: "Lumiere, It's no birthday party without America's hottest candle!"

1995: "Woody, Buzz, and the 'Toy Story Parade' took Disney-MGM Studios to infinity and beyond!"

1996: "Grown-up taste takes center stage at McDonald's with the Arch Deluxe sandwich."

2. Light blue mouse ears on dark blue at top, yellow Arches on red at bottom; "Fantasy" in large red and yellow letters. "In 25 years we've made some fantastic friends!"

1971: "The Hamburglar, Grimace, and Mayor McCheese came to McDonaldland as new friends of Ronald McDonald."

1971: "Chip 'n' Dale."

1994: "Pumbaa and Timon in *The Legend of the Lion King.*"

1996: "For the Walt Disney World 25th Anniversary, the Cinderella Castle will be magically transformed into the biggest birthday cake ever!"

1996: "The magic is back for grown-ups...with McDonald's Arch Deluxe sandwich!"

DISNEY "COME REMEMBER THE MAGIC!", *FLUBBER*, AND *GEORGE OF THE JUNGLE* CUPS

Left: 1996 "McDonald's celebrates 25 years of magic at the Walt Disney World Resort," a set of two 6³/₈" cups.

These cups invite the customer to "Come Remember the Magic!" They are quite similar in design and purpose to the larger 7" cups described on page 107. Various Disney World and McDonald's milestones are featured on the cups. Both cups have Coca-Cola logos. $2.00 – 5.00 each.

1. Light blue mouse ears on yellow at top, yellow Arches on red at bottom.

1989: "Minnie Mouse, Minnie gets carried away...at Typhoon Lagoon!"

1995: "Ice Gator at Blizzard Beach, Way Cool!"

1996: "McDonald's now operates in 93 countries."

1996: "More and more grown-ups are taking the plunge into the summer's hottest sandwich: McDonald's Arch Deluxe sandwich!"

2. Yellow Arches on blue at top, light blue mouse ears on yellow at bottom.

1975: " 'TwoAllBeefPattiesSpecialSauceLettuceCheesePicklesOnionsOnASesameSeedBun' was the phrase of the day at McDonald's. Can you still say it?"

1982: "Figment, Take a 'Journey Into Imagination' with Figment."

1994: "Honey, I Shrunk The Audience. You won't believe your size in 'Honey, I Shrunk The Audience.'"

1996: "America discovers a taste just for grown-ups: McDonald's Arch Deluxe sandwich!"

Right: *Flubber* and *George of the Jungle* cups.

1. 1997 "Disney's *Flubber*, Bouncing into Theatres Everywhere!," a 7" cup with green blob-like Flubbers all over it and a large McDonald's logo. I presume this cup came in other sizes as well. $2.00 – 4.00 each.

2. 1997 "Watch Out! Disney's *George of the Jungle* at theatres everywhere!," a 5" cup with two "My McDonald's" logos and heavy promotion of their fruit pie: "Swing into McDonald's and swing out with that Treeeeat! Baked Fruit Pie. Grab hold of a delicious Baked Fruit Pie!" This cup probably came in other sizes. $2.00 – 4.00.

MISCELLANEOUS DISNEY PAPER CUPS

Row 1.

1. 1999 "Celebrate 2000 with Walt Disney World Resort." This medium-sized soft drink cup promotes the Millennium, Disney World, and McDonald's Walt Disney World 2000 Commemorative Glassware. A panel on the cup shows the four glasses which were distributed in October of 1999. $0.50 – 1.00.

2, 3. Large and Supersize Inspector Gadget cups.

1999 "Quarter Pounder with Cheese Code Name Game, Starring Disney's Inspector Gadget, Play To win $1,000,000 Instantly." These colorful cups (the large size and the super size) had game stamps on them which were to be applied to a game board, sort of like the Monopoly game, and the idea was to collect three code letters in a series to win prizes. Large cup: $1.00 – 3.00; Super size cup: $2.00 – 4.00.

4. 1999 "Disney Pixar *Toy Story 2* Only in Theaters Starts Nov. 26th." This medium-sized drink container which came out at Thanksgiving promotes the Disney movie and McDonald's six Happy Meal toys, which patrons are urged to collect "While Supplies Last." $0.50 – 1.00.

Row 2.

1. 2000 "*Disney's 102 Dalmations* Only in Theatres!," a 6³/₈" cup promoting Disney's fall 2000 movie and, of course, another game with slogans such as "102 Reasons McDonald's Is Your Spot," "Win on The Spot Game!," "3 of the same wins the game!," and "Woof! the Fun Begins Nov. 21, 2000!" Some of the prizes: "102 Brand New Puppy Toys," "CD Jukebox," "High tech DVD Player," "1st Class to London!," and "More Cash on the spot prizes than ever!" "Game is scheduled to end 12/21/00." Co-sponsored by Coca-Cola. $0.50 – 1.00.

2, 3. Large and Supersize 7" 102 Dalmations cups.

©2000 "*Disney's 102 Dalmations* Only In Theatres!," a set of two paper cups (large and super size). These cups have game pieces which customers are urged to peel off and scratch off to win prizes. Each cup features a large dalmation graphic under which is "Play Win on the Spot!" The prizes shown on these cups are a "Land Rover Discovery with 102 Fill-ups!," a "First Class London Trip For 4 plus $102.00 spending money per day!," "Fetch $102,000 Cash!," "One Million Cash on the Spot Prizes, $1.00, $5.00 or $10.00." The super size cup shows one additional prize: a "Kenwood 200 Disc CD Changer with 102 Cds of your choice!" Both cups have a Coca-Cola logo, an Arch logo, and a larger "Smile" logo. "Legal Beagle Stuff" is listed in small black print on the seam. "Game is scheduled to end 12/21/00." $1.00 – 2.00 each; deduct $0.50 for missing game pieces.

4. ©2002 "100 Years of Magic Walt Disney World Glassware Bring home a fun reminder of the celebration! Each glass is a McDonald's exclusive that features Disney trivia and lots of your favorite characters." This large 6³/₈" cup promotes the March 2002 four-glass set. This cup shows the four glasses in the set and also has the "smile" and Coca-Cola logos. $1.00 – 2.00.

VARIOUS EARLY McDONALD'S PAPER CUPS AND A PLASTIC TRAY

Row 1.

1. 3³/₄" paper coffee cup with folding handles, slashed Arch logo on one side, and "The All American" meal on the other side. The inside rim of the base contains the following information in white print on blue background: "8 FL. OZ. Prac. Cap. No. 4338 By Dixie Cup Div. of American Can Co., Easton, PA. Made in U.S.A. Edfal Rev. Wrap." On the seam in yellow (almost invisible) writing the following appears: "TM ® McDonald's Corporation, Illinois." $15.00 – 25.00.

2. Slashed Arch logo side of cup.

3. "The All American" meal side of cup.

3¹¹/₁₆" paper cup with the slashed arch logo on one side and "The All American" meal on the other. The inside rim of the base has the following in blue: "7 FL. OZ. PRAC. CAP. NO. 77 BY DIXIE CUP DIV. OF + AMERICAN CAN CO., EASTON, PA. MADE IN U.S.A.E." Next to the seam in red lettering: "McDonald's Corporation. Trademarks Reg. U. S. Pat. Off." $10.00 – 15.00.

4. 4⁵/₈" paper cup featuring Speedee holding his "Custom Built Hamburgers" sign with "McDonald's" above in red and "Coast To Coast" on blue band around the bottom. Red and blue deco on white background. Same design both sides. On the inside rim of the base: "+ A 8 R-12 , By Sweetheart Cup Div. Of Maryland Cup Corp., Baltimore, MD U.S.A. S-42849 +." I can't date this cup. It may be a reproduction of an early McDonald's cup, or it may be an early original. $8.00 – 12.00.

Row 2.

Plastic car window tray and 4⁵/₈" paper cup showing the early slashed Arch McDonald's logo within a blue circle on both sides of the cup. Inside rim on base says "©R-12, 12 oz., by Sweetheart Cup Div. of Maryland Cup Corp., Baltimore, MD U.S.A. +." In red appearing vertically along the seam we have: "McDonald's Corporation Trademarks Reg. U.S. Pat. Off." A thin yellow line encircles the cup about a half inch below the rim. From the 1960s. I show this cup here with a plastic tip tray from the same period. The tray was made by "Art Combed Plastics By demaree, Kokomo, Indiana." The tip tray was designed to attach to the window slot in the door, and it has a raised circular plastic rim for the cup to fit into. There's also a raised rim around the surface of the tray. The protoypical McDonald's brothers restaurant from the 1950s is depicted on the surface of the tray and described as "the drive-in with the arches." Cup: $10.00 – 15.00; Plastic Tray: $15.00 – 20.00.

1. Plastic car window tray.

2. Slashed arch Sweetheart cup.

1986 3⅝" Ronald McDonald with right hand raised and "Please Put Litter In Its Place" in yellow above his head; McDonald's logo in red lined box with "Please Put Litter In Its Place" in yellow on other side. Red and yellow decoration on white. The 1986 copyright date appears in red on the inside bottom rim. Some of these cups have black printing on the inside bottom rim. I guess we can call that a variation. $5.00 – 10.00 each.

3. Ronald side of 1986 cup.

4. Logo side of 1986 cup.

5. 3¾" laughing Ronald McDonald on both sides of cup with red and black decoration on white. Black lettering on inside bottom rim: "7 Fl. Oz. Prac. Cap. No. 77 Dixie Cup By American Can Co. Easton, PA. Made In U. S. A. E." $3.00 – 5.00.

PAPER NFL CUPS

Row 1: 1993 and 1994 paper NFL cups.

©1993 "Kickoff Payoff" set of two cups with "Pull Here" game pieces. The idea was for players to drink lots of Coke and accumulate points which could be redeemed for "NFL Player Trading Cards or Officially Licensed NFL Merchandise." The cups have a football jersey design with Coke and NFL logos. $2.00 – 4.00; deduct $1.00 for missing game pieces.

1. 6³/₈" Kickoff Payoff #21 cup
2. 7" Kickoff Payoff #32 cup

©1994 National Football League 6³/₈" wax-coated paper cup series. On each cup: "McDonald's is the Official Restaurant of the NFL." The name of the team appears in large letters, and there are generic player images in striking color combinations. Each cup has Coke, NFL, and McDonald's logos. I assume that there's a cup for most of the NFL teams. $3.00 – 7.00 each.

3. Bears, featuring a quarterback preparing to pass (has "Questions? Comments? See the Manager" graphic)
4. Eagles, featuring a running back
5. Falcons, featuring a quarterback preparing to pass

Row 2: 1994 and 1995 paper NFL cups.

©1995 National Football League 6³/₈" wax-coated paper cup series. On each cup: "McDonald's is the Official Restaurant of the NFL." Graphics are virtually the same as the 1994 cups with Coke, NFL, and McDonald's logos. One of the cups shown here has all the NFL team names on it, so I assume that a cup is available for each team. $3.00 – 7.00 each.

1. All NFL teams listed, quarterback preparing to pass.
2. St. Louis Rams, quarterback preparing to pass.

1994 Super-Size Your Way to the Super Bowl at McDonald's, a set of two 7" paper cups showing NFL players in gridiron action and promoting the "200 Ultimate Superbowl XXIX Trips-for-2" giveaway sponsored by "Fox NFL Sunday." A panel on the side of each cup explains the rules. The main idea was to get customers to "Super-size any Extra Value Meal to get your Super ticket" on Super-Size Fry boxes and then to watch the "Pregame Show to see if you have a winning number." Coke, Fox NFL Sunday, and NFL logos appear on the cup along with the McDonald's "Questions ? Comments? See the Manager or Call 1-800-244-6227" and "Please Put Litter In Its Place" notices. $3.00 – 5.00 each.

3. Kansas City Chiefs Quarterback #12 being rushed by #95 Detroit Lions lineman.
4. Reverse of Kansas City Chiefs cup.
5. Buffalo Bills running back being tackled by #73 and #3 of the Rams.
6. Reverse of Buffalo Bills cup.

MISCELLANEOUS PAPER CUPS
Row 1.

1. 1987 5" milk shake cup with three bands of Arch logos in yellow, orange, and brown encircling it. Two "Please Put Litter In Its Place" notices in yellow appear on opposite sides of the cup in yellow just below the brown "Milk Shake" label. McDonald's logos in brown-outlined boxes appear on opposite sides of the cup, and a "Real" icon appears centered under "Milk Shake" just between those logos. Copyright date is on inside rim of base. $10.00 – 15.00.

1987 wax-coated paper cup like the one to its left listed above with three bands of yellow, orange, and brown arches encircling it, McDonald's logos in brown-outlined squares, and almost unreadable "Please Put Litter In Its Place" notices. This cup, however, does not have the "Milk Shake" label on it or the "Real" icon. It's the same in every other respect. This cup came in various sizes. I show the $3^3/_4$" and 5" cups here. $6.00 – 10.00 each.

2. $3^3/_4$" cup (no date or other information on inside bottom rim),

3. 5" cup (1987 copyright date and other information on inside bottom rim),

4. 1990 "Fun," "Food," and "Folks," a $4^5/_8$" courtesy cup featuring multicolored graphics of a hamburger, French fries, and a drink cup with a childlike drawing of Ronald McDonald on it. "Please Put Litter In Its Place" appears twice just below the rim. Obviously a cup for kids. Copyright date is on inside rim of base. $2.00 – 5.00.

5. 1990 McDonald's and Coca-Cola, a $6^3/_8$" cup with a predominantly red background showing a cheeseburger, French fries with McDonald's logo on them, and a Coke. Same design on both sides. Copyright date is on inside rim of base. $3.00 – 6.00.

Row 2.

1990 McDonald's logo with cheeseburger, French fries with McDonald's logo on them, and a Coca-Cola on a 5" cup. This scheme is repeated two and two-thirds times (there wasn't room for a third Coke). There appear to be at least two variations of this cup: some have "Please Put Litter In Its Place" on the seam in red letters, and others have the message in an almost unreadable yellow. The red probably replaced the yellow. Copyright date is on inside rim of base. Red litter message: $2.00 - 4.00; yellow litter message: $3.00 – 5.00.

1. 5" cup with "Please Put Litter In Its Place" in red on seam.

2. 5" cup with "Please Put Litter In Its Place" in yellow on seam.

©1990 "McDonald's" in red script at 45 degree angle with French fries above to left and cup of Coke below to right. This design is repeated twice on the cup. "Please Put Litter In Its Place" appears vertically near the seam on the cup, but on some cups that message is in red lettering, and on others it is in yellow. The yellow is almost unreadable so my guess is that it was replaced by the red. I show the 7" cups here; other sizes surely exist. Red litter message: $2.00 – 4.00; yellow litter message: $3.00 – 5.00.

3. 7" cup with red litter message.

4. 7" cup with yellow litter message.

MISCELLANEOUS PAPER CUPS

Row 1.

1. 1991 "McDonald's" in red and lavender script at 45 degree angle three times around this 3³/₄" courtesy cup with red and lavender confetti in background. Cup dated on inside rim of base in red. $2.00 – 3.00.

2. 1991 "McDonald's" in red script on 6³/₈" cup at 45 degree angle with cheeseburger above and to the right, French fries just below, and cup of Coke at the bottom. This design is repeated twice. "Put Litter In Its Place" appears in red vertically by the seam. But the interesting thing about this cup is that it has a pair of red Deluxe Monopoly game pieces on it (see "Monopoly" category). The earliest Monopoly cups I know of are the 1995 paper cups with game pieces. I'm not sure when the McDonald's Monopoly games started. The inside bottom rim of this cup has a 1991 copyright date. It's possible that the copyright date is not the actual issue date and that cups like this were used for the Monopoly promotions when stores ran out of Monopoly cups. Still, this is an odd cup. $5.00 – 10.00.

3. 1992 "McDonald's" in red script on 7" cup at 45 degree angle with French fries above and to the left and cup of Coke at the bottom right. This design is repeated twice. Just above one of the Coke cups are two red Monopoly Deluxe game pieces. This is a strange combination since the earliest Monopoly paper cups I know of date from 1995. The inside bottom of the rim of this cup has a 1992 copyright date. My inclination is to think that the copyright date is not the actual distribution date, and that cups like this were pressed into service when stores ran out of regular Monopoly contest cups. Another anomaly cup. $5.00 – 10.00.

4. ©1992 2¹/₈" sundae cup with "McDonald's" in red script, lavender brushstrokes in background, two McDonald's Arch logos in red blocks, and a childish line drawing of Ronald McDonald. Copyright date and other information appear in lavender on inside bottom rim. $4.00 – 7.00.

Row 2.

1. ©1992 Houston Livestock Show and Rodeo "sparkling for 60 years...February 15, March 1, 1992," a 6³/₈" cup commemorating the 60th anniversary of the show and promoting the show as "the largest livestock exhibition in the world with more than 25,000 entries annually." Texas McDonald's logos appear twice on the cup. $5.00 – 10.00.

2. ©1993 "Houston Livestock Show and Rodeo February 20, March 7, 1993," a 6³/₈" cup showing a McDonald's "Ranch" logo on the front along with the McDonaldland characters (Ronald, Grimace, Early Bird, Hamburglar, and fry creatures) in a rodeo context. The cup's reverse panel informs us that "The McDonald's Restaurants of the Greater Houston area are proud to be riding into the second decade as a supporter of the Houston Livestock Show and Rodeo." $5.00 – 10.00.

©1994 McDonald's in script at 45 degree angle beside cheeseburger, French fries with McDonald's logo on them, and Coca-Cola on one panel, a "Questions? Comments? See The Manager" logo on a second panel, and a cheeseburger and Coke on the third panel. But that's not all! This venerable design has undergone some other changes. "Please Put Litter In Its Place" appears in red in a wavy line near the seam. "Comments?" appears in a half circle lavender script above the Coke's straw on one panel; "Questions?" appears in a half circle lavender script just to the left of "McDonald's" on the main panel; and "See the Manager Or Call 1-800-244-6227" appears just to the left of the Coke on the main panel. But wait, there's an additional consideration: yellow/gold pigments were omitted during the printing of some of these cups resulting in a second cup with a remarkably different appearance. This "error" cup, having no yellow pigmentation, has an overall red, lavender, plum-colored look, actually quite attractive. Put the two versions of this cup side by side, and you will see what I mean. I assume that the cup without the normal yellow color is rarer than the "standard" cup and hence more desirable. (These cups may also be available in other sizes.) Full color cup: $2.00 – 4.00; cup without yellow color: $4.00 – 7.00.

3. 6³/₈" cup with full color.

4. 6³/₈" cup without yellow screening.

THREE MID 1990S PAPER CUPS

1. ©1994 "McDonald's" in red script at 45 degree angle with French fries above and Coke below; a large "Questions? Comments? See The Manager" graphic; and "McDonald's" once more with a cup of Coke below it. "Questions?" and "Comments?" appear in lavender text half circles, and "See The Manager Or Call 1-800-244-6227" appears as a linear two-line message in lavender. "Please Put Litter In Its Place" appears near the top of the cup in red in a wavy line. I show the 7" cup here, but there were probably other sizes as well. $3.00 – 5.00.

2. ©1995 "Buy Recycled and Save," a 5" cup which focuses on the benefits of recycling and even provides the address of McDonald's Department of Environmental Affairs. The front of the cup is standard for the mid 1990s, showing the then popular burger, Coke, and fries images along with the "Questions? Comments? See the Manager" logo. $5.00 – 10.00.

3. ©1996 "McDonald's Official Sponsor of the Ferris Wheel at Navy Pier," a 6" cup encouraging the patron to "Bring This Coupon to Navy Pier Park (in Chicago) to Receive One (1) FREE Ferris Wheel ride with the purchase of another Ferris Wheel Ride for $2.00." The customer had to cut the coupon out of the cup to get the free ride. Offer expired June 30, 1996. $4.00 – 7.00.

GENERAL PURPOSE PAPER CUPS

©1996 and ©1999 series of general purpose cups with large Arches and Coca-Cola sponsorship, red, blue, and yellow decoration, red measuring markings. Date in red on inside rim of bottom. Red litter icon near base. These cups come in at least four sizes and are dated either 1996 or 1999. The fifth cup shown here is a courtesy cup which shares the same general design but without the two Coca-Cola logos the other cups have. These cups have had a long run. They must have made a zillion of them. Collecting all the variations would be a serious challenge. $0.50 – 1.00.

Row 1: Five general purpose cups from the 1990s.

1. $4^5/_8$" cup (date not readable).
2. $6^3/_8$" cup (1996).
3. 7" cup, 4" mouth diameter (1996).
4. 7" cup, $4^1/_4$" mouth diameter (1999).
5. $4^5/_8$" courtesy cup, no Coca-Cola logos (date in black not readable).

Row 2: Two general purpose cups from England.

(2001) English version of cups shown above with large arches and Coca-Cola sponsorship (on .4 and .5 litre cups), red, blue, and yellow decoration. These cups are undated, but I got them in London in the summer of 2001. They are almost identical to the American cups of the same design, but these have metric fill line markings in red near the top and "www.mcdonalds.co.uk" vertically in blue on the seam. These cups also have two different recycling icons near the bottom in red: a circle (the earth) with an arrow on it and a person putting litter into a collection basket. Inside bottom rim information is in red and includes "Food Safe" along with various production numbers. $2.00 – 3.00 each.

1. .4 litre cup, $5^3/_8$" with Coca-Cola logo.
2. .5 litre cup, $6^9/_{16}$" with Coca-Cola logo.

GENERAL PURPOSE CUPS FROM ENGLAND AND AUSTRIA

English cups obtained in London in December of 2002. The smaller ("courtesy") water cup is 3½" high and has the Arches with red and yellow color blocks repeated three times in different sizes. Recycling and litter disposal icons appear near the bottom, and there is blue production information on the inside bottom rim. All in all, a very plain cup. The 4½" .25 litre cup to the right shares the same basic design with three different-sized Arch logos and the recycling and litter icons, but it also has a .25 litre fill line in red, a small red and yellow block logo, and McDonald's website address (www.mcdonalds.co.uk) in blue. Cup production information appears in red on the inside bottom rim. $1.00 – 2.00.

1. 3½" English "courtesy" cup (2002).
2. 4½" .25 litre English water cup (2002) left front view.
3. 4½" .25 litre English water cup (2002) reverse view with fill line.
4. Austrian version of English cup shown to left with large Arches and red, blue, and yellow graphics (without Coca-Cola logo). The small .25 litre cup (4⅝") shown here I found in Salzburg, Austria, in the summer of 2001. It also comes in .4 and .5 litre sizes with Coca-Cola logo. The cups have one recycling icon showing a person throwing recyclables into a collection basket. Inside bottom rim information is in red and includes no date but has "Food Safe" and various code numbers. $1.00 – 2.00 each.

PAPER CUPS FROM THE LATE 1990S

Row 1.

1. ©1997 "did somebody say McDonald's?," a 6³/₈" cup showing a grandmotherly-looking figure supervising a youngster riding a tricycle. A thought bubble with a McDonald's logo is shown coming out of the youngster's mouth. The "did somebody say McDonald's?" slogan appears vertically in red on a yellow panel on the cup. $3.00 – 6.00.

2. ©1997 3³/₄" courtesy cup with block logo, litter icon, and three variously sized newer Arch logos. Dated in red on inside bottom rim of base. Still being used and available as of January 2001. $0.25 – $0.50.

3. ©1997 5" cup urging the customer to "Start a Butterfly Garden" along with instructions on how to do it along with the admonition that "Helping the environment starts in your own backyard!" In fine print on this panel of the cup there is information about The National Wildlife Federation and McDonald's "Big Help" program. The front of the cup is less interesting since it just shows the late 1990s McDonald's logo, an older McDonald's block logo and the "Always Coca-Cola" logo. $4.00 – 7.00.

Row 2.

1998 "Cafe Blend McDonald's," 4¹/₈" and 5³/₈" paper coffee cups with white plastic sipping lid. On the seam in red: "Caution: Contents Hot!" On the reverse: "McDonald's Cafe Blend is a rich blend of 100% Arabica beans from Columbia, Costa Rica, and Guatemala — roasted dark and freshly ground for a bold, aromatic, delicious cup of coffee." $1.00 – 3.00.

1. 4¹/₈" cup. Inside bottom rim in black: "111-040 ©1998 McDonald's Corporation Printed In The U.S.A. (14396)."

2. Reverse view of above cup,

3. 5³/₈" cup. Inside bottom rim in black: "187-033 ©1998 McDonald's Corporation Printed In The U.S.A. (14396)."

4. 1999 "One Day. One Big Difference for the Kids." This medium-sized soft drink cup promotes "Happy Deal Day, October 4th, 1999." There's the usual late 1990s Arches on the front with a Ronald McDonald House Charities logo on the side, and the opposing panel gives details about the promotion: "$1.00 from every Big Mac Extra Value Meal will go directly to benefit Ronald McDonald House Charities! You can help make a difference in our community." This was a relatively short-lived, date specific promotion. $1.00 – 3.00.

TWO DIFFERENT SETS OF HAPPY MEAL PAPER CUPS

Row 1.

1999 Happy Meal cups featuring Hamburglar and Birdie the Early Bird, Ronald McDonald, and Grimace. These three 4¹/₂" cups feature the four most popular late nineties characters: a very young Hamburglar and equally young Birdie on one cup, Ronald, and Grimace along with two McDonald's logos and the www.ronald.com Internet address on the seam. There are slight variations in these cups. Some are more glossy than others; some are more waxy. Be prepared for inconsistencies and subtle variations. $0.50 – 1.00.

1. Hamburglar (front)
2. Birdie the Early Bird (reverse of cup to left)
3. Ronald McDonald
4. Grimace

Row 2.

2000 (redesigned) Happy Meal cups featuring the same characters as the 1999 lineup but slightly redesigned to include the vertical blue and white "We love to see you smile" slogan on the seam and the new "Smile" logo (also redesigned to look like it was executed by a child) to the upper left of each character's head. These cups came out in late 2000, but as I write this in 2004 I notice that the 1999 cups are back, and the "Smile" cups are no longer in use. $1.00 – 3.00.

1. Hamburglar and Birdie
2. Ronald McDonald
3. Grimace
4. Grimace (showing slogan and "Smile" logo of cup to left)

"OFFICIAL RESTAURANT" OLYMPIC CUP

1999 6³/₈" medium-sized soft drink cup with Olympic flame above the Golden Arches and the five Olympic rings below the Arches. "Official Restaurant" appears beneath the rings, and there's a round red Coke bottle logo on one side near the top. This red, blue, and yellow decorated cup is very similar in design to its ubiquitous late nineties predecessor, but it is slightly different in that it has a duller more waxy surface. There's also a less waxy paper version which has an obvious glossy surface. It probably comes in other sizes as well. (The date appears in blue on the inside of the bottom rim.) $0.50 – 1.00.

1. Olympic logo side (waxy surface)
2. Round Coca-Cola logo side (glossy surface)

1998 & 1999 MCFLURRY CUPS

These wax-covered thick paper cups are not actually drink containers but cups for the thick ice cream, nut, and candy concoction McDonald's calls the "McFlurry." I include them here because they look like cups and may in the future be regarded as cups. The cups come in two sizes: 3⁷/₈" and 4⁷/₈", but when the white plastic cap is applied, the cups stand an additional inch and a half higher. The cap has a 1⁷/₈" cutout in the top so that the McFlurry can be spooned out with a sturdy clear 7¹/₄" plastic spoon. Same design on both sides: a McDonald's logo above a whirling vortex-Milky Way Galaxy design in light and dark blue. The date appears on the inside bottom rim of the cups along with manufacturing and copyright information. Some of the cups were made in 1998 and have red printing on the inside bottom rim; others were made in 1999 and have blue writing on the inside bottom rim. We are warned near the bottom of the 1999 cups that this product "May contain nut products." The 1998 cups say that the McFlurry "May contain peanuts." Finally, I discovered when looking at the 3⁷/₈" cups closely that the 1999 cup easily fits inside the 1998 cup. When I measured their liquid capacity, I discovered that the 1999 cup holds about one tablespoon less liquid. $0.25 – 1.00; with cap and spoon add $0.50.

1. 3⁷/₈", 1998, "May Contain Peanuts," red writing on inside bottom rim.

2. 3⁷/₈", 1999, "May Contain Nut Products," blue writing on inside bottom rim.

3. 4⁷/₈", 1998, "May Contain Peanuts," red writing on inside bottom rim.

4. 3¹/₄", McFlurry cup from London, England (Summer 2001). This cup is undated and has the same white plastic cap that the US versions have, but the graphics are significantly different. On the inside bottom rim in red: "WRIN 06373-078 (91902) Fuer Nahrungsmittel – Food Safe – Pour Contact Alimentaire" which tells us that this cup is used in English, French, and German speaking European countries. $1.00 – 2.00.

A VARIETY OF PAPER CUPS

1. 3⁴/₈" courtesy cup. I first found this gayly decorated cup at the Slippery Rock, Pennsylvania, McDonald's in February of 2000. The designs on this "modern" millennium cup show a shake, fries, and Ronald McDonald, but the renderings are playfully childish and suggestive, rather than exact, especially those of Ronald. "Please put litter in its place" appears twice in a wavy black line on the cup. Colors are lavender, red, black, and yellow. Black print on inside rim of bottom is unfortunately not readable. This cup very closely resembles the ©1992 2¹/₈" cup described and pictured on page 114, row 1, #4. $0.50 – 1.00.

2. 3⁵/₈" courtesy cup found in Salzburg, Austria, summer 2001. This undated cup shows Ronald stepping out and waving his arms three times around the cup in three different sizes. On the inside rim of the bottom in black: "Per Alimenti - Wrin No 00101-076 — For Food Use — W.S.I. No.41915 — Pour Contact Alimentaire" which indicates that this cup was used in several European countries. $1.00 – 2.00.

©1999 "McDonald's Arching Into Education, Scholarship Program For NY Tri-State Students," 6³/₈" medium soft drink cup. Front of cup shows a graduating boy and girl in a circular frame along with a McDonald's logo. The reverse shows a larger McDonald's logo and small Coca-Cola logo along with this information: "McDonald's Restaurants In The NY Tri-State Area Give Students More Money For College. Ask Your Guidance Counselor For An Application Or Visit Our Website: www.mcdonaldsnymetro.com." In very small print near the bottom of the cup: "McDonald's offers more scholarship money in 2000 than in 1999." There's a 1999 copyright and other production information on the inside rim of the bottom of the cup. I found these cups in New York City and in western New Jersey in late February, 2000. $0.50 – 1.00.

3. Front view of "Scholarship" cup.

4. Reverse view of "Scholarship" cup.

5. ©Nov. 1999 25th HK Anniversary, Made in Hong Kong 5" cup. This wax-coated paper cup was available in Hong Kong from late 1999 into the first three months of 2000. It has red and yellow decoration with a large McDonald's logo and 25th HK Anniversary with some Chinese characters. $5.00 – 10.00.

©1999 "Join the Great American Cleanup," a 4³/₄" wax-coated paper cup which promotes "the nation's largest litter cleanup, beautification and community improvement program in cities and towns all across the country." The cup has the standard late 1990s graphics and Coca-Cola co-sponsorship. $0.50 – 1.00.

1. Reverse with "American Cleanup" graphics.

2. Front view of "Cleanup" cup with logo.

3. ©2000 "McDonald's Celebrates Black History Month." This large 7" cup has a large McDonald's logo on the front along with a small Coca-Cola logo. On the reverse there's a ten-question "It pays to know black history" quiz and an address to send one's answers to. The deadline for entries was March 19, 2000, and the prize was "a Premier Family Cruise." I found this cup in western New Jersey. It was probably distributed in New York also. 50¢ – 1.00.

©1999 "Try A New! Triple Thick Milkshake" set of two cups with clear plastic igloo caps with McDonald's Arches in the igloo doorways. These cups come in the standard late 1990s design with Coca-Cola co-sponsorship, but the milkshake graphics are new. Actually, though these cups have a 1999 copyright date on the inside rim of the base, they first appeared at McDonald's stores in January of 2001. $0.25 – $0.75.

4. Small 4³/₄" milkshake cup.

5. Medium 6¹/₄" milkshake cup.

"SMILE" LOGO PAPER CUPS

Left.

©2000 "we love to see you smile" drink cup with large McDonald's "Smile" logo and Coca-Cola and (Sydney Summer) Olympic sponsorships. The "Smile" logo was a summer 2000 introduction, and it lasted until late 2003/early 2004 when the "I'm lovin' it" slogan replaced it. "We love to see you smile" appears on a broad blue vertical strip on the seam of the cup. All cups are identical in design. $0.50 - $1.00.

1. Small size, 4³/₄", "Smile" cup.
2. Small size, 4³/₄", "Smile" cup, reverse view .
3. Medium size, 6³/₈", "Smile" cup.
4. Medium size, 6³/₈", "Smile" cup, another view.
5. Large size, 7", "Smile" cup.
6. Super size, 7", "Smile" cup.

Right.

©2001 "we love to see you smile" drink cup with large McDonald's "Smile" logo, blue vertical strip with "we love to see you smile" slogan," USA Proud Partner Olympic rings logo, and Coke logo. The cup design here is basically identical to the ©2000 issue, but there's one noticeable difference: this general purpose cup now shows a curved Coca-Cola contour bottle on its side with "Coca-Cola" superimposed on it. The cup comes in four sizes: small, medium, large, and super size. I show the small and medium cups here. $0.50 – $1.00.

1. Small size, 4³/₄", "Smile" cup.
2. Medium size, 6³/₈", "Smile" cup.

MISCELLANEOUS PAPER CUPS

Left.

2000 Ronald McDonald "Courtesy Cup" from Australia, summer 2000. This 3³/₄" paper cup features Ronald on one side with right hand raised. "Courtesy Cup" appears in red caps just above the Australian McDonald's logo on the reverse. A band of yellow Arches encircles the base of the cup. This cup is undated, but the person I got it from at the 2000 McDonald's National Convention in Chicago in early July assured me that it had just come from Australia. $4.00 – 8.00.

1. Ronald McDonald on front of Australian Courtesy cup.

2. Australian Courtesy cup showing Australian McDonald's logo.

3. 2000 "Britney Spears, The Music event of the summer…starting Aug 4," a medium-sized 6³/₈" cup promoting the "new music and video footage from both NSYNC & BRITNEY SPEARS" and "hot, new CDs" from "the Groove Collection" and "the Rhythm Collection." Right below the large "we love to see you smile logo" the customer is encouraged to "Buy this CD or Video at McDonald's 'Your #1 Requests…And More!' and you could Win!" Co-sponsored by Coca-Cola. $1.00 – 2.00.

2000 "Play to Win $1,000,000 Instantly…Taste Trials Game," a set of two cups featuring a gold Olympic game piece on a soccer ball hitting a player's forehead. The three most recent McDonald's logos appear on these cups along with a Coca-Cola logo and a USA Olympic logo. The cups promote the "Great Taste" of the Big Xtra, Crispy Chicken, and the Chicken McGrill. Both cups show the same prizes: "a trip to anywhere in the world," "Pontiac or GMC vehicles," a "Replay TV Showstopper from Panasonic and a PanaBlack TV," and "Over 200,000 prizes from At&T Prepaid…10 Free Minutes in U.S. Calls." Fine print near the seam informs us that the "Game is scheduled to end 10/12/00." $1.00 – 2.00; deduct $0.50 for missing gamepiece.

4. Large 7" Taste Trials cup.

5. Super size 7" Taste Trials cup.

Right.

2000 "McFamily Night," a 6³/₈" cup with the new "Smile" logo and co-sponsored by Sprite and the NBA and promoting special deals for families to go see various NBA "McFamily Night" games. The cup I show here promotes the Cleveland Cavaliers, has a large "CAV'S cavs.com" logo, and the pitch is as follows: "4 Cavs tickets, 4 McDonald's Meals, 1 single use Giant Eagle camera. All for $52.00…Choose from 19 exciting McFamily Night games, including: Celtics, Sixers, Raptors, Heat, Bucks, Knicks, Suns. For More Information Call 216.420.CAVS." I assume that there is a different cup offering the same deal for each of these teams and perhaps others not listed on this particular cup. So this could be a series much larger than the eight teams listed on this cup. Date and cup production information in blue on bottom inside rim. $1.00 – 3.00.

1. McFamily Night, front view with large family graphic.

2. McFamily Night, reverse view with promotion details and "Smile" logo.

2002 "McFamily Night," a 6³/₈" cup with a "We're here to help you" logo, toll-free telephone number, and Coca-Cola, Sprite, and NBA sponsorship promoting special deals for families to go see various NBA games. This cup, which closely resembles the 2000 cup shown to its left, came out in western Pennsylvania and highlights the Cleveland Cavaliers. The "McFamily Night" graphics on this cup are the same as the ones on the 2000 cup, but they are much smaller. The deal here is slightly different from the earlier one: "4 Cavaliers tickets, 4 McDonald's Meals, 1 single-use Giant Eagle camera. All for $56.00…Choose from 10 exciting games. Magic, Trail Blazers, Jazz, Pistons, Nuggets, Suns, Hornets, Hawks, Grizzlies. For More Information Call 1.800.332.CAVS." I assume that there is a different regional cup offering the same deal for each of these teams and perhaps others not listed on this particular cup. So this could be a series much larger than the ten teams listed on this cup. Date and cup production information in red on bottom inside rim. $1.00 – 3.00.

3. McFamily Night with small family graphic, promotion details, and city skyline graphic.

4. McFamily Night with large Arch logo and "We're here to help you" slogan.

5. 2003 "McFamily Night," a 6³/₈" paper cup promoting "4 Cavalier tickets" and "4 McDonald's Meals All For $64.00." The design of the cup is generally similar to its two predecessors, but there is less graphic clutter. The Cavaliers' logo has changed and is smaller, and now we have the "how are we doin'?" tagline and no Smile logo. The biggest change is that the cost of this night has risen to $64.00, and the number of games families can choose from has increased to "15 exciting games." Sprite is absent and Coca-Cola is back. $1.00 – 3.00.

MISCELLANEOUS PAPER CUPS

Left.

©2000 "Play Win on the Spot!," "McFlurry Play to Win a 102 Dalmations Poo-Chi Instantly!," a set of two paper cups which promote the November/December 2000 Disney *102 Dalmations* movie. These cups have "Heel! Peel! Play!" scratch-off game pieces which affirm that "3 of the SAME wins the Game INSTANTLY!" Patrons could win Tiger Electronics products. The game is "scheduled to end 12/21/00." $0.50 – 1.00 each.

1. Small McFlurry 102 Dalmations cup.

2. Large McFlurry 102 Dalmations cup.

3. ©2000 "A New Spin on Yo-Yos! from Yomega," a 4³/₄" paper cup promoting "6 Extreme Designs Awesome Colors Only $1.99 each + tax with any food purchase." This cup has the Smile logo and is co-sponsored by Coca-Cola. The six different yo-yos occupy most of the space on this cup which tells us that the promotion starts on November 21, 2000 "While supplies last at participating McDonald's. Recommended for ages 8 and up." $1.00 - $2.00.

4. ©2001 "new tastes Menu!," a 6³/₈" cup aimed at teenagers and urging them to "Take a break for a light quick bite!" Also on the cup: "Moms love it, too!," "Cool New Stuff," "Fun Favorites Made Just for You!," "A well deserved sweet treat." There's a Coca-Cola logo, two "Smile" logos, a large blue vertical "we love to see you smile" tagline strip, and McDonald's web address. I've found two variations of this cup: one with blue writing on the inside rim of the base and one with red writing on the inside rim of the base. A 7/23/04 *Wall Street Journal* article (A-11) reports that McDonald's second quarter profits for 2004 "increased 25%, driven by a wave of new menu items" and that income was up "47¢ a share…from 470.9 million, or 37¢ a share a year earlier. Revenue rose 10% to 4.73 billion, and systemwide sales…increased 11%." A good move for McDonald's. You can bet we'll see more cups that feature new menu items. $0.50 – 1.50.

5. ©2001 "Who Wants To Be A Millionaire…Play at McDonald's Starting April 19," a 6³/₈" paper cup which promotes the ABC Network game. The cup has a Coca-Cola logo, a picture of Regis pointing at us, and several happy people who have (presumably) won a million. There's also a large "Smile" logo and vertical "we love to see you smile" panel. The game pieces advertised on this cup were not available on other (plastic) cups but on French fry packages. The game was scheduled to end on 5/17/01. $0.50 – 1.00.

Right.

©2001 "Discover Two Worlds, One of taste. One of mystery. new tastes Menu!," a 6³/₈" cup promoting McDonald's New Tastes Menu and Disney's *Atlantis, The Lost Empire*. This cup pitches "Hearty Eggs Benedict McMuffin" and "Savory Hot Ham 'n Cheese." The cup has the "smile" logo on it along with a Coke logo and a vertical "we love to see you smile" slogan. $0.50 – 1.00.

1. New tastes menu front view.

2. New tastes menu reverse view.

3. 2001, 3⁵/₈", "McMorning All American Breakfast" paper cup with red, white, and blue stars and stripes design and folding paper handles (found in Munich, Germany, summer 2001). This cup has the metric fill line and number (0.2 litre) and warning in German: "Vorsicht, heisses Getrank!" A cute detail appears in black on the inside bottom: "I feel me so leer." On the inside of the bottom rim in red: "Pour Contact Alimentaire WSI No 41811 Food Safe Wrin 00232-117 Per Alimenti." $2.00 – 4.00.

4. 2001, 3$^{1}/_{2}$" paper coffee cup with brown and black graphics from Salzburg, Austria (summer 2001), with "McCafe Classico" on one side and "McCafe Jacobs" on the other. On the inside bottom rim in black: "Food Safe Wrin No 00232-189 WSI. No 13343." $2.00 – 4.00.

5. 2001, 6$^{3}/_{8}$" medium sized paper cup promoting "Upromise College Savings Accelerator" at "www.upromise.com." This is the ubiquitous McDonald's cup with large Arch design, "Smile" logo, and Coca-Cola contour bottle graphic. Date appears in blue on inside bottom rim. This cup was distributed in the fall of 2001. $0.50 – 1.00.

MISCELLANEOUS PAPER CUPS FROM 2001 AND 2002

Left.

1. 2001, 6$^{3}/_{8}$" medium sized paper cup promoting McDonald's "new M tastes menu!" Christmas tree lights adorn the top of the cup along with the injunction to "Turn on the Flavor with Merry — Good Tastes!" There's also the Coca-Cola Contour Bottle logo, McDonald's Smile logo, and USA Olympic Proud Partner logo. This cup was issued in December of 2001. $0.50 – 1.00.

2. ©2001, "Careful! It's really hot," a 3$^{5}/_{8}$" thick paper coffee cup from England with spiral galaxy design in brown and red with pitch in, hot, and recycling icons. On the vertical seam: "00232-255 (27798) ©2001 McDonald's Corporation." This cup is covered by a maroon plastic lid and was still in circulation in London in December of 2002. $1.00 - 3.00.

3. 2002, "Reach for it!," 6$^{3}/_{8}$" medium sized paper cup promoting the Salt Lake City Winter Olympics. This cup features a snowboarder in a red diamond along with the Salt Lake 2002 Proud Partner logo, USA Proud Partner flag, Salt Lake 2002 banner, and Coca-Cola script. $0.50 - $1.00.

4. 2002, "Dip the Chicken, Dig the Sauce!," a 6$^{3}/_{8}$" medium sized paper cup promoting McDonald's "new taste menu" and "New Chicken Select Strips." The front panel has the familiar Arches, "Smile" logo, and Coca-Cola in script; the reverse has a detailed listing of the chicken strips, sauces, and dips. $0.50 – 1.00.

Right.

2002 "how are we doin'? 1-800-244-6227 www.mcdonalds.com," 6$^{3}/_{8}$" medium and 7" large sized paper cups which came out about the same time as the 2002 Winter Olympics in Park City, Utah, obviously an attempt to deal with internal problems and marketing woes, the Monopoly scandal, mad cow disease fear in Europe, and falling stock value. The cups have the Coca-Cola script, Olympic "Proud Partner" graphics, and pitch in icon on them. $0.50 – 1.00 each.

1. Medium sized cup, red writing around inside rim of base.

2. Large cup, blue writing on inside rim of base.

3. 2002, "You're up late, so we're up late," 6$^{3}/_{8}$" medium sized paper cup which also features the "how are we doin'?" question with toll free number (1-800-244-6227) and Coca-Cola script. $0.50 – 1.00.

4. 2002, "Now on our New Tastes Menu! New! Grilled Chicken Flatbread Sandwich," a 6$^{3}/_{8}$" medium sized paper cup with the "how are we doin'?" question and toll free number and the Coca-Cola script. $0.50 – 1.00.

5. 2002, "Disney's Lilo & Stitch Only In Theatres! www.disney.com/stitch," a 6$^{3}/_{8}$" paper cup with the "how are we doin'?" question and toll free number and the Coca-Cola script. $0.50 – 1.00.

2002 WINTER OLYMPICS CUPS

2002, "how are we doin'? 1-800-244-6227 www.mcdonalds.com," 7" large and super size paper cups which came out in the winter of 2002 during the Olympics. These cups are almost identical to the medium cups shown on page 120, but these have the "Contour" Coke bottle on the side instead of the round Coke logo with Coca-Cola script. $0.50 – 1.00.

1. 7" large cup with "Contour" Coke bottle.
2. 7" super size with "Contour" Coke bottle.

MISCELLANEOUS PAPER CUPS

Left.

1. 2002 "November 20 at McDonald's, Save the date to help the world's children," a 6³/₈" paper cup promoting World Children's Day and McDonald's Ronald McDonald House Charities. The cup is crowded with other messages: "upromise," "how are we doin'?," Coca-Cola script, and the pitch in icon. $0.50 – 1.00.

2002 "pop & text 2 win!...popstars the rivals...win prizes only at McDonald's," a 6⁵/₈" English cup promoting a game with "McChoice" food prizes. This was a December 2002 promotion with a January 15, 2003, prize claim deadline date. Players tear out a perforated half-moon chunk of the cup near the rim to reveal a code which can be accessed by a mobile phone to see if they have won. Phoneless players can access the website: www.itu.com/pop stars to see if they have won. The promoter of this game was McDonald's Restaurants Ltd, 11 – 59 High Road, East Finchley, London N2 8AW. The cup came in medium and large sizes. $3.00 - 5.00.

2. English McChoice 5¹/₄" medium cup.

3. English McChoice 6⁵/₈" large cup front panel.

4. English McChoice 6⁵/₈" large cup side panel.

Right.

2003 "McDonald's Wants To Make You A V.I.P.," large and super size 7" cups which offer patrons "a chance to dine with basketball celebrities, watch a high-profile game, and groove at an all-star concert" by logging on to "mcdonalds.com or 365blackhistory.com for your shot to win!" by the sweepstakes end date of 5/19/03. These by now very familiar cups also have the "how are we doin'?," Coca-Cola, "Smile" logo, website address, and pitch in visuals on them. Date and other information in black on inside bottom rim. Large and super sizes. $0.50 – 1.00.

1. Large V.I.P. cup, sweepstakes end date 5/19/03 (reverse view).

2. Super Size V.I.P. cup, sweepstakes end date 5/19/03 (reverse view).

2003 "McDonald's Wants To Make You A V.I.P.," large and super size 7" cups which offer patrons a chance to "Score a getaway with 2 tickets to an NBA Opening Night Game!" by logging on to "mcdonald's.com, 365blackhistory.com, or NBA.com for your chance to win your NBA Platinum Pass!" by sweepstakes ending date of 7/21/03. These cups are generally similar to the cups listed above, but there are noticeable graphical design differences and of course the contest's expiration date is different. New to these cups are the NBA.com graphic and omission of the McDonald's website address at bottom of cup. Like its predecessors these cups have the "how are we doin'?," Coca-Cola, "Smile" logo, and pitch in visuals on them. Large and super sizes: $0.50 – 1.00.

3. Super size V.I.P. cup, sweepstakes end date 7/21/03 (reverse view).

(Not shown: large V.I.P. cup, sweepstakes end date 7/21/03).

2003 PAPER CUPS

Row 1.

1. 2003 "Disney — Pixar *Finding Nemo* May 30...SEA the movie! Then get a FIN-tastic Happy Meal toy!," a 6³/₈" medium sized cup with Coca-Cola, "how are we doin'?" and pitch in visuals but no "Smile" logo/tagline, which McDonald's abandoned in the fall of 2003 for the hipper "I'm Lovin' It" tagline. Date and other copyright information on bottom inside rim in red. $0.50 – 1.00.

2. 2003 "New! Premium Fresh Salads...They're a fresh new reason to come to McDonald's!," a medium sized 6³/₈" cup proclaiming McDonald's "deathbed conversion to more healthful food" (*Business Week*, 8/25/03, page 46). As McDonald's followers know, 2002 was a disappointing year for the franchise which "announced its first ever quarterly loss on Dec. 17" and shut down 175 outlets worldwide (*Business Week*, 1/13/03, page 50). Fast food patrons are no doubt aware that McDonald's came late to the salad party which Wendy's and other sandwich chains were so successfully hosting. According to *The Wall Street Journal* (6/12/03), "strong demand" for the salads "resulted in a 6.3% increase in May comparable-unit sales in the U.S." The usual motifs, minus the "Smile" logo appear: "how are we doin'?," Coca-Cola, and pitch in icon. Date and copyright information in red on inside bottom rim. $0.50 – 1.00.

3. 2003 "Taste what's in! New McGriddles Breakfast Sandwiches," a medium sized 6³/₈" cup promoting what *Business Week* (8/25/03, page 46) describes as a "gut-busting" sandwich containing "550 calories, 33 grams of fat, and 260 milligrams of cholesterol," a sandwich which has "sparked a cult-like fascination" and sent "McDonald's morning sales soaring," making June "the highest breakfast sales month for McDonald's in thirteen years." The cup has the "how are we doin'?" tagline, Coca-Cola script, and pitch in icon. Date and copyright information in dark blue on inside bottom rim. $0.50 – 1.00.

4. 2003 "Are You Mac Enough? You bet your sesame seed bun!," a medium sized 6³/₈" cup offered in the summer of 2003 to stimulate interest in the franchise's revitalized offerings. The cup has the "how are we doin'?" tagline, Coca-Cola script, and pitch in icon. $0.50 – 1.00.

Row 2.

1. 2003 "Triple Thick Milkshake...New! Raspberry," a 4³/₄" cup touting "the thickest, most delicious milkshake McDonald's has to offer." This small cup, which came out in the spring of 2003, carries the Smile logo and Coca-Cola script. Date is in red on inside bottom rim. $0.50 – 1.00.

2. 2003 "I'm lovin' it," 6⅜" paper cup showing a mom blowing bubbles for her daughter. The bubbles materialize on the cup as spheres with McDonald's new tagline in a selection of the world's major languages. There's also the Olympic Proud Partner logos (Athens 2004), Coca-Cola contour bottle, two Golden Arch logos, and a "how are we doin'?" panel. Although this cup bears a 2003 copyright on its inside bottom rim (red printing), it did not appear in most stores until well into January of 2004. This cup also comes in a small 4¾" size, shown below. It is my belief that this cup and the one listed below were the first "I'm lovin' it" cup designs to be introduced. $0.50 – 1.00.

3. 2003 "I'm lovin' it," 6⅜" paper cup showing a youngster on roller blades on a path composed of McDonald's new tagline slogan in a selection of the world's most used languages. There's also the Olympic Proud Partner logos (Athens 2004), Coca-Cola contour bottle, two Golden Arch logos, and a "how are we doin'?" panel. Although this cup bears a 2003 copyright on its inside bottom rim (on some cups the printing is red, on others blue), it did not appear in most stores until well into January of 2004. $0.50 – 1.00.

2004 "I'M LOVIN' IT" CUPS

Spring 2004 "I'm lovin' it" cup explosion! By the spring of 2004 this series of cups had grown greatly with an amazing variety of sizes and graphics, all with the same basic elements (described above). Most of the cups bear 2003 copyright dates, and 2004 versions have begun to carry advertising for various promotions. I cannot presume to guess how many different cups there might be in this issue and design, but it's clear that it has found favor with the public and will be around for some time. The 2004 Athens Olympics undoubtedly gave these cups additional lift. I show a variety of the cups below. $0.50 – 1.00 each.

Row 1.

1. Small 4¾": mom blowing bubbles for child (©2003 blue rim writing).

2. Small 4¾": mom blowing bubbles for child (©2004 red rim writing) with smaller front graphic and reverse of cup with graphic of Neopets Happy Meal Promotion "May 28th thru June 24th" (front view).

3. Reverse view of Neopet Happy Meal promotion.

4. Small 4¾": Soccer goalie in midair making save (©2003 red rim writing).

5. Medium 6⅜": Soccer goalie in midair making save (©2003 blue rim writing).

Row 2.

1. Large 7": Female gymnast (©2003 red rim writing).

2. Small 4¾": Smiling woman standing in rain catching raindrops (©2003 red rim writing).

3. Medium 6⅜": Smiling woman standing in rain catching raindrops (©2003, comes in both blue and red rim writing).

4. Super size 7": Smiling woman standing in rain catching raindrops (©2003 red rim writing).

5. Medium 6⅜": Smiling woman doing stair climbing exercise on front; "finally, a Happy Meal for me — Go Active Happy Meal, for adults" on reverse (©2004 red rim writing).

6. Reverse view of "Go Active" cup listed above and shown to left.

PAPER CUPS PROMOTING MOVIES

Row 1.

1. 1991 "E. T. Adventure at Universal Presented by AT&T, Universal Studios Hollywood, and USAir," a 6³/₈" cup with game piece, same graphics both sides. $7.00 – 11.00.

2. 1992 "Universal Studios McMovie Magic," a 6³/₈" cup with Universal Studios-McMovie Magic game piece. Some of the prizes listed: 1992 Mercury Sable LS, Southwest Airlines flights, and Extra Value Meals. $6.00 – 9.00.

3. 1993 "Yabba-Dabba-Doo! Roc Donald's," a 7" cup which promotes the 1993 *Flintstones* movie. Co-sponsored by Coca-Cola. $4.00 – 7.00.

1995 *Batman Forever*, a set of two 7" cups featuring a Gotham City background and the major Batman movie characters. "Always Coca-Cola; Questions? Comments?" and McDonald's logos appear on each cup. $3.00 – 8.00.

4. Batman and Robin.

5. Two-Face and Riddler.

Row 2.

1. 1996 "*James and the Giant Peach*, Only at a theatre near you!," a 5" cup with "Enjoy Hi-C" co-sponsorship. $2.00 – 4.00.

1996 "Warner Brothers Space Jam, McDonald's Is The Place For Space Jam Characters," a set of two 7" cups featuring Michael Jordan and various Warner Brothers cartoon characters. Patrons are encouraged to "Collect All 6" Space Jam stuffed characters. $4.00 – 7.00.

2. Michael Jordan, Tasmanian Devil, Bugs *Space Jam* cup

3. Frankenstein and space monsters *Space Jam* cup

4. 1996 "Warner Bros. *Space Jam*, Watch the Looney Tunes Slam Dunk the Monstars…With A Little Help From Michael Jordan!," a 6³/₈" cup which advises "Earthlings" that "Stuffed Characters From the Movie *Space Jam* Have Landed At McDonald's" and that they should "Collect All 6." $4.00 – 7.00.

OLYMPIC PAPER CUPS

Left.

©1987 McDonald's USA, Sponsor of the 1988 U.S. Olympic Team/Proud Partners In The Olympic Dream. These red, blue, and yellow decorated cups came in several sizes and were used widely for several months during the Olympic games in 1988. I show the 4½" and 5" sizes here. $5.00 – 10.00.

1. 4½" 1988 Proud Partner cup.

2. 5" 1988 Proud Partner cup.

3. 1989 US Olympic Festival Torch Run, a 7" cup with "U.S. Olympic Festival '89 Tickets Call 1-800-USA-OK89" around the top rim and "Discover Oklahoma 1-800-652-6552 Tourism Information" around the bottom. The cup shows Olympic athletes in action against a purple and white striped background. Co-sponsored by Coca-Cola Classic. $5.00 – 10.00.

1991 "McDonald's Helping Olympic Dreams Come True," a set of three cups featuring the well-known format of the cheeseburger, French fries, and Coke. "Helping" is positioned right above "Olympic" in small blue letters, and "Come True" is positioned right below "Dreams" in small blue letters. "Please Put Litter In Its Place" appears in a blue wavy line right below the upper package of French fries and again in a red wavy line below the cup's largest cheeseburger. These cups also feature, near the bottom, a blue globe with a McDonald's block logo and USA Olympic rings logo on it. $4.00 – 7.00 each.

4. 4¾" Olympic Dreams cup.

5. 5" Olympic Dreams cup.

6. 6⅜" Olympic Dreams cup.

Right.

1. ©1995 (on inside rim of base) "Atlanta 1996 McDonald's Olympic Games Giveaway, Official Break of The Olympic Games," a 7" cup with a "Pull To Play" McDonald's Olympic game piece on its front. "Atlanta 1996" appears vertically in large blue letters on one panel along with a "Questions? Comments?" logo and an "Always Coca-Cola" logo. Another panel lists the prizes that players can win. $2.00 – 4.00; deduct $1.00 for missing game piece.

©1996 Atlanta Olympics "when the USA wins, you win!," a set of two 7" cups with attached game pieces urging McDonald's patrons to "Play for Millions of prizes!" Icons depicting Olympic summer sports encircle the top of each cup. The "Always Coca-Cola" logo appears near the bottom of each cup. $2.00 – 4.00 each; deduct $1.00 for missing game piece.

2. Green band at top, purple background below. Prizes listed: "$1,000,000, All New 1997 Pontiac Grand Prix, Trips for four to any Sea World or Busch Gardens Park, Free McDonald's Food, Free Coca-Cola for One Year, $5 in McDonald's Gift Certificates."

3. Purple band at top, green background below. Prizes listed: "$1,000,000; Sports Illustrated 1996 Summer Games Commemorative Magazines; $10,000, $500 & $25 Cash Prizes; Hanes Licensed 1996 U.S. Olympic Team T-Shirts; Free McDonald's Food."

©1996, "Atlanta 1996...Proud Sponsor...Official Break of the Olympic Games," a set of 7" cups with "Always Coca-Cola" logos and large McDonald's Olympic logos. Each cup has an icon which highlights a specific Olympic sport. There are almost certainly other cups in this series. $1.00 – 3.00 each.

4. Athletics.

5. USA Basketball.

OLYMPICS PAPER CUPS

Left.

©1996 "Atlanta 1996...Proud Sponsor...Official Break of the Olympic Games," a series of 6^3/$_8$" cups, each of which features an icon which represents an Olympic sport. One panel of the cup has a large "Proud Sponsor" McDonald's logo, and there's also an "Always Coca-Cola" logo near the top by the seam. I'm not sure how many cups make up this set. $1.00 – 3.00 each.

1. Athletics.

2. USA Basketball.

3. USA Gymnastics.

1996 Atlanta Olympics "when the USA wins, you win!," a set of two 6^3/$_8$" cups with attached game pieces. Three icons of various Olympic summer sports appear on each side of the game piece. There's also a "2 Ways to Play & Win!" panel and a panel showing some of the prizes. "Always Coca-Cola" and McDonald "Proud Sponsor" logos appear near the bottom of the cups. The prizes shown on each of the cups are different, and the predominant background color of each of the cups is different also. $2.00 – 4.00 each; deduct $1.00 for missing game piece.

4. Predominantly purple cup; prizes shown: $1,000,000; IBM Aptiva Multimedia Computer Systems; Panasonic Mini Systems with CD Changer; Kodak Cameo Motor EX Cameras; Free McDonald's Food.

5. Predominantly green cup; prizes shown: $1,000,000; All New 1997 Pontiac Grand Prix; Trips for Four to any Sea World or Busch Gardens Park; Champion Licensed U.S. Olympic Team Replica Jackets; Free McDonald's Food.

Right.

1. 1998 Nagano "Official Restaurant Where the World's Best Come Together," co-sponsored by Coca-Cola Worldwide Olympic Partner 1928 – 1998, a 6^1/$_2$" cup with red, yellow, and blue decoration. $1.00 – 3.00.

©2000 McDonald's Proud Partner Summer Australian Olympic Series with "Enjoy Coca-Cola" co-sponsorship. These cups feature generic images of athletes performing along with quoted personal statements by former Olympic medal winners. These are very striking cups with nice graphics. I don't know how many different cups or sizes there were, but I assume it was a very large promotion. $3.00 – 5.00 each.

2. 5", "Modern Pentathlon tested my every resolve, every fibre of my body from the tip of my hair to the soles of my feet...At the end of competition I knew I had faced a great test and survived." Peter Macken, Olympian Modern Pentathlon.

3. 6^5/$_8$", "Participating in the Olympic Games gives you the opportunity to stand up one day in your life...and ask the question, 'am I good enough.'" Justin Lemberg, Olympian Swimming.

4. 6^5/$_8$", "For me the Olympic Games are like your final exam at Secondary School. It is the ultimate test to determine how you will be rewarded...after years of learning, training, and sacrifices." Russell Mark, Olympian Shooting.

5. 6^5/$_8$", "Every athlete who trains and competes in the Olympic Games...is a winner." Jeff Van De Graaf, Olympian Swimming.

2004 "GET INTO THE GAMES" PAPER CUPS

2004 "get into the games at McDonald's" Athens Olympics paper cups series. These 6³/₈" medium size cups began appearing in June of 2004, just in time for the Athens Olympics. They are strikingly similar to the "I'm lovin' it" cups, but that tagline does not appear on them. Olympic hopefuls are pictured with appropriately clever text designs. I do not know how many different cups there will be in this set. Coca-Cola contour bottle and Olympic rings appear on the reverse along with the "how are we doin'?" tag line. $0.50 – 1.00.

1. Tim Duncan, Olympian. Thirsts for victory.
2. Diana Munz, Olympian. Speedy in liquid.
3. Carly Patterson, U. S. Gymnast. Flips for McDonald's.
4. Reverse view of Carly Patterson cup

2004 "GET INTO THE GAMES" PAPER CUPS

The 2004 "get into the games" series now includes small and large cups featuring additional sports. The Tim Duncan medium size cup has been modified to carry McDonald's "when you're up, we're up" advertising slogan on its reverse. The "get into the games" tagline does not appear on this redesigned Tim Duncan cup, but all the design elements appearing on the Tim Duncan cup above are present here, although they are slightly rearranged. $0.50 – 1.00.

1. Marion Shirley, U.S. Paralympion. Never runs on empty (small 4³/₄" cup).
2. Steven Lopez, Olympian. Gets a kick out of McDonald's (large 7" cup).
3. Misty May and Kerri Walsh, Olympians. Dig McDonald's (large 7" cup).
4. "when you're up, we're up," a 6³/₈" cup with Olympian Tim Duncan on the other side.

TWO 1994 WORLD CUP SOCCER CUPS

1. 1994 World Cup USA, 6³/₈" cup featuring soccer player in black and white and with little red, blue, and yellow squares and rectangles in the background. McDonald's USA World Cup 94 and Coke logos also appear on the cup. $3.00 – 6.00.

2. 1994 McDonald's World Cup USA, "Trophy Watch" 7" cup featuring a player in black and white. A "Trophy Watch" panel on the reverse lists the champions from 1970 through 1990 and suggests that Germany is the "team to beat" but that the "U.S.A. can't be counted out!" Co-sponsored by Coke. $3.00 – 6.00.

PITCHERS

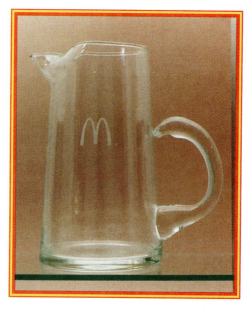

McDonald's pitchers are uncommon and were available only through company catalogs, by chance at meetings and conventions, or as special premiums to employees.

8⁵/₈" clear glass pitcher with one-inch high frosted McDonald's logo on side to left of handle. $50.00 – 75.00.

FIVE PLASTIC CHRISTMAS CUPS

Set of three undated 5½" cups with Christmas motifs and "Enjoy Coca-Cola" logo. On the bottom: "The Collectibles, Canada Cup Inc., Toronto. Made in Canada." $3.00 – 5.00 each.

Row 1.

1. Santa waving.

2. Snowmen wearing colorful scarves.

3. Reindeer.

Row 2.

1. 1992 McDonald's Christmas. A red 5⅝" red-ribbed cup with green holly boughs and McDonald's name in gold with black-outlined script and silver bars at a 45 degree angle made by Sterling Products, Winchester, Virginia. Barely visible on this cup are small gold Coca-Cola Classic and McDonald's logos below the central graphic. $2.00 – 4.00.

2. 1994 McDonald's Christmas. This is a jumbo red 6¾" cup with the same design as its 1992 predecessor: "McDonald's" in gold outlined in black, holly sprig below, gold Coca-Cola Classic and McDonald's logos, and silver decorated bars at a 45 degree angle. Made by Sterling Products, Winchester, Virginia. $2.00 – 4.00.

MINUTE MAID JUICE CUPS AND A CHILD'S TRAY AND CUP SET

Row 1.

1. McDonald's 6 oz. "Minute Maid Premium 100% Pure Squeezed Orange Juice" plastic cup with foil seal. This little plastic tumbler has twelve indented arched vertical columns with McDonald's Arches embossed into the top of each one. A colorful foil seal with a 1998 copyright date serves as a peel-off cap. On the bottom: "109 Sweetheart Plastics, INC. J73M." A cup identical to this one comes with apple juice in it. I don't know if these will ever be collectible or if anyone will go to the trouble of putting some of them aside, but someday someone might want to know about them. I show the cups lying on their sides in order to show the top foil covers which are much easier to photograph than the foggy plastic cups! $0.50 – 2.00.

2. McDonald's 10 oz. "Minute Maid Premium 100% Pure Squeezed Orange Juice" plastic cup with a foil seal. This foil seal serves as a peel-off cap and has a 1998 copyright date. The plastic tumbler has three bands of arches encircling it and a McDonald's block logo on opposite sides. On the bottom: "M-60 J1OM 77 0593 (recycling symbol 6) PS." My guess is that it won't occur to most people to save cups like this, so if you do, you could very well be in the "Catbird Seat" in 2099! $0.50 – 2.00.

Row 2.

Red 2^1/$_8$" plastic cup with yellow Arches encircling it. This cup set was designed for kids, and it sits in an indented circular enclosure on a yellow plastic food tray with a gray sponge base. There are no markings anywhere on this set, so dating and manufacturing identification are problematical. My guess is that this set was issued in the late 1990s. $2.00 – 6.00.

EARLY TO MID 1970s McDONALDLAND CHARACTERS ON PLASTIC CUPS
Row 1.
McDonaldland characters in static poses, undated set of six 5" cups. These yellow cups show the McDonaldland characters in static early to mid-seventies poses. They are probably contemporaneous with the mid-seventies glass tumblers showing the same images, but they may have been issued as early as 1973 when the 5th Anniversary Hawaiian set appeared (page 140 bottom). The character's name and a McDonald logo appear on the back of each cup. The McDonald's Arch logo is embossed on the bottom of each cup. There's also a Canadian version of this series with the same character images but with the name of each character in French on the reverse. Hard to find in nice condition. American versions: $7.00 – 15.00 each; Canadian versions: $10.00 – 25.00 each.
1. Ronald McDonald
2. Ronald McDonald (reverse view)
3. Hamburglar
4. Captain Crook

Row 2.
1. Captain Crook (reverse view)
2. Big Mac
3. Mayor McCheese/Maire-Au-Fromage (Canadian version)
4. Mayor McCheese/Maire-Au-Fromage (reverse of Canadian version)
(Not shown: Grimace, if he exists as part of this series. It may be that in 1973 the McDonaldland character lineup was not completely established.)

REVERSE VIEWS OF CANADIAN PLASTIC McDONALDLAND CUPS
1. Hamburglar/Pique-Burger (reverse of Canadian version)
2. Ronald McDonald (reverse of Canadian version)

THREE HAWAIIAN 5TH ANNIVERSARY McDONALDLAND CUPS
These 5" yellow plastic cups have the same character images that the U.S. and Canadian versions have, but there's location-specific information on the reverse celebrating McDonald's presence on the various islands that comprise Hawaii. I'm not sure how many cups there are in this set (I believe the fourth cup may be Captain Crook), but I do know that these cups are quite rare. Some of these cups have McDonald's Arch logo on the bottom, and others don't. Of the ones I show here, Ronald and Hamburglar have the logo on the bottom, and Big Mac does not. Reverse of cups shown here since the character images are the same on the American and Canadian versions. Since 1993 was McDonald's 25th Anniversary in Hawaii, these cups date from 1973. $15.00 – 25.00 each.
1. 5th Anniversary in Hawaii, McDonald's In Kahului, Big Mac
2. 5th Anniversary in Hawaii, McDonald's In Lihue, Hamburglar
3. 5th Anniversary In Hawaii, McDonald's On Oahu, Ronald McDonald
Not shown: 5th Anniversary in Hawaii, McDonald's, Captain Crook (?)

1978 CHARACTER-ZOO ANIMAL INTERACTION SERIES

©McDonald's System, Inc. 1978 set of four. These yellow plastic cups, which come in both 5" and 3³/₄" versions, show the McDonaldland characters in playful interaction with animals at the zoo. Condition is everything with these cups as with the earlier ones shown. The shorter version is quite hard to find and commands a much higher price. 5" version, $5.00 – 10.00; 3³/₄" version, $10.00 – 25.00.

Left.
1. Ronald McDonald jumping rope with two monkeys turning the rope.
2. Hamburglar taking picture of himself with zebra.
3. Hamburglar taking picture of himself with zebra (short version).
4. Grimace in tug of war with elephant.
5. Captain Crook in boat playing toss the ball with a seal.

Right.
1. Monkeys on back of Ronald McDonald cup.
2. Camera on back of Hamburglar cup.
3. Pink elephant on back of Grimace cup.
4. Seal on back of Captain Crook cup.

WHITE 1980 CHARACTER-ZOO INTERACTION SERIES

©McDonald's System, Inc. 1980 set of four white cups. These cups share the same motifs and designs with the 1978 yellow plastic set, but these cups are a bit shorter at 4³/₄". They are also much harder to find than the yellow ones. If a 3³/₄" version exists, it is quite rare. An inscription on the bottom of these cups says "Nichols-Kusan, Inc. Jacksonville, Texas." $10.00 – 15.00 each.
1. Grimace in tug of war with elephant.
2. Variation of #1 above: Elephant on reverse is filled in with pink color.
3. Hamburglar taking picture of himself with zebra.
4. Ronald McDonald jumping rope with two monkeys turning the rope.
5. Captain Crook in boat playing ball with seal.

TWO PLASTIC CHARACTER SETS FROM THE 1990S

Row 1: 1993 set of four acrylic juice tumblers.

1993 4¼" thick clear acrylic juice tumbler set of four showing the McDonaldland characters in a circus context. These little tumblers were part of a kids' dinner service set. Made in Taiwan. Hard to find in nice condition. $4.00 – 8.00 each.

1. Ronald & Hamburglar in front of Ferris wheel, Grimace in front of tent with balloon (Ronald and Hamburglar view).
2. Grimace, tent, and balloon view of #1 above.
3. Ronald McDonald and Birdie with balloons and confetti.
4. Ronald McDonald, Hamburglar, and Grimace on roller coaster.
5. Hamburglar and Birdie on carousel.

Row 2: 1996 set of four Australian "Crazy Feet" mugs.

1996 McDonald's Australia Ltd., set of four McDonaldland "Crazy Feet" mugs for kids. These 3½" plastic mugs were made in China for McDonald's of Australia. Each mug features the head of a McDonaldland character and came in a sealed plastic envelope which said "McDonaldland Crazy Feet Mug" and had black line drawings of the four characters in the series. "©1996 McDonald's/China" appears at the center of the base of each cup. $4.00 – 7.00. each with plastic wrapper intact; $3.00 – 5.00 without plastic.

1. Birdie (rose with yellow feet).
2. Grimace (all purple).
3. Hamburglar (orange with white feet).
4. Ronald McDonald (yellow with red feet).

EARLY PLASTIC McDONALDLAND CHARACTER CUPS

Left.

1. Uncle O'Grimacey, early to mid 1970s 5" plastic cup depicting our purple US Grimace's green Irish uncle wearing a shamrock vest and brandishing a walking stick. This cup was used in the US for St. Patrick's Day beverage (shamrock milkshake) promotions. According to John Love (*Behind the Arches*), "the idea originated in the early 1970s with Hal Rosen, a franchisee in Connecticut" (311). It is a fairly difficult cup to find in good condition. $10.00 – 25.00.

2. Ronald McDonald standing with hands outspread on a yellow plastic cup. This is an early version of Ronald probably from the late 1960s to the early 1970s. On bottom: "PAT. PEND./2/5117." Another, seen on eBay, had "Mutual Plastics, La Mirada, California CD-16-2" on bottom. $10.00 – 15.00.

3. Ronald McDonald running over the countryside after a hamburger-like flying saucer on a 5" yellow plastic cup. On the bottom: "PT. NO. 3300 16 OZ. LPO (logo) Chicago Ridge ILL." Another early version of Ronald. $10.00 – 15.00.

Right.

1. McDonaldland characters on a 5" yellow plastic cup made by "Somerville Plastics" in "Bramalea, Ont. Canada/860." This early cup probably dates to the early 1970s and features early versions of the McDonaldland characters in static poses. Characters shown are a pear-shaped Ronald McDonald, McCheese (not Mayor McCheese), Gobblin, Apple Pie Tree, a rather nasty looking Hamburglar, Captain Crook, and Big Mac. $10.00 – 15.00.

2. McDonaldland characters on a 5$^1/_{16}$" early 1970s yellow plastic cup that, the bottom tells us, was "Made in U.S.A." This cup's graphics are identical to those on the Canadian version listed above and to its left, but this cup's shape is different: it has a wide lip which protrudes very noticeably and a $^3/_4$" high slightly indented band around the bottom. $10.00 – 15.00.

3. McDonaldland characters on 5$^1/_4$" yellow plastic cup which closely resembles the two cups listed above and shown to its left. However, close examination reveals that the graphics are larger, and "McCheese" is now "Mayor McCheese." Finally, because of the larger graphics, the Apple Pie Tree had to be sacrificed. This cup has a $^3/_8$" high slightly indented band around the base. The only writing on the bottom is numbers: "5392" on one side of the base and 62 on the other. $10.00 – 15.00.

MISCELLANEOUS 1980s PLASTIC MUGS AND CUPS

Row 1.

1. 1980 McDonald's Canada party cup with Ronald on a tricycle with Gobblins in background and a grid on one panel for children to draw picture of Ronald. $5.00 – 8.00.

2. 1981 Ronald McDonald Valentine Cup showing Ronald in a heart-shaped frame with Grimace and Hamburglar releasing hearts into the air with "I Love You" and "Be My Valentine." $2.00 – 4.00.

3. 1981 Ronald McDonald yellow plastic figural mug. $5.00 – 10.00.

4. Ronald McDonald, a $3^5/8$" thick white Canadian plastic mug showing Ronald McDonald's head and upper body. The Arches on Ronald's pocket have a maple leaf beneath them, so we know this is a Canadian mug. Bottom says: "Dishwasher Safe, Top Rack Only, Made in Canada." Mug is not dated but probably belongs to the early to mid 1980s. $8.00 – 15.00.

5. 1982 "Happy Birthday Cup," a $5^1/8$" Sweetheart cup showing Grimace, Fry Guys, and Hamburglar with balloons and Ronald with a birthday cake all in the context of "Happy Birthday Cup" repeated around the cup in large letters. $5.00 – 10.00.

Row 2.

1. 1983 Happy Birthday, a white plastic cup with McDonaldland characters following Ronald in a parade over the words "Happy Birthday." Characters shown: Ronald McDonald beating a "Party Parade" drum, Gobblins, Hamburglar, Mayor McCheese, Grimace, and Birdie the Early Bird. $4.00 – 7.00.

2. 1983 "McDonald's + You!," a $5^1/8$" Sweetheart cup showing Birdie, Ronald, Hamburglar, Grimace, and Fry Guys under a tree that has "McDonald's + You!" on its trunk. A Fry Guy is holding a watering can and pouring hearts from it onto white flowers in the foreground. $4.00 – 7.00.

3. 1983 McDonald's Fun Cup, a white plastic cup with McDonaldland characters on amusement park rides, Gobblin and Hamburglar on Ferris wheel; Birdie, Grimace, Ronald, and Gobblin on roller coaster. $4.00 – 7.00.

4. 1983 McDonald's "Going Places Cup" showing Ronald driving truck with Fry Guy, Big Mac in Harbor Patrol Boat, Grimace in red car, and Birdie in airplane. $3.00 – 6.00.

5. 1983 McDonald's Colorado, a $5^1/8$" Sweetheart cup showing Birdie, Grimace, Ronald, and Hamburglar in winter gear posing in front of a ski resort in the mountains. $8.00 – 12.00.

MUGS, CUPS, AND A BOWL FROM THE 1980S

Row 1.

1 & 2. 1983, thick-walled plastic mug with figure eight handle and sipping lid with spout and cover. Lid has a "My Mug" space for the owner to write his or her name. There's also a white McDonald's logo on the lid. The mug and its accompanying plastic bowl show Mayor McCheese, Grimace, Captain Crook, Hamburglar, Ronald McDonald, and a Gobblin (but not Big Mac). Mug: $3.00 – 5.00, Bowl: $3.00 – 5.00.

3. 1983, thick-walled plastic mug with figure eight handle and sipping lid. This mug features the Hamburglar who is shown twice on the mug spreading his cape. $3.00 – 5.00.

4. 1983, thick-walled plastic mug with orange figure eight handle and sipping lid showing Hamburglar spreading his cape. This mug is special because it advertises a "Free Sundae Sampler through May 31, 1983. Bring this mug to any participating McDonald's for a free 3 oz. Sundae sampler. Offer limited to kids 12 years old and under when accompanied by a parent or adult. Only one sampler per child per visit. ©1983 McDonald's Corporation. The names, characters and designs are trademarks owned by the McDonald's Corporation." Made by Whirley Industries, Warren, Pennsylvania. $10.00 – 15.00.

5. 1983, thick-walled plastic mug with figure eight handle and sipping lid. This mug shows Grimace spreading his flippers in the same pose three times. $3.00 – 5.00.

Row 2.

1. 1983, thick-walled plastic mug with figure eight handle and sipping lid. This mug features one picture of Ronald McDonald with his arms spread wide. $3.00 – 5.00.

2. 1984, "We Wish You A Merry Christmas," a 5⅛" Sweetheart cup featuring Grimace, Ronald, Hamburglar, and two Fry Guys singing Christmas carols. $3.00 – 5.00.

3. 1985, thick-walled plastic mug with orange figure-eight handle and orange sipping lid. This mug features Mayor McCheese, Grimace, Captain Crook (and his parrot), Hamburglar, a couple of hamburgers, and Ronald McDonald (but not Big Mac). $3.00 – 5.00.

4. 1985, Happy Birthday to You!, a white plastic Sweetheart cup with McDonaldland characters (Ronald, Grimace, Birdie, Hamburglar, and Gobblins) interacting in outer space, driving miscellaneous space vehicles, with a huge birthday cake in the center. $4.00 – 7.00.

MISCELLANEOUS PLASTIC ISSUES FROM THE MID 80S

Row 1.

1. 1985, Happy Birthday to You!, the same cup I picture on p. 145, only this cup's graphics are on a pink panel. $4.00 – 7.00.

2. 1985, Happy Birthday! To You, a white plastic cup featuring Ronald, Grimace, Birdie, and Hamburglar and various zoo animals riding on the "Happy Birthday Express" train. $4.00 – 7.00.

3. 1985, Ronald McDonald's head in red and black colors wearing a party hat on a white plastic cup sitting on red plastic feet base. $6.00 – 10.00.

4. 1986, "Happy Birthday To You!," a $5\frac{1}{8}$" Sweetheart cup showing Ronald leading a parade of dinosaurs. Hamburglar, Grimace, and Fry Guys are riding on the dinos, and "Happy Birthday To You!" is erupting from a volcano in the background. $4.00 – 7.00.

Row 2.

1. Ronald McDonald's head in red and black, Ronald's signature in black in line with his right ear, white plastic cup with red plastic feet base, no date, but probably 1985. $5.00 – 9.00.

2. Grimace plastic cup sitting on plastic feet base, no date, but probably 1985. This cup and the one above may belong to a set of character mugs. $6.00 – 10.00.

3. 1987, McKids "This bank belongs to…" white plastic cup with McDonaldland characters posing and blank space for kids to write their own name on the cup. Cup comes with plastic lid with slot in it for coins. This cup was originally available from Sears with a clothing purchase at their McKids department. $4.00 – 7.00.

A 1987 CHILD'S SET AND FOUR PLASTIC CUPS

Row 1.

1, 2, 3. 1987, plastic mug with orange two-finger handle and orange sipping lid featuring McDonaldland characters in tug of war: Captain Crook with parrot, Hamburglar, Ronald vs. Grimace, Birdie, and the Professor measuring results with ruler. This mug is part of a set. With it comes a thick plastic bowl with a plastic lid and the same designs. Finally, there's a three-compartment tray, also with the same design. Mug, $3.00 – 5.00; Bowl, $3.00 – 5.00; Tray, $4.00 – 7.00.

Row 2.

1. 1987, thick plastic 3^3/$_8$" cup with yellow Arch logo showing tug of war between Hamburglar, Ronald, and Goblin on one side and Grimace, Gobblins, and Birdie on the other side. $3.00 – 4.00.

2. 1988, Ronald with party hat sitting on star, Birdie flying, Grimace sitting on moon, and Fry Guys sitting on clouds. This is a heavy 4^3/$_8$" plastic cup made by Louisiana Plastics in St. Louis, Missouri. $3.00 – 5.00.

3. 1988, 5^1/$_8$" Sweetheart birthday cup showing Ronald and Fry Guy riding dinosaur with birthday cake on dino's tail, Birdie dropping gifts from her airplane, Hamburglar on ground catching gifts, Grimace in party hat, Fry Girl riding horse. Huge rainbow in background. $3.00 – 5.00.

4. 1990, Ronald in playland with rabbit, squirrel, birds, butterflies, and happy smile rising sun. This is a 4^3/$_8$" heavy plastic cup made by Louisiana Plastics in St. Louis, Missouri. $3.00 – 5.00.

PLASTIC MCDONALDLAND CUPS FROM THE 1990S

Row 1.

1. 1991, McDonald's Canada plastic party cup showing Hamburglar, Grimace, Ronald, and Fry Guys with balloons riding on magic rainbow carpet in various space machines. $3.00 – 4.00.

2. 1991, plastic mug showing Ronald McDonald carrying a McDonald's recycling flag and leading Hamburglar, Grimace, Birdie, and Fry Guys along a path through rolling hills in the country in support of Earth Day activities. On the bottom: "Dishwasher Safe, Made in USA, Top Rack Only." $5.00 – 8.00.

3. 1992, plastic Sweetheart party cup showing Ronald leading parade of dinosaurs with Fry Guys, Grimace, and Hamburglar riding the dinos. Large rainbow over mountain in background and McDonald's logo on kite. Very similar to the 1986 Happy Birthday cup, shown on page 146. $2.00 – 4.00.

4. 1992, plastic party cup showing Ronald, Grimace, Hamburglar, Birdie, and Fry Guys playing soccer with seven kids with the Golden Arch goal net in the background. $3.00 – 6.00.

Row 2.

1. 1994, "Happy Birthday" cup, 5$\frac{1}{8}$" high, showing Ronald as drum major followed by Grimace playing a trombone, Hamburglar playing a drum, and Birdie blowing a trumpet. This cup, the bottom tells us, was made by Sweetheart. $2.00 – 4.00.

2. 1995, "Play Place" plastic party cup with confetti at top and bottom and Ronald's head in center "Play Place" banner with Golden Arches. Same decoration on both sides and "Sweetheart" on the bottom. $2.00 – 5.00.

3. 1995, Happy Birthday cup, 5$\frac{1}{8}$", showing Ronald, Birdie, Grimace, Hamburglar in space suits along with Fry Guys and various space creatures having a party on a pink planet. Made by Sweetheart. $2.00 – 5.00

4. 1996, plastic cup showing Grimace, Ronald, Hamburglar, and Birdie sitting on a picnic blanket taking a break from playing baseball and eating McDonald's products. This unusual 4$\frac{3}{4}$" cup is composed of a silver-flecked thick plastic, and it has a wide, flanged mouth. On the bottom: "Marketed by Whirley Industries, Inc. Warren, PA, U.S.A." $5.00 – 8.00.

5. 1997, "Ronald McDonald y sus amigos," a 4$\frac{3}{4}$" glittery sports cup from Mexico showing Ronald, Grimace, Hamburglar, and Birdie having a picnic on a checked blanket. On the reverse, there's a block logo with McDonald's Mexico. This cup had a cap (not shown) and is "Marketed by Whirley Industries, Warren, PA." $8.00 – 12.00.

MISCELLANEOUS PLASTIC CUPS AND MUGS

1. 1997, heavy plastic cup measuring 3⅝" and showing a tug of war with Hamburglar, Fry Guy, and Ronald on one side and Grimace, Fry Guy and Girl, and Birdie on the other. The ⅜" high base is slightly indented. This cup is very similar to the 1987 version shown previously on page 147, but this cup has the Arches in a red block. Made by Whirley Industries in Warren, Pennsylvania. $1.00 – 3.00.

2. 1997, "Play Place," a 5¼" plastic tumbler with red cap and clear flex straw. "Play Place" appears in large multicolored decoration on one side; the other has a large graphic showing Ronald's head. On the bottom: "Marketed by Whirley Industries, Warren, PA." $3.00 – 5.00.

3. 2000, "Proud Partner" plastic tumbler with red cap and clear flex straw. This 5¼" tumbler shows Ronald, Hamburglar, Birdie, and Grimace down under in front of the Sydney Opera House supporting the 2000 summer Olympics. Ronald is wearing an Aussie hat and carrying a Proud Partner flag which consists of Arches with a flame above and the Olympic five-ring logo. On the bottom: "Marketed by Whirley Industries, Inc., Warren, PA, USA." $2.00 – 4.00.

4. 2000, "Short Sport" 9¾" plastic Halloween cup with orange pumpkin figural top with straw hole. This Halloween cup was not distributed everywhere, so it's fairly rare. There are two panels on the body of the cup. One shows Grimace, Ronald, and Hamburglar floating in space with a bunch of pumpkins and the moon in the background with bats; the other panel shows jack-o-lanterns. Made by Whirley in Warren, Pennsylvania. $5.00 – 10.00.

5. McDonaldland characters in space on a 6⅛" plastic tumbler with red cap and flex straw. Ronald, Hamburglar, and Grimace are wearing clear space helmets, and there are stars and planets in the background. A six-armed space creature is shown doing cartwheels on a yellow panel around the bottom. The bottom tells us this is a "Short Sport" tumbler made by Whirley in Warren, Pennsylvania. $2.00 – 4.00.

6. Mid to late 1990s?, double-walled plastic mug from McDonald's of Cancun, Mexico, with "Made in USA, Pat. Pend" on base. This mug shows Birdie, Grimace, Hamburglar, and Ronald. $8.00 – 12.00.

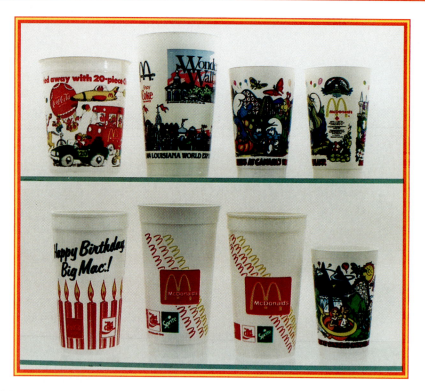

PLASTIC CUPS FROM THE 1980S

Row 1.

1. 1983, "Get carried away with 20-piece Chicken McNuggets & Coke," a 5¹/₂" wide-bodied cup with wild graphics promoting Chicken McNuggets. $5.00 – 8.00.

2. 1984 Louisiana World Exposition, May 12 – November 11, 1984, a 6³/₄" Sweetheart cup featuring the Wonder Wall and other attractions at the Exposition. "Enjoy Coke" and black McDonald's logos appear twice on opposite sides of the cup. There's also a large 1984 Expo logo. $10.00 – 15.00.

1985 "Smurf Fun Begins At Canada's Wonderland," a 5¹/₈" Canadian cup made by Styroware in Canada showing the Smurfs having fun at McDonald's Canadian theme park. $10.00 – 15.00.

3. Smurf cup front

4. Smurf cup reverse

Row 2.

1. 1986 "Happy Birthday Big Mac!" co-sponsored by Coca-Cola Classic and Diet Coke. Red and yellow birthday candles encircle the bottom of the cup. The Big Mac Sandwich was introduced in 1968. $3.00 – 5.00.

1986, with large McDonald's logo, lines of Arches in red, orange, and yellow at 45 degree angle, and Coca-Cola Classic, Diet Coke, and Sprite logos near the bottom, same design on both sides. This cup comes in two versions: a 7¹/₈" cup with flared top made by "The Collectibles" and a 6³/₄" cup made by Louisiana Plastics. $3.00 – 5.00 each.

2. 7¹/₈" cup with flared top

3. 6³/₄" cup

4. 1987, Canada Wonderland "The Jetson Family at Canada's Wonderland," a 5¹/₄" plastic cup showing the Jetsons and other Hanna-Barbera characters in spaceships at Canada's Wonderland. There's a maze on one side of the cup with a spaceship in the middle, and the caption: "Can you help the Jetsons find their spaceship?" Made by "The Collectibles, Canada Cup Inc., Toronto." $8.00 – 12.00.

MISCELLANEOUS 1987 – 1990 PLASTIC CUPS

Row 1.

1. 1987, "The Smurf Family at Canada's Wonderland," a 5¹/₈" plastic cup featuring several Smurfs looking for flowers in Smurf Forest. Papa Smurf says, "Smurfette, how many flowers are there in Smurf Forest?" and Smurfette replies, "Gee Papa Smurf, Let's count them together." Made by "The Collectibles" in Toronto. $8.00 – 12.00.

2. 1987, "The Ozarks" co-sponsored by Coca-Cola, Diet Coke, and Sprite. This cup promotes the attractions of the Ozarks and shows representative scenes from a number of Ozark locations including Monett, Mt. Vernon, Springfield, Marshfield, Lebanon, Camdenton, Ozark, Branson, Lakeview, Harrison, Eureka Springs, Mountain Home, West Plains, Mountain Grove, St. Robert, and Salem. $3.00 – 5.00.

3. 1988, "Super Size," a 6³/₄" cup with red and yellow decoration and Coca-Cola, Diet Coke, and Sprite logos on one side. "Please Put Litter In Its Place" in yellow near top of cup. Made by Louisiana Plastics, St. Louis. $2.00 – 3.00.

4. 1988, "The Smurfs Visit Racing Rivers at Canada's Wonderland," a 5¹/₈" Canadian cup showing 14 Smurfs at Racing Rivers. The cup has a Canada's Wonderland logo and a Canadian McDonald's logo along with a question to keep the kids busy: "Can you count the Smurfs?" Made by Canada Cup Inc., Toronto and part of The Collectibles series. $8.00 – 12.00.

Row 2.

1. 1989, "Canada's Wonderland, The one for all the fun!," a 5¹/₈" Canadian cup featuring The Flintstones engaged in various leisure activities. Canada's Wonderland and a Canadian McDonald's logo appear on the cup along with various copyright information. Made by Canada Cup Inc. in Toronto and part of The Collectibles series. $8.00 – 12.00.

2. 1989, "McDonald's" in white at 45 degree angle on red background with blocks outlined in yellow and white, Coca-Cola Classic and McDonald's logo with McDonald's in red script on white vertical panel on one side of cup. $2.00 – 4.00.

3. 1989 McDonald's and Coca-Cola Classic celebrate the Grumman F14 Tom Cat on a 5¹/₂" cup made by Louisiana Plastics in St. Louis, Missouri. A neat cup with unusual subject matter! Probably from Bethpage, NY, where Tom Cats are made. $8.00 – 12.00.

4. 1990 ,"McDonald's Presents New Kids On The Block Magic Summer," a 6³/₄" plastic cup showing pictures of the five New Kids in the then-popular group. Signatures of the "Kids" appear above and below them on the yellow background. $4.00 – 8.00.

5. 1990, "McDonald's Presents New Kids On The Block Magic Summer," a 6³/₄" plastic cup showing the "New Kids" posing as a group against a predominantly neon green background. $4.00 – 8.00.

1990 – 1991 PLASTIC CUPS

Row 1.

1. 1990, orange plastic cup with silver decoration co-sponsored by Coca-Coca-Classic. The McDonald's name appears in large silver script on this 6³/₄" cup. Made by Sterling Productions, Winchester, Virginia. $2.00 – 4.00.

2. 1990, lime-green/yellow plastic cup with silver decoration co-sponsored by Coca-Cola Classic. The McDonald's name appears in large silver script on this 6³/₄" cup. Made by Sterling Productions, Winchester, Virginia. It's possible that this cup and the one listed above are part of a set of three or four. $2.00 – 4.00.

3. 1990, lime/green yellow 7" vertically ribbed cup with silver decoration. "McDonald's" appears in large silver letters. Co-sponsored by Coca-Cola Classic. Made by Sterling Products, Sterling, Virginia. $2.00 – 4.00.

Row 2.

1991 McDonald's, a set of four 6³/₄" plastic cups with black line decoration co-sponsored by Coca-Cola Classic. Made by Sterling Productions, Winchester, Virginia. $2.00 – 4.00 each.

1. Pink cup
2. Yellow cup
3. Orange cup
4. Green cup

1991 PLASTIC CUPS

Row 1.

1. 1991, $6^7/_8$" supersized cup showing cups of Coke and French fry packages with red and yellow decoration co-sponsored by Coca-Cola. "Please put litter in its place" and "Please recycle or reuse this cup" appear vertically in large red capitals on opposite sides of the cup. The date appears in black letters near the bottom of the cup. Made by Sweetheart. $2.00 – 4.00.

2. 1991, $6^7/_8$" supersized cup showing cups of Coke and French fry packages with red and yellow decoration, very similar to the cup above. This cup has "Please put litter in its place" in very small red letters on one side of the cup only. There is no date, but I assume from the cup's graphics that it is 1991. Made by Sweetheart. $2.00 – 4.00.

3. 1991, Nostalgia McDonald's, a $6^3/_4$" cup with multicolored decoration (the same on both sides) featuring party paraphernalia: guitars, saxophones, records, musical notes, roller skates, and soft drinks. A diamond-shaped grid covers the whole cup. Made by Sweetheart. $3.00 – 5.00.

4. 1991, McDonald's in white script at 45 degree angle on purple background with green and white "spots" floating around. This $7^1/_8$" cup has two green Coca-Cola Classic logos on it and was made by Louisiana Plastics, St. Louis, Missouri. $2.00 – 4.00.

Row 2.

1. 1991, McDonald's "Downtown Express, Thank You For Your Business, Downtown McDonald's Owners." This $6^3/_4$" cup features a cartoonish drawing of downtown Chicago's famous skyline looking north towards Lake Michigan. On the other side there's a commuter train with a McDonald's logo on its nose and a line-drawing of a city skyline in the background. $5.00 – 10.00.

2. ©1991 McDonald's, red Crayola shaped $6^3/_4$" plastic cup with black decoration, co-sponsored by "Kay-Bee America's Toy Store." On the bottom: "The Collectibles, Made in Toronto Canada." $6.00 – 10.00.

1991, "Let's Get Growing America," a green $4^3/_{16}$" plastic cup with black decoration and white interior featuring a child planting a tree. Another panel has a black McDonald's logo with "Please recycle or reuse this container" below it, and the third panel has on it "Global Releaf, The American Forestry Association." $5.00 – 10.00.

3. "Let's Get Growing America ©1991 McDonald's Corporation" view of cup.

4. McDonald's logo view of cup.

MISCELLANEOUS 1990s PLASTIC CUPS

Row 1.

1992 supersize 7" plastic cup set of four. Each cup features "McDonald's" in black at a 45 degree angle on a random-looking color splash. Co-sponsored by Coca-Cola Classic. The date appears vertically in black above a black block logo. $2.00 – 5.00 each.

1. Orange cup
2. Neon green cup
3. Magenta cup
4. Neon yellow cup

Row 2.

1. 1992, "McDonald's Walk Thru" plastic Sweetheart party cup showing frolicking dinosaurs playing musical instruments in a prehistoric McDonald's playland setting. $4.00 – 7.00.

2. 1993, "McDonald's Summer" co-sponsored by Coca-Cola Classic with multicolored decoration showing people engaged in summer sports such as golf, jet skiing, cycling, basketball, and sunbathing. $2.00 – 4.00.

3. 1993, McDonald's logo in block against checkerboard background, a supersize 7" gray cup with an "Always Coca-Cola" logo showing on one side a red and yellow McDonald's block logo in front of a blue and yellow checkerboard and on the other a black and yellow logo in front of a pink and yellow checkerboard. Colored circles appear all around the cup. Made by Sterling Products, Winchester, Virginia. $2.00 – 4.00.

4. 1996, "Welcome to Fabulous Las Vegas Nevada," a supersize $6^7/_8$" cup co-sponsored by Coca-Cola and Mr. Pibb showing a variety of Las Vegas motifs and attractions. $3.00 – 6.00.

1997 – 2000 PLASTIC CUPS

Row 1.

1. 1997, 30th "Anniversario" of McDonald's in Puerto Rico 1967 – 1997 co-sponsored by Coca-Cola, a colorful 6³/₄" cup featuring Puerto Rican motifs. A bright yellow swirling sun appears twice on the cup and seems to establish the tone. "Packing Resources" appears on the bottom. $4.00 – 6.00.

2. Walt Disney World Animal Kingdom Opens Spring 1998, co-sponsored by Coca-Cola. Made by "Berry Plastics, Sterling." $3.00 – 5.00.

3. "Cows on Parade Commemorative Cup, June 15 – October 31, 1999, in Chicago," a 6⁵/₈" cup featuring gaily decorated flying cows and drawings of Chicago's skyline. Chicago is said to have initiated this unusual type of entertainment. Made by Berry Plastics, Sterling. $3.00 – 5.00.

4. 1999, "Celebrate the Millennium in New York City," a 6⁷/₈" plastic cup featuring Times Square Millennium images, fireworks, clocks, the Waterford ball, etc., co-sponsored by Coca-Cola. Available only in the New York City area and still being distributed in late February 2000 by New York McDonald's. $3.00 – 5.00.

Row 2.

2000, "Smile" logo plastic cup set of two with cup holder bases and "Contour" Coke bottles and French fries graphics. The 7" 32 oz. cup is made by Whirley of Sandusky, Ohio, and has seven rings on a 2" section of its base. The larger supersized cup comes in two versions, one of which has no manufacturer's name on the bottom and another which is 7³/₈" high and lists Sweetheart as the manufacturer and has Sweetheart's web address (www.sweetheart.com). The rings on the Sweetheart cup continue up the base and stop just short of the red panel whereas the seven rings on the cup with no manufacturer's name are confined to about 2" of the cup holder base. The coloration of the supersize cups is subtly different also with the 7³/₈" cup having a decidedly orange tint to its graphics. $1.00 – 2.00 each.

1. Large 7", 32 oz. cup, Whirley, 2" section with 7 rings on base.

2. Supersize 7", 42 oz. cup, no manufacturer named, 2" section with seven rings on base.

3. Supersize 7³/₈", 42 oz. cup, Sweetheart, rings continue up to the red panel.

4. 2000, "Smile" logo plastic cup with cup holder base and "Contour" Coke bottles and French fry graphics. This 7", 32 oz. cup at first glance looks identical to the 7" cup listed just above and shown to the left, but closer inspection shows that this cup's base is quite different: it has a plain, smooth base which yields to four graduated rings which come outward progressively just below the graphics panel. On the bottom: "Sweetheart 32 oz." $1.00 – 2.00.

2000 – 2001 PLASTIC CUPS

Row 1.

1. 2000 "Play to Win $1,000,000 Instantly…McDonald's Taste Trials Game," a 7" cup featuring a gold Olympic Taste Trials game piece with Olympic rings just to the right of a female runner. The three most recent McDonald's logos appear on the cup along with a Coca-Cola logo and a USA Olympic logo. The cup promotes the "Great Taste" of the Big Xtra, Crispy Chicken, and the Chicken McGrill and shows the following prizes: "a trip to anywhere in the world," "Pontiac or GMC vehicles," a "Replay TV Showstopper from Panasonic and a PanaBlack TV," and "Over 200,000 prizes from At&T Prepaid…10 Free Minutes in U.S. Calls." Fine print on the side panel informs us that the "Game is scheduled to end 10/12/00." Made by Sweetheart. $1.00 – 2.00; deduct $0.50 for missing game piece.

2. ©2000 "Frozen Coca-Cola," a 5¾" clear plastic cup with dome lid and red spoon-straw which fits through a 1" hole in the dome's top. There are two Frozen Coca-Cola logos and two large "Smile" logos. On the bottom: "Sweetheart (with a #6 recycling symbol) PS 24T." Frozen Coca-Cola is one of the latest additions to McDonald's drink menu. $0.50 – 1.00.

3. ©2001 African American Legacy of Music, a large 7" cup which celebrates the contributions of African musical traditions to American music: "McDonald's And Coca-Cola Proudly Celebrate Black History All Year Long." The cup's graphics depict African contributions to Big Band, Blues, Gospel, and Hip Hop musical styles. The cup also has a "Smile" logo and a vertical "we love to see you smile" strip. Made by Whirley in Sandusky, Ohio. $1.00 – 2.00.

4. ©2001 McDonald's and Walt Disney World Present "The Best of Latin Music," a large 7" cup which promotes a concert to be broadcast on October 27, 2001, by Latino musicians Elvis Crespo, Luis Fonsi, and MDO. Consumers are urged to log on to terra.com to learn about the concert and to qualify for a Disney World vacation or passes to the October 13, 2001, taping of the concert. Text on the cup is Spanish and English, and there are both Coca-Cola and Terra Network logos. A #6 recycling triangle with "PS" beneath it and the number string 41213 – 97 are all that appear on the bottom. $1.00 – 2.00.

Row 2.

©2001 "new tastes Menu!," a pair of cups aimed at teenagers and urging them to "Chill with friends & tasty treats," to "Take a break for a light quick bite!" and to "Grab a savory sandwich on the go!" There's a Coca-Cola logo and two "Smile" logos, a blue vertical "we love to see you smile" strip, and www.mcdonalds.com. Close inspection of these cups reveals that there are actually at least three different ones involving subtle design differences described below. $0.50 – 1.00.

1. Large 7" cup made by Whirley in Sandusky, Ohio, 7 rings on cup holder base.

2. Supersize 7³/₈" cup made by Sweetheart, 11 rings going up to the wide part of the cup.

3. Large 7" Sweetheart 32 oz. showing view of guy. Three rings just under the wide part of the cup.

4. Cup to left with view showing girl.

2001 – 2003 PLASTIC CUPS

Row 1.

1. ©2001 "McDonald's Extra Value Meals" supersize 42 oz. cup showing a burger, fries, and Coke which all add up to the Extra Value Meal. Also on the cup: Smile logo, Olympic Pround Partner logo, and blue vertical "we love to see you smile" band. Made by Sweetheart whose web address (www.sweatheart.com) appears on the bottom. $1.00 – 2.00.

2. ©2001 supersize 42 oz. cup with Coca-Cola and Olympic sponsor logos promoting the winter 2002 Olympics in Salt Lake City. This cup shows the Coke contour bottle and Coca-Cola Worldwide Olympic Partner logo, mountains and blue skies, and French fries with red, white, and blue decoration, USA Proud Partner logo and McDonald's web address, nothing of note on the bottom. $1.00 – 2.00.

3. ©2001 large 32 oz. cup with McDonald's logos, Coca-Cola script, and circular graphic featuring fries and Coke contour bottle. This cup has 16 vertical panels on its tapered base. Information on the bottom tells us it was made by Berry Plastics. $1.00 – 2.00.

Row 2.

©2002 "Chill Out" 32 oz. large and 42 oz. supersized plastic cups which promote McDonald's "McValue Menu" consisting of cones, sundaes, and shakes. These cups have the "Smile" logo and "Coca-Cola" script and feature graphics of an ice cream cone, a sundae, and triple thick milk shakes. The date appears vertically in red above the pitch-in anti-litter graphic. The bottoms indicate that both cups were made by Sweetheart. $1.00 – 2.00 each.

1. Medium size "Chill Out" cup

2. Super size "Chill Out" cup

©2003 "Winning Time" plastic cup set of two, large and supersize, promoting "Lots of Chances To Win Instantly!" Carnival Cruise Lines prizes and computers and AOL memberships. Each cup has a pull-tab game piece which promises players "Winning Time." Vertical print in English and Spanish informs the consumer that the "Game ends 4/21/03." White Coca-Cola script on each cup. No maker indicated on bottom. $0.50 – 1.00 each, less for cups without game pieces intact.

3. Large cup, "Winning Time," "Play & You Might Win a 4-Day Cruise on Carnival."

4. Supersize cup, "Winning Time," "Play & You Might Win a Computer & a 1-Year America Online membership."

5. 2003, "Disney's Kim Possible — The Secret Files On Disney DVD And Video September 2," a $4^3/_8$" kids' cup with Ronald McDonald on one side and Kim Possible promotional matter on the other. $0.50 – 1.00.

2003 "I'M LOVIN' IT" PLASTIC SPORTS CUPS

©2003 "I'm lovin' it" plastic cups featuring McDonald's newest tagline-slogan which was launched in late 2003 and really got going in early 2004. These cups share the same overall design of their more prolific paper counterparts, but so far I've only been able to find two different plastic cups. On them appear the Coke contour bottle, "how are we doin'?" message, Olympic "Proud Partner" Athens 2004 graphics, and pitch in icon. The slamming basketball player on the supersize cup is not represented on the paper cups as far as I know. Bottom information tells us that these cups were made by Berry Plastics. $1.00 – 3.00.

1. 32 oz. cup showing soccer goalie in mid air making save in "I'm lovin' it" net frame.
2. 42 oz. cup showing a slam dunker on one side and lady standing in rain on other.
3. Reverse of cup listed above and shown to left showing lady catching raindrops.

2004 EXTENDED HOURS / ATHENS OLYMPIC CUP

©2004 "up at 6 AM or Earlier/when you're up, we're up./Open Till Midnight or Later," a large 32 oz. plastic cup carrying graphics appropriate for the advertising message on one side and Carly Patterson, U.S. Gymnast, on the other. This cup combines McDonald's two most current marketing thrusts: the 2004 Athens summer Olympics and extended hours for Americans who work the overnight shift. As of July 17, 2004, according to an article in *The Wall Street Journal*, "12% of its (McDonald's) roughly 13,000 U.S. outlets are now open 24 hours a day…About 75% of its U.S. restaurants are open an hour or two beyond the traditional 6 a.m. to 10 p.m. hours" (*WSJ*, 7/15/04, B1&2). The cup, made by Berry Plastics, also sports the contour Coca-Cola bottle logo, Olympic Proud Partner logo, pitch in icon, and "how are we doin'?" tagline. $1.00 – 2.00.

1. Extended hours graphics featuring sun and moon.
2. "Carly Patterson, U.S. Gymnast. Flips for McDonald's" panel of cup.

MISCELLANEOUS UNDATED PLASTIC CUPS

Row 1.

1. 6¼" thin plastic cup with the classic triple band of Arches in gold, orange, and brown around the center and large Arch logo enclosed by a brown line. "Ayude A Mantener Limpia La Ciudad" appears in gold on both sides just below the top. In English this means "Help keep the city clean." This cup could be from any Spanish speaking country. It is too thin to have held hot drinks. It was probably for milk shakes and soft drinks. It dates from the 1980s when coffee cups with this design were popular. No markings on the bottom. $8.00 – 12.00.

2. Sea World of Ohio "Shark Encounter," a 7⅛" cup showing sharks, fish, and an eel in a beautiful aquarium setting. Made by Louisiana Plastics, St. Louis, Missouri. $3.00 – 5.00.

3. 5½" Canadian plastic cup with Coca-Cola logo showing people recreating at a swimming pool. It could be a spring break kind of scene with kids on rocket-powered boogie boards, a musclebound hunk showing off his physique, a good looking woman with big hair and pink bathing suit, and a guy with electric hair driving a hot rod dune buggy. The bottom of the cup tells us that this is a Collectibles cup made in Toronto. $3.00 – 6.00.

4. 5½" Canadian plastic cup with English/French Coca-Cola logo with brightly colored mod decoration showing seashore imagery: fish, palm trees, sunglasses, suntan lotion, beach ball, boat, airplane, helicopter, and sports car. A guy wearing winter clothes and carrying a suitcase seems to be heading towards a mermaidish figure on the beach. A "Collectibles" cup made in Toronto. $3.00 – 6.00.

Row 2.

1. "Blast Off With The Taste Of Mr. Pibb Every Day Value At (McDonald's logo)." This undated 6½" cup shows a rocket with a Mr. Pibb logo on its side. Made by Louisiana Plastics in St. Louis, Missouri. Mr. Pibb is fairly rare on McDonald's cups and is offered mainly in the southwestern states. $5.00 – 10.00.

"Kente Kup™ By Dobson Products P.O. Box 496027 Chicago, IL 60649," a set of three 5½" cups co-sponsored by Coca-Cola Classic featuring neatly arranged blocks of striped Kente cloth designs. Kente cloth is a hand woven cloth from Ghana. Warren T. Dobson II (aka "The Kupman") worked for a company which supplied McDonald Happy Meal containers, cups, and premiums. He came up with the idea of marketing a plastic tumbler with Kente cloth designs to African Americans. Before his efforts, drinkware had not specifically been marketed to African Americans. His marketing company was named Dobson Products. The designs are the same on all three cups, but each cup has a different background color. Made by Cups Illustrated, Lancaster, Texas. $5.00 – 10.00 each.

2. Beige background Kente cloth cup

3. Orange background Kente cloth cup

4. White background Kente cloth cup

5. "McDonald's" in red script at 45 degree angle on 6⅞" cup with cup holder base and variously colored confetti, two cheeseburgers, and two French fry packages on the front with a McDonald's logo and "just say 'Super-Size'" and "Enjoy Coke To Go" graphic on the reverse. Made by Sterling Products in Winchester, Virginia. This cup is difficult to date because its main graphic was put to heavy use all through the 1990s. $1.00 – 3.00.

TWO 1988 HONEY I SHRUNK THE KIDS AND WHO FRAMED ROGER RABBIT PLASTIC CUP SETS

Left.

Honey, I Shrunk the Kids, ©1988 Buena Vista Pictures Distribution, Inc. and McDonald's Corporation, co-sponsored by Coca-Cola. This set of three cups features scenes showing the shrunken Szalinski and Thompson kids coping with the implications of their miniscule size. $2.00 – 3.00 each.

1. Rick Moranis as mad professor Wayne Szalinski looking through magnifying glass at the friendly ant which fought off a scorpion and saved the Thompson and Szalinski kids.

2. The kids on the kitchen table with the family dog assisting.

3. The kids dealing with the honeybee.

Right.

Who Framed Roger Rabbit, ©1988 The Walt Disney Company, Amblin Entertainment, Inc., McDonald's, and Coca-Cola. This set of three cups shows scenes and characters from one of the best family films of the 1980s which features Roger Rabbit and detective Eddie Valiant who team up to save Toon Town from Judge Doom who plans to erase the town by inundating it in 5,000 gallons of heated dip shot out of a water cannon. The film received four Academy Awards and made over 150 million dollars. For trivia buffs: it's the only movie to ever have appearances by both Looney Tunes and Disney characters. $2.00 – 3.00 each.

1. Front view of Benny the Cab with Eddie Valiant at the wheel and Jessica Rabbit sitting on the fender. Roger is standing by left front fender of cab. Hollywood sign in background to left of Jessica.

2. Roger and Detective Eddie Valiant in Benny the Cab screeching to a stop at the bus stop in Toon Town where Jessica is standing.

3. Judge Doom and one of the Weasels in cowboy hat chasing Roger.

SET OF THREE *DICK TRACY* MOVIE CUPS

Dick Tracy, ©1990 Disney, co-sponsored by McDonald's and Coca-Cola. This set of three brightly colored cups features scenes and characters from the movie. $2.00 – 4.00 each.

1. Dick Tracy
2. Flattop
3. The Kid

SET OF SIX *BATMAN RETURNS* PLASTIC CUPS

Batman Returns, ©1992 DC Comics, Inc., co-sponsored by McDonald's and Coca-Cola. This set of six cups has vivid and detailed graphics of characters and scenes from the popular sequel to the 1989 *Batman* movie. In the earlier movie, Batman's antagonist was The Joker; in this movie it's The Penguin. Michael Keaton is Bruce Wayne/Batman. Michelle Pfeiffer is Selena Kyle/Catwoman. Danny DeVito is Oswald Chesterfield Cobblepot/Penguin. Each cup has a vertically printed title on it (below in parentheses) and came with a colored plastic "Frisbee Bat Disk" cap in black, silver, or neon green. $2.00 – 4.00 each, add $1.00 for frisbee cap.

Left.

1. Batman running (*Batman*)
2. Batmobile (*Batman Returns*)
3. Catwoman (Catwoman)

Right.

1. Michael Keaton and Michelle Pfeiffer dancing (*Batman Returns*)
2. The Penguin with microphones (The Penguin)
3. Penguin and rubber duck (*Batman Returns*)

SET OF SIX *JURASSIC PARK* PLASTIC CUPS

Jurassic Park, ©1992 Universal City Studios, Inc. and Amblin Entertainment, Inc. and co-sponsored by McDonald's and Coca-Cola. This set of six numbered cups has elaborate graphics and an informational panel which provides information about the plot of the movie and the various dinosaurs in it. McDonald's official pitch was "a Free *Jurassic Park* Collector Cup when you buy any DINO-SIZED Extra Value Meal or Large Soft Drink." $2.00 – 4.00 each.

Left.
1. JP 1 Tyrannosaurus Rex
2. JP 2 Gallimimus
3. JP 3 Dilophosaur

Right.
1. JP 4 Triceratops
2. JP 5 Velociraptor
3. JP 6 Brachiosaur

THE *FLINTSTONES* MOVIE CUPS FROM CANADA

The *Flintstones* ©U.C.S. And Amblin. TM H-B Prod., Inc., a set of six unnumbered and undated 6³/₄" Canadian cups promoting the 1993 *Flintstones* movie. The US got the glass mugs and Canada got these. Actually, these are neat cups with lots of color and great images! Co-sponsored by Coca-Cola, each cup has the Canadian McDonald's logo with maple leaf. $5.00 – 10.00 each.

Left.
1. "The Flintstones and Rubbles Enjoy Eating At Everyones Favourite Bedrock Hangout." (Flintstones and Rubbles at "Roc Donald's Over 19 Dozen Sold.")
2. "Newly Promoted, Fred Is Unaware Of Cliff And Miss Stone's Plot Against Him." (Fred as Vice President of Industrial Procurement.")

Right.
1. "Fred 'Twinkle Toes' Flintstone Leads the Water Buffalos to Another Bowling League Championship!" (Fred and Barney bowling.)
2. "Barney Is Catapulted to Rescue Pebbles and Bamm Bamm From Danger." (Barney flying through the air towards Pebbles and Bamm Bamm.)
3. "Only Chores For Betty and Barney After They Move in with the Flintstones." (Barney mowing the lawn with lobster mower.)
Not shown: "Quitting Time…" (I have not actually seen this cup, but it has been described to me.)

ALADDIN MOVIE PLASTIC SET OF FOUR

1993 *Aladdin*, ©Disney, a set of four 4³/₈" cups featuring characters and scenes from the movie. Each cup is capped by a 3³/₄" plastic figural head that matches the character on the cup. A straw fits through a hole at the top of each head. A black McDonald's logo appears near the bottom of each cup on the vertical side panel. The bottom of each cup tells us that these cups were made in Italy and printed in Germany and that Simon Marketing Int., Dreieich oversaw the promotion. I'm told that these were distributed in England. $10.00 – 15.00 each.

1. Aladdin and Abu riding the magic carpet. Aladdin's head in beige.
2. Princess Jasmine and "Prince" Aladdin riding the magic carpet. Jasmine's head in green.
3. Jafar riding horse and holding cobra-headed staff. Jafar's head in red.
4. Genie holding Aladdin and Princess Jasmine in his hand. Genie's head in blue.

102 DALMATIANS PLASTIC CUPS

2000 "Disney's *102 Dalmatians* Only In Theatres!," a set of two plastic cups promoting Disney's latest cinematic offering and promising fabulous prizes for customers who "Heel! Peel! (and) Play!" Each cup has a game piece which involves peeling and scratching. We are informed that "3 of the Same Wins the Game Instantly!" The prize at the end of this contest on the super size cup is a "First Class London Trip For 4 plus $102 spending money per day!" The large cup shows a "Land Rover Discovery with 102 Fill-ups!" Small vertical print on the cup informs us that the "Game is scheduled to end 12/21/00." The bottom of the super size cup has only a #6 recycling symbol with "PS" under it. The large cups were made by at least two different companies. The bottom of one of them says "Sweetheart (with a #6 recycling symbol) PS 32 oz." This cup has a plain base with three rings going around the cup just below the wide top. The other one says "Whirley Sandusky, Ohio USA TC-32CM" (with a smaller #6 recycling symbol in the center). This cup has seven bands on the base. Co-sponsored by Coca-Cola. $1.00 – 2.00 each; deduct $0.50 for missing game pieces.

1. Large Sweetheart cup with three rings on base, Smile logo, and 102 Dalmations panel.
2. Large Whirley cup with seven bands around base, prize panel view with Land Rover.
3. Super size cup with seven bands around base, First Class London Trip panel.
4. Super size cup showing game piece panel.

MISCELLANEOUS PLASTIC AUTO RACING CUPS AND MUGS

Row 1.

1. 1990 McDonald's All-Star Race Team, co-sponsored by Coca-Cola. This plastic cup shows Rick Mears, Emerson Fittipaldi, and Michael Andretti posing on the front. The McDonald's All-Star Race Team logo and "CART" (Championship Auto Racing Teams) appear on the reverse along with the signatures of the three drivers. CART's history goes all the way back to 1909; in 1990 fans voted for the first All-Star Race Team composed of these drivers. $4.00 – 7.00.

2. 1992 McDonald's Racing, NHRA Championship Racing, co-sponsored by Coca-Cola and Larry Minor Motorsports. This cup features a McDonald's funny car and a top fuel dragster. $2.00 – 5.00.

3. 1993 McDonald's All-Star Race Team featuring Bill Elliott and co-sponsored by Coca-Cola Classic and NASCAR. This cup has a nicely detailed picture of Bill Elliott, and on the reverse there's biographical information and 1992 season results. $2.00 – 5.00.

4. 1993 McDonald's Racing Team, Inaugural Race #27 Daytona February 14, 1993, co-sponsored by Coca-Cola Classic. This cup shows a large picture of Junior Johnson, car owner, and Hut Stricklin, driver, standing beside their red Ford Thunderbird. $2.00 – 5.00.

Row 2.

1. 1994 "McDonald's Ford Thunderbird," a 6³/₄" cup featuring car #27 along with a short biography of the car. Co-sponsored by Coca-Cola and made by Sterling Products, Winchester, Virginia. $2.00 – 4.00.

2. 1998 Bill Elliott, co-sponsored by Coca-Cola and NASCAR. This 6⁷/₈" cup shows Bill in his red driving suit holding a Coke; Bill's signature appears in large white letters along with the number 94 against a black and gray checkered background. Made by Berry Plastics, Sterling. $2.00 – 4.00.

3. McDonald's Racing Team, a 6¹/₈" thick plastic mug with red, yellow, and black decoration and red plastic sipping cap. $2.00 – 5.00.

4. Trackside Limited Edition clear plastic mug with McDonald's #27 model race car in false bottom. This may or may not be a McDonald's sponsored item, but it is certainly interesting! Made by Howw Mfg. Inc. $8.00 – 15.00.

TIGERS, ROYALS, AND TWINS PLASTIC BASEBALL CUPS

Row 1.

1. 1984 Detroit Tigers "Bless You Boys," co-sponsored by McDonald's and Coca-Cola. The front of this large cup shows a tiger with a bat in his mouth. The reverse says "Tigers 84." $2.00 – 5.00.

2. 1986 "Royals and Me" medium-sized plastic cup with all kinds of people (including animals) depicted on it. Co-sponsored by McDonald's and Coca-Cola. $3.00 – 5.00.

3. Undated "Royals and Me" cup with blue and gold decoration on white. Co-sponsored by McDonald's and Coca-Cola. $2.00 – 3.00.

4. Undated "Royals and Me" light blue plastic cup with dark blue and gold decoration. Co-sponsored by McDonald's and Coca-Cola. $2.00 – 3.00.

Row 2.

©1988 McDonald's, MLBPA and Coca-Cola Classic Minnesota Twins 1987 World Champions. Each of these plastic cups features large colored photographs of two Twins' players and very brief 1987 statistics. $3.00 – 8.00 each.

1. Bert Blyleven, Pitcher/Kent Hrbek, First Base
2. Tom Brunansky, Right Field/Jeff Reardon, Pitcher
3. Greg Gagne, Shortstop/Dan Gladden, Left Field
4. Steve Lombardozzi, Second Base/Kirby Puckett, Center Field

TORONTO BLUE JAYS AND MARK MCGWIRE PLASTIC CUPS

Left: Three Toronto Blue Jays plastic baseball cups.

1. ©1990, MLBPA ©MSA, Toronto Blue Jays, co-sponsored by Coca-Cola Classic. This 6⁷/₈" cup made in Canada under "The Collectibles" imprint, shows three Blue Jays players: George Bell, Tony Fernandez, and David Wells. $5.00 – 10.00.

(1997) Toronto Blue Jays Trivia set of three numbered 7⁷/₁₆" cups. Each cup has nice graphics of Blue Jay players along with questions about their baseball exploits. Each cup has a Canadian McDonald's logo and an "Always Coca-Cola" logo. Answers appear upside down near the base of each cup. There's also a Blue Jay 20 year logo below the home run hitters. The cup is undated, but the number 20 tells us that its their 20th anniversary. They played their first regular season game on April 7, 1997, so this is a 1997 cup. On the bottom: "The Collectibles, Made in Toronto Canada." $4.00 – 8.00 each.

2. Cup 2 in a Series of 3 Toronto Blue Jays trivia cups. The big question on this cup is "Name the 6 players, what record they set, against what team and when?" The answer is "Rance Mulliniks, George Bell, Lloyd Moseby, Rob Ducey, Fred McGriff & Ernie Whitt set a Major League Record of 10 home runs in one game, on Sept. 14th 1987 versus Baltimore." The other question is "In 1987 what 2 awards did George Bell win?" The answer is "American League MVP & Major League Player of the Year."

(Not pictured: Cups 1 and 3 in a series of 3)

3. 1997 McDonald's of Canada/Toronto Blue Jays/Coca-Cola "The Rocket Takes Flight." The tall cup with red cap is #2 of a series and shows three nice graphics of Clemons in various stages of pitching. A panel on one side of the cup provides biographical information and career highlights. $4.00 – 8.00.

Right: Set of three Mark McGwire cups.

1999 McDonald's "Welcome to Big Mac Land," Mark McGwire unnumbered set of three. These large cups were available only in St. Louis. Each has the new "Did someone say McDonald's?" logo and shows a picture of McGwire and has a facsimile autograph. Made by Berry Plastics, Sterling. $4.00 – 8.00 each.

1. McGwire eating a Big Mac.
2. McGwire in warm-up jersey.
3. McGwire swinging the bat.

MISCELLANEOUS PLASTIC BASEBALL CUPS

Left: Three Chicago baseball cups.

1. 1998 "Slammin" Sammy Sosa 66 home run cup. This cup, available only in the Chicago area, shows the Cubs' star running and batting. Made by Berry Plastics, Sterling. $4.00 – 8.00.

2. 1999 "Summer Sizzles with Sammy!" This large plastic cup which was available only in the Chicago area shows Sammy Sosa running and batting. Made by Berry Plastics, Sterling. $4.00 – 8.00.

3. 2000 Chicago (image of white sock) Sox, a 6³/₄" super size plastic cup with small cup-holder base, Coca-Cola logo, and McDonald's "Smile" logo. White, black, and gray decoration. $1.00 – 3.00.

Right: Three plastic baseball cups.

1. 2000 Chicago Cubs, a 6⁴/₈" cup with red, white, and blue decoration showing a player swinging the bat, a Cubs logo, and a McDonald's "Smile" logo. Made by Berry Plastics, Sterling. $1.00 – 3.00.

2. 2000 Pedro Martinez shown in three poses pitching on a 6⁵/₈" cup with the new McDonald's Smile logo. A brief biography box on one side of the cup highlights Martinez's accomplishments in the 1997 – 1999 seasons. Made by Berry Plastics, Sterling. $2.00 – 4.00.

3. Cleveland Indians Inaugural Year/Good Luck Indians, a 6³/₄" large plastic cup showing Cleveland's Jacob's Field which opened in 1994. Made by Louisiana Plastics. $2.00 – 4.00.

CLEVELAND INDIANS BASEBALL CUPS

1. Sandy Alomar, Jr., Catcher, Cleveland Indians, a 6³/₄" large plastic cup showing two poses of Sandy Alomar and on the reverse a detailed biographical career profile. Made by Louisiana Plastics. $2.00 – 5.00.

2. Cleveland Indians Winter Home 1994 Schedule, Chain-O-Lakes Stadium, City of Winter Haven, Florida, a 6³/₄" large cup showing the stadium and on the reverse the 1994 Home Spring Schedule. Made by Louisiana Plastics. $2.00 – 4.00.

3. Louis Sockalexis; The Cleveland Indian (1871 – 1913), a 6³/₄" large plastic cup featuring a photograph of Louis Sockalexis. On the reverse: "In 1914 a Cleveland newspaper held a contest to rename the team. The winning entry was 'Indians' as a testament to Sockalexis, the game's first American Indian." Made by Louisiana Plastics. $2.00 – 5.00.

ARKANSAS RAZORBACKS BASKETBALL CUPS

1. 1993 – 1994 Arkansas Razorbacks National Basketball Champions, a 7$\frac{1}{8}$" cup showing the red Arkansas Razorback and the caption "Hog Wild." Co-sponsored by Coca-Cola. Made by Louisiana Plastics in St. Louis. $4.00 – 7.00.

2. 1995 Arkansas Razorbacks "Hog Wild," a 6$\frac{7}{8}$" cup showing the Arkansas hog in basketball action, co-sponsored by Coke to Go. Made by Sterling Products, Winchester, Virginia. $3.00 – 5.00.

HIGHSCHOOL BASKETBALL CUPS

Left.

1. 1988 City League Classic, Toledo, Ohio, Savage Hall, November 25, 1988, co-sponsored by McDonald's and Coca-Cola Classic. The logos of six participating teams appear on this 5$\frac{3}{8}$" cup. $3.00 – 6.00.

2. 1990 Jammin' Jubilee, 1990 McDonald's All American High School Basketball Game, Market Square Arena, Indianapolis, Indiana, a 6$\frac{3}{4}$" cup co-sponsored by Coca-Cola Classic. Made by Louisiana Plastics, St. Louis, Missouri. $3.00 – 6.00.

3. 1991 "Get the Spirit at McDonald's, Go Indians!," a 6$\frac{3}{4}$" cup with the Mukwonago (Wisconsin) High School Boys Varsity Basketball Schedule 1991 – 1992 on the reverse. Co-sponsored by Coca-Cola Classic and made by Louisiana Plastics. $3.00 – 7.00.

Right.

1. 1992 "Bring This Cup Back To McDonald's And Receive Free Refill Anytime you purchase a large Sandwich and Large Fry," with Larkin High School Varsity & JV Boys Basketball 1992 – 1993 Home Games and Larkin High School Girls Basketball 1992 – 1993 Home Games on the reverse. "Go Royals!" appears near the base. Elsewhere we are informed that the "Offer Expires 4/1/93" and "Offer Good at McDonald's 1480 Larkin Ave. Elgin, IL" $3.00 – 7.00.

2. 1992 "Get the Spirit at McDonald's, Go Indians!," a 6$\frac{3}{4}$" cup co-sponsored by Coca-Cola showing the Mukwonago (Wisconsin) High School Varsity & JB Boys Basketball Schedule 1992 Home Games along with the Mukwonago High School Varsity Football Schedule 1992 Home Games. Made by Louisiana Plastics. $3.00 – 7.00.

3. 1996 "Pittsburgh March 31, 1996, McDonald's All American High School Basketball Game" at the Civic Arena. The cup also promotes a March 28, 1996, "Slam Jam Contest and 3 Point Shootout" at Fitzgerald Field House at the University of Pittsburgh. This 6$\frac{5}{8}$" plastic cup was made by Berry Plastics and is sponsored by Sprite. $3.00 – 5.00.

SIX 1992 "OLYMPICS DREAMS" NBA PLASTIC CUPS

1992 USA Basketball sponsored by McDonald's and USA Basketball, "Helping Olympic Dreams Come True," numbered set of ten, plus two unnumbered cups (added later) with "Commemorative Collector Cup Series" labels on them. Each of these cups shows an NBA player in nice detail and color and has a statistics box devoted to career highlights. Dates of the promotion: July 17 to August 13, 1992. "The Collectibles, Made in Canada" appears on the bottom of each cup. These cups could be collected at McDonald's restaurants with Coca-Cola in them, but they could also be ordered as a set from FAC Services Group, 834 N. Church Rd., Elmhurst, Illinois 60126. $3.00 – 5.00 each for numbers 1 – 10; $5.00 – 7.00 each for Drexler and Laettner.

Left.
1. #1 of 10 Charles Barkley
2. #2 of 10 Larry Bird
3. #3 of 10 Patrick Ewing

Right.
1. #4 of 10 Magic Johnson
2. #5 of 10 Michael Jordan
3. #6 of 10 Karl Malone

SIX 1992 "OLYMPICS DREAMS" NBA PLASTIC CUPS

Left.
1. #7 of 10 Chris Mullin
2. #8 of 10 Scottie Pippen
3. #9 of 10 David Robinson

Right.
1. #10 of 10 John Stockton
2. Clyde Drexler
3. Christian Laettner

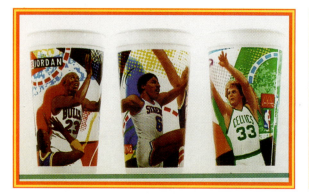

1993 – 1994 "NOTHING BUT NET" MVP CUPS

1993 McDonald's and Coca-Cola, ©1994 NBA Properties, Inc. "Nothing But Net MVPs" numbered set of six. These colorful cups feature NBA MVPs in action, and there's a brief description of the player's exploits in a particular series or game. These cups are made in Canada and are part of "The Collectibles" series. In addition to the plastic cups, there was at least one wax-coated medium-sized paper cup ©1993 McDonald's, ©1994 NBA Properties. This cup, co-sponsored by Coca-Cola, has generic basketball player images and says "Nothing But Net," "Official Restaurant of the NBA." I show the paper cup here because of its connection with the plastic set. Plastic cups, $4.00 – 7.00 each; wax-coated paper cup, $5.00 – 8.00.

Left.

1. 1 of 6 Michael Jordan, Chicago Bulls
2. 2 of 6 Julius Erving, Philadelphia 76ers
3. 3 of 6 Larry Bird, Boston Celtics

Right.

1. 4 of 6 Moses Malone, Philadelphia 76ers
2. 5 of 6 Charles Barkley, Phoenix Suns
3. 6 of 6 Bill Walton, Portland Trail Blazers
4. 1993 Nothing But Net 6³/₈" wax-coated paper cup

SIX 1994 DREAM TEAM II PLASTIC CUPS

1994 Dream Team II sponsored by McDonald's and Coca-Cola, a numbered set of 13 cups and one extra added later with action shots of players and brief player profiles. An interesting fact about this set: at least five different manufacturers were involved with making the cups, and there are even minor but noticeable differences in the cups made by each manufacturer. For example, some of the Miner cups have Lenexa, KANS. on the bottom, and others have Lenexa, KS. Additional confusion is created by the fact that two manufacturers made some of the cups. Here's what I know based on the copies I have in my collection: Cups #1, 5, 6, 9, 10, and 13 were made by The Collectibles in Toronto, Canada. Cups #7, 8, and 11 were made by Miner Container Inc. in Lenexa, Kansas. Cup #11 was also made by Louisiana Plastics. Cups # 3 and 4 were made by Sweetheart. Cup #12 was made by both Louisiana Plastics and Miner. The Kevin Johnson cup was made by Louisiana Plastics in St. Louis, Missouri. Cup #2 was made by Cups Illustrated in Lancaster, Texas, and also by the Collectibles. My guess is that each of these companies may have made its own set of the cups for various regions of the country since this was such a large promotion. $3.00 – 5.00 each for #1 – 13; #14 Kevin Johnson, $5.00 – 10.00.

Left.

1. #1 of 13 Isaiah Thomas, Guard, Detroit Pistons
2. #2 of 13 Larry Johnson, Forward, Charlotte Hornets
3. #3 of 13 Shawn Kemp, Forward, Seattle SuperSonics

Right.

1. #4 of 13 Dan Majerle, Guard/Forward, Phoenix Suns
2. #5 of 13 Dominique Wilkins, Forward, Los Angeles Clippers
3. #6 of 13 Derrick Coleman, Forward, New Jersey Nets

EIGHT 1994 DREAM TEAM II PLASTIC CUPS

Left.

1. #7 of 13 Alonzo Mourning, Center, Charlotte Hornets
2. #8 of 13 Steve Smith, Guard, Miami Heat
3. #9 of 13 Joe Dumars, Guard, Detroit Pistons
4. #10 of 13 Mark Price, Guard, Cleveland Cavaliers

Right.

1. #11 of 13 Shaquille O'Neal, Center, Orlando Magic
2. #12 of 13 Reggie Miller, Guard, Indiana Pacers
3. #13 of 13 Tim Hardaway, Guard, Golden State Warriors
4. #14 (not numbered), Kevin Johnson, Guard, Phoenix Suns (added to set late in the promotion and available by mail order only)

1995 NBA LOONEY TUNES "ALL-STAR SHOWDOWN" CUPS

1995 McDonald's and Sprite NBA Looney Tunes All-Star Showdown, ©1995 NBA Properties and 1995 Warner Brothers unnumbered set of seven. The dates of this promotion were from April 1 to April 30, 1995. Customers could get the cups in two ways: by supersizing any Extra Value Meal and by purchasing any large soft drink. These cups, referred to in official McDonald's promotions as All-Star Showdown Cups, show NBA stars in action along with a Warner Brothers character and in some cases, a humorous caption. For some reason, not all of the cups have a Sprite logo, and for more obvious reasons, not all of them have clever commentaries. This was a big promotion, so there were also at least two medium-sized wax-coated 6³/₈" paper cups involved in it. The colors on the paper cups are subdued, and the players are shown in black and white along with line drawings of the Warner Brothers cartoon characters. These cups are much harder to find than their larger plastic counterparts. Plastic: $4.00 – 7.00 each; wax-coated paper cups: $5.00 – 10.00 each.

Left.

1. Charles Barkley (Phoenix Suns) and the Tasmanian Devil.

2. Larry Bird (Boston Celtics) and Sylvester (no Sprite logo): "Sufferin' Succotash! That's the BIGGEST BIRD I've ever seen!"

3. Patrick Ewing (New York Knicks) and Yosemite Sam: "Hey! That's some ROOTIN' TOOTIN' Hoop Shootin'!"

4. Larry Johnson (Charlotte) and Wile E. Coyote.

Right.

1. Michael Jordan (Chicago Bulls) and Bugs Bunny (no Sprite logo): "C'Mon, doc! Dunk one right over the plate!"

2. Shawn Kemp (Seattle Supersonics) and Daffy Duck: "The only defense for this guy is to duck!"

3. Reggie Miller (Indiana Pacers) and Road Runner (no Sprite logo): "Playerus Maximus!"

1995 NBA Looney Tunes All-Star Showdown wax-coated paper cups featuring views of players.

4. Reggie Miller, Shawn Kemp, Patrick Ewing, and Michael Jordan shown with Wile E. Coyote, Daffy Duck, and Yosemite Sam.

5. Larry Bird, Charles Barkley, and Larry Johnson shown with Tasmanian Devil, Bugs Bunny, Road Runner, and Sylvester.

1995 NBA LOONEY TUNES ALL-STAR SHOWDOWN CUPS REVERSE VIEWS FEATURING WARNER BROTHERS CARTOON CHARACTERS

Row 1.

1. Tasmanian Devil
2. Sylvester
3. Yosemite Sam
4. Wile E. Coyote

Row 2.

1. Bugs Bunny
2. Daffy Duck
3. Road Runner
4. Wile E. Coyote, Daffy Duck, Yosemite Sam
5. Tasmanian Devil, Bugs Bunny, Road Runner, Sylvester

TWO NBA PLASTIC CUP SETS

Left: Set of four 1996 Dennis Rodman cups.

1996 Dennis Rodman set of four. This set shows the Chicago Bulls' player in various poses and action shots with various hair colors. When cold beverages are poured into these cups, Rodman's hair changes color. A small McDonald's logo appears near the bottom of each cup under Rodman's picture on each side of the cup. These cups were distributed in the Chicago area for a fairly limited time. $6.00 – 8.00 each.

1. Dennis Rodman in defensive posture with blue star in background, green hair, same image both sides of cup.
2. Close-up of Rodman's head, same image both sides, green hair one side, pink hair other side.
3. Upper body shot of Rodman with white hair, front view on one side, back view on other.
4. Rodman with green hair on one side and on the other a view of the back of Rodman's head with pink hair and a beige McDonald's logo centered on the back of his head. When this cup is filled with ice cubes and water, the McDonald's logo becomes clearer and more visible.

Right: Set of four 1996 Australian NBA cups.

1996 McDonald's Australia Limited, set of four temperature sensitive NBA cups. These 6³/₄" plastic cups feature four NBA stars in action. Each player's number and broadcast slogan or name becomes activated and more visible when ice cubes and cold liquid are put into the cup. The McDonald's Arches appear in a red block with "Official Restaurant of the NBA" below. There's also an NBA logo near the bottom of each cup. On the bottom: "The Collectibles Made in Toronto Canada." $5.00 – 10.00 each.

1. Charles Barkley, Rockets, #4, "Sir Charles."
2. Grant Hill, Pistons, #33, "From Downtown."
3. Shawn Kemp, #40, Seattle Sonics, "Jamm City."
4. Luc Longley, #13, Chicago Bulls, "Luuuc!"

TWO 1996 GRANT HILL NBA PAPER CUPS

1996 McDonald's U.S. Olympic Dream Team paper cups featuring Grant Hill. This cup comes in medium and large sizes. $2.00 – 4.00.
1. Medium sized Grant Hill cup
2. Large sized Grant Hill cup

MISCELLANEOUS PLASTIC AND PAPER NBA CUPS

Left: Three plastic Chicago Bulls cups.

1. 1991 NBA World Champions Chicago Bulls, a medium-sized plastic cup co-sponsored by McDonald's and Coca-Cola Classic. On the reverse: "There's just no stopping a herd of charging Bulls" along with the crossed-out names of the teams defeated by the Bulls in the playoffs. $3.00 – 7.00.

2. 1997 Chicago Bulls Championships, a $6^7/_8$" cup co-sponsored by "Sprite To Go," showing the Bulls logo on the front and a large red bull against a large basketball background on the reverse. A "Did somebody say McDonald's?" thought bubble appears below the Sprite logo. Made by "Berry Plastics, Sterling." $2.00 – 4.00.

3. 1999 Chicago Bulls, a $6^5/_8$" cup with a Bulls logo against a blue Chicago skyline background with "Jordan" in large red letters. Jordan's records appear in a white band below the Bulls logo, and Michael appears on the reverse wearing a plain red tank-top and black basketball pants getting ready to stuff it. Made by Berry Plastics, Sterling. $3.00 – 5.00.

Right: Four NBA cups, three plastic and one paper.

1. 1993, a $5^1/_2$" cup with "Utah All-Star NBA Weekend Feb. 19 – 21, 1993, Delta Center" on one side and "All-Star NBA Jam Session Presented By Fleer Feb. 18 – 21, 1993 Salt Palace" on the other. McDonald's and "Enjoy Coca-Cola Classic" logos both appear at the bottom of each side. Made by Louisiana Plastics. $3.00 – 6.00.

2. 1995, a $6^7/_8$" cup with "All Star NBA Weekend Phoenix February 10 – 12, 1995 America West Arena" on one side and "All-Star NBA Jam Session Presented by Fleer, Feb. 9 – 12, 1995 Phoenix Civic Plaza" on the other. Co-sponsored by "Coke To Go" and Sprite and made by Sterling Products in Winchester, Virginia. $3.00 – 5.00.

3. 1996 McDonald's, Sprite, and the NBA, "Vote for All-Star Guys!" The large paper cup shows Grant Hill, Charles Barkley, and Scottie Pippen stuffing NBA All-Star ballot boxes with their own names and encouraging fans to vote "today at McDonald's: Official Headquarters of NBA All-Star Balloting!" Penny Hardaway is shown holding an order of fries, and Shawn Kemp is shown at the drive-thru window. $3.00 – 5.00.

4. 1999 McDonald's/Sprite Grant Hill 1990 McDonald's All American High School Basketball Game, Catch Tomorrow's Superstars! March 24, 1999, Hilton Coliseum, Ames, Iowa. This $6^7/_8$" plastic cup celebrates Grant Hill, a 1990 McDonald's All American. $5.00 – 10.00.

TWO PLASTIC COLLEGE FOOTBALL CUPS

1. 1978 LSU Tigers Football Schedule, a 6¹³⁄₁₆" cup with purple and yellow decoration. The front shows the LSU Tiger logo with "Go Tigers!" below. The reverse shows the schedule with "Go Tigers!" below it. No identifying information on bottom. $10.00 – 15.00.

2. 1981 Arkansas Football Schedule, a 5" cup showing the Razorbacks' schedule on one side and the McDonald's logo along with a Dr Pepper logo on the other. $8.00 – 12.00.

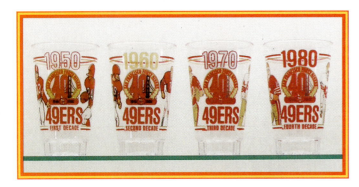 

SAN FRANCISCO 49ERS AND CHICAGO BEARS CUPS

Left: Set of four San Francisco 49ers NFL cups.

San Francisco 49ers 1946 – 1986. This set of four clear plastic cups with red, gold, and white decoration came out in 1986. The set covers four decades: the 1950s, the 1960s, the 1970s, and the 1980s. Each cup pays tribute to two 49er greats. There is considerable detailed biographical information for each of the players and a white McDonald's logo on the reverse. These cups in nice condition are getting pretty hard to find. $10.00 – 15.00 each.

1. 1950 First Decade: Joe Perry (Fullback) and Hardy Brown (Linebacker)
2. 1960 Second Decade: Leo Nomellini (Defensive Tackle) and Hugh McElhenny (Halfback)
3. 1970 Third Decade: Dave Wilcox (Linebacker) and John Brodie (Quarterback)
4. 1980 Fourth Decade: Ronnie Lott (Cornerback-Safety) and Joe Montana (Quarterback)

Right: Chicago Bears cups.

1990 Chicago Bears Schedule, a set of two 6³/₄" supersize plastic cups, one with the Bears' logo on the front and the other with a Bears helmet. The Bears' 1990 schedule is on the reverse; the "Bear" cup has a helmet with the schedule, and the "helmet" cup has a bear with the schedule. The cup is co-sponsored by Diet Coke and the NFL. $2.00 – 4.00 each.

1. Bears cup with Bear on front
2. Bears cup with Bear on front (reverse view showing schedule)
3. Bears cup with helmet on front

BILLS, PACKERS, AND 1995 LOONEY TUNES PLAYS PLASTIC CUPS

Left: Bills and Packers cups.

1. 1991 – 1992 AFC Champion Bills, ©1992 McDonald's and co-sponsored by Coca-Cola and the NFL, a medium-sized white ribbed cup. On the reverse: Superbowl XXVI (logo), Sunday, January 26, 1992, Hubert H. Humphrey Metrodome Minneapolis, Minnesota. $2.00 – 5.00.

2. 1993 Green Bay Packers, 1919 – 1993 Celebrating 75 Years of Pro Football, a large plastic cup with a brief history of the team and its 1993 schedule on the reverse, co-sponsored by Coca-Cola and the NFL. $2.00 – 4.00.

3. 1996 Green Bay Packers 7" cup featuring the Packers gridiron with McDonald's and Packers pennants and three McDonald's thought bubble logos. Made by Packaging Resources. $2.00 – 4.00.

4. 1997 Green Bay Packers Superbowl XXXI Champs, a 6⁷⁄₈" "Superbowl Champion Collector Cup" featuring a Packers helmet along with "Coke To Go" and NFL logos. Bottom says: "Berry Plastics/Sterling/Patent Pending." $2.00 – 4.00.

Right: Set of four NFL Looney Tunes Plays plastic cups.

McDonald's/Coke Looney Tunes Plays (1995) ©McDonald's, Looney Tunes, Warner Brothers, and NFLP Plastic Cup Series, set of four "To Go Cups." These large 32 oz. plastic cups with bold graphics feature NFL stars and Warner Brothers characters in action. Customers could get these cups by super sizing any extra value meal. $4.00 – 7.00 each.

1. Drew Bledsoe/Wile E. Coyote, "The Long Bomb."
2. Dan Marino/Daffy Duck, "Forgot to Duck, Loss of Down."
3. Barry Sanders/Tasmanian Devil, "The Sweep" (front view).
4. Barry Sanders/Tasmanian Devil, "The Sweep" (reverse view).
5. Emmitt Smith/Bugs Bunny, "The Draw."

SEVEN SUPER BOWL CUPS AND ONE VIKINGS CUP

Left.

1. ™/©1993 NFL, Super Bowl XXVIII, Sunday, January 30, 1994, Georgia Dome, Atlanta. This 6³/₄" cup is co-sponsored by Coca-Cola Classic and shows the Super Bowl logo on one side and the 1994 NFL Experience logo on the other. Made by Sterling Products, Winchester, Virginia. $3.00 – 6.00.

2. 1995 Superbowl XXX, a 5¹/₂" cup with dark green background showing the 30th Superbowl logo along with the McDonald's logo on the front and Coca-Cola logo on the other. Below the Coke logo are the dates "January 19 – 21, 25 – 28, 1996, ASU Sun Devil Stadium/Tempe." $3.00 – 5.00.

3. ™/© 1995 NFL, Super Bowl XXX, a 6³/₄" super size cup co-sponsored by Coca-Cola. Predominant color is green with southwestern-flavored graphics including a playing field with cactuses on it and a hot-looking sun rising over an air-borne football. Under the Coca-Cola "NFL Experience" block, we find the following information: "January 19 – 21, 25 – 28, 1996 ASU Sun Devil Stadium/Tempe." Made by Packer Plastics, Lawrence, Kansas, and Reno, Nevada. This cup and the one listed above are probably partners in a series. $3.00 – 5.00.

4. ™/© 1995 NFL, Super Bowl XXX, a 6³/₄" super size cup co-sponsored by Coca-Cola and showing football players in action. Made by Packer Plastics, Lawrence, Kansas, and Reno, Nevada. $3.00 – 5.00.

Right.

1. ™/© 1995 NFL, Super Bowl XXX, a 6³/₄" super size cup co-sponsored by Coca-Cola. Same design on both sides with one large vertical "Enjoy Coca-Cola" block between the sides. Orange and brown are the predominant colors. Made by Packer Plastics, Lawrence, Kansas, and Reno, Nevada. $3.00 – 5.00.

2. ™/© 1995 NFL, Super Bowl XXX, a 6³/₄" super size cup co-sponsored by Coca-Cola. Same design on both sides is broken by "Enjoy Coca-Cola" and a large McDonald's logo. Predominant color is olive green. Made by Packer Plastics, Lawrence, Kansas, and Reno, Nevada. $3.00 – 5.00.

3. 1998 Minnesota Vikings 7" cup showing a Viking in an explosive graphic and with "Vikings" repeated six times in blue on the reverse. Made by Berry Plastics, Sterling. $2.00 – 4.00.

4. ©1998 Superbowl XXXII Sunday January 25, 1998, San Diego, California, Packers vs Broncos, a 7" cup with Packers and Chargers helmets, Coke to Go logo, NFL logo, and McDonald's thought bubble logo. Made by Berry Plastics, Sterling. $3.00 – 5.00.

MISCELLANEOUS NFL PLASTIC CUPS

Left.

1. 1999 Kansas City Chiefs, a 5" cup which promotes McDonald's McFlurry. $1.00 – 3.00.

2. 2000 Chicago Bears with graphics celebrating the teamwork of Marcus Robinson and Cade McNown, a 7" cup with "Smile" logo and Coca-Cola contour bottle logo. Made by Sweetheart. $1.00 – 3.00.

3. "2001 • Inaugural Season • 2002 Heinz Field," a 32 oz. 7" cup showing a graphic of the Steelers' new stadium. There's also a large Steelers logo, a Coke contour bottle logo, and the logo of FM 102.5 WDVE. Obviously distributed in western Pennsylvania in October 2001 for the Steelers' home opener. On the bottom: "Sweetheart, 32 oz. www.sweetheart.com." $1.00 – 3.00.

Right.

Clear thick $5^3/_8$" acrylic cups showing an NFL helmet on the front with McDonald's and Coke logo on the reverse. The two cups I show here are probably members of a much larger series. These cups are undated, but their style indicates a mid to late 1980s date, and they are pretty hard to find. $5.00 – 10.00 each.

1. San Diego Chargers

2. Los Angeles Raiders

THREE PLASTIC GOLF CUPS

1. ©1985, a 5¹/₈" Sweetheart cup showing on its front a golf ball with a McDonald's logo on it on a tee with "McDonald's Championship" around it and "Help make a tough course easier for kids" at the top. On the reverse "McDonald's Championship" appears again at the top. In the middle we have: "Come and see the top women golfers in the nation compete to benefit Ronald McDonald Childrens Charities and help make a tough course easier for kids. June 4 – 9, 1985, White Manor Country Club, Malvern, PA." $8.00 – 13.00.

2. 1988 McDonald's Championship, a 6³/₄" cup promoting the LPGA and showing pictures of winners of the Championship from 1981 through 1987. At the bottom are the dates for the 1988 Championship: June 23, 24, 25, 26, 1988. Co-sponsored by Coca-Cola and made by Louisiana Plastics. $7.00 – 10.00.

3. McDonald's Championship, LPGA, a 5¹/₈" Sweetheart cup with McDonald's LPGA Championship logo on both sides and "Enjoy Coca-Cola Classic" logo repeated twice. No date. $5.00 – 8.00.

THREE HOCKEY CUPS

1. 1991 Brett Hull cup, co-sponsored by McDonald's and Coca-Cola. This medium-sized cup shows Brett Hull in action in a St. Louis Blues uniform and reviews the highlights of his (then) 25 year career. $5.00 – 10.00.

2. 1993 Dallas Stars Inaugural Year Commemorative Cup, a 5³/₄" cup with McDonald's logo and these additional co-sponsorships: WBAP Radio 820, Spirit of Texas WFAA-TV 8, Dr Pepper, and 96.3 KSCS. Made by Pescor Plastics, Ft. Worth, Texas. $3.00 – 6.00.

3. 1995 Western NHL Conference Central Division, a 6³/₄" medium-sized Canadian plastic cup showing the logos of NHL Central Division teams. Team logos shown are Dallas Stars, Winnipeg Jets, Toronto Maple Leafs, St. Louis Blues, and Detroit Red Wings. Co-sponsored by Coca-Cola and made in Toronto by The Collectibles. The Canadian McDonald's logo appears just above the Red Wings logo. $4.00 – 8.00.

MISCELLANEOUS SPORTS

1983 Kentucky Derby with Ronald McDonald House co-sponsorship, May 7, 1983. This cup is considered rare and desirable because it was issued in limited quantities at only one location. $25.00 – 75.00.

1. Front view of 1983 Kentucky Derby cup (photo courtesy of David and Kathy Clark).

2. Reverse view of 1983 Kentucky Derby cup showing Ronald McDonald House logo (photo courtesy of David and Kathy Clark).

MISCELLANEOUS SPORTS CUPS

Left.

1. National Sports Festival VI, Baton Rouge 1985, July 24th – August 4th. The front of the 5⅛" cup shows United States athletes performing and receiving medals; the reverse has a large McDonald's logo, "Coke," and "Not just better athletes, better kids." $8.00 – 12.00.

2. 1986 Illinois Home of the Fighting Illini, a 6¾" cup co-sponsored by Coca-Cola Classic, Sprite, and Diet Coke. The cup shows the Illini stadium, a football player, and a basketball player. Made by Louisiana Plastics. $8.00 – 12.00.

3. 1986, Indianapolis 500-Mile Race 75th Anniversary 1911 – 1986, a 6¾" large cup co-sponsored by Coca-Cola with a list of Indy 500 winners from 1911 to 1985 on the reverse. Made by Louisiana Plastics. $8.00 – 12.00.

Right.

1. 1987, Tenth Pan American Games, Indianapolis 7 – 23 August 1987, a 6¾" large cup featuring the ©1985 Indianapolis Pan American Games logo on one side and a McDonald's logo, games dates, and "Enjoy Coca-Cola Classic" logo on the other. Made by Louisiana Plastics. $4.00 – 8.00.

2. ©1988, USA Diving, Summer 1988, a 6¾" cup co-sponsored by Coca-Cola featuring a diving board and ribbon of water. I'm not sure what level of diving is being promoted here, perhaps summer Olympics or American qualifying events (?). Made by Louisiana Plastics in St. Louis. $6.00 – 10.00.

3. 1989, a 5½" cup co-sponsored by Coca-Cola Classic showing Cal Ripken, Jr. of the Baltimore Orioles on one side with the caption "The Home Run Meal" and Charles Mann of the Washington Redskins on the other with the caption "The Quarterback Sack Meal." Made by Louisiana Plastics. $8.00 – 13.00.

4. 1994, Kentucky Derby 120, Churchill Downs, Louisville, Kentucky May 7, 1994, a 6¾" large cup with KD 120th logo on front and a large McDonald's logo with "What you want is what you get" on the reverse. Made by Comet in Chelmsford, Mass. $8.00 – 12.00.

MISCELLANEOUS SPORTS CUPS

Left: Two Australian Rugby League cups.

1995 Australian Rugby League "6 of the Best," a set of six 5¾" cups showcasing six of Australia's best rugby players. There's a nice picture of each player in action along with a fair amount of personal and career information. These cups are hard to come by in the United States, so I can only show two of them. Made in Toronto and marketed as the "Collectibles." $10.00 – 15.00 each.

1. Allan Langer, Half Back, Brisbane Broncos
2. Rod Wishart, Wing, Illawarra Steelers

Right: Ohio and Oklahoma sports cups.

1. 1998 Ohio Bobcats, a 7" cup featuring the 1998 Bobcats' football schedule, along with the "Always Coca-Cola" logo and McDonald's thought bubble logo. Made by Berry Plastics, Sterling. $2.00 – 4.00.
2. Oklahoma, "McDonald's All-State Games, McDonald's proudly salutes the best high school athletes in Oklahoma," a 6¾" super-sized cup made by Pescor Plastics in Ft. Worth, Texas (no date). Sports named on the cup include basketball, cheerleading, Tennis, baseball, golf, football, and wrestling. $5.00 – 9.00.

FOUR OLYMPICS CUPS

1. Undated 4³/₄" Olympic poster cup with McDonald's and Coca-Cola logos on two sides and Olympic posters from the 1928 Amsterdam games and the 1959 Helsinki games on the other two sides. $5.00 – 10.00.

2. 1984 Los Angeles Summer Olympics, a 4³/₄" plastic cup with 1984 Olympic and McDonald's logo. $5.00 – 8.00.

1984 Los Angeles Summer Olympics, 5¹/₈" cups featuring Sam the Olympic Eagle participating in various revents at the 1984 Olympics. ©1980 Los Angeles Olympic logo, Olympic ring logo, and McDonald's logo appear on the reverse. This plastic set is probably what the glass set of four promised on the 1984 owner-operator's tumbler would have looked like (see page 226). Informed sources tell me that there are four cups in this set which share the same designs as several different (non-McDonald's) 1984 Olympic glass sets. These cups are hard to find in any condition! Made by Sweetheart. $10.00 – 15.00 each.

3. Sam jumping hurdle (Track)

4. Sam preparing to swim (Swimming)

Not pictured: Gymnastics and Basketball

SIX 1988 U.S. OLYMPIC TEAM CUPS

1988 U.S. Olympic Team sponsored by McDonald's and Coca-Cola/Diet Coke, set of twelve. These large plastic cups (shown here in alphabetical order) feature summer Olympic sports along with an account of the United States' achievements in these sports in previous Olympics. $2.00 – 4.00 each.

Left.

1. Basketball
2. Boxing
3. Cycling (Diet Coke)

Right.

1. Diving (Diet Coke)
2. Gymnastics, rings (Diet Coke)
3. Gymnastics, women's, featuring the balance beam (Diet Coke)

 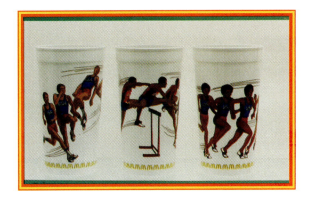

SIX 1988 U.S. OLYMPIC TEAM CUPS
Left.
1. Gymnastics, women's, featuring floor exercises
2. Soccer
3. Swimming (Diet Coke)

Right.
1. Track & Field, high jump
2. Track & Field, men's hurdles
3. Track & Field, running (Diet Coke)

1992 BARCELONA AND ALBERTVILLE OLYMPIC CUPS

1992 Barcelona Olympic Summer Games, 5³/₈" cups, co-sponsored by Coca-Cola. These cups feature a large Barcelona Olympic logo along with Olympic posters going back to 1896. Each cup covers different years. I believe there may be three cups in this set. Made by Louisiana Plastics in St. Louis. $7.00 – 12.00 each.
1. 1896 – 1924. Posters from 1896, 1900, 1904, 1908, 1912, 1920, 1924
2. 1932 – 1964. Posters from 1932, 1936, 1948, 1952, 1956, 1960, 1964
1992 Albertville Winter Olympic Games, 5¹/₈" Sweetheart cups showing the Albertville logo, the English/French "Enjoy/Savourez" Coca-Cola logo, and colorful graphics depicting various winter sports. I'm not sure how many cups there are in this set, but there are almost certainly more than two. $7.00 – 12.00 each.
3. Ice Hockey
4. Ice Skating

OLYMPIC GAMES POSTER SERIES CUPS

1996 Centennial Olympic Games Poster Collection, co-sponsored by Coca-Cola, "Official Soft Drink Of The 1996 Olympic Games." Each of these 6³/₄" super-sized cups features two different historic Olympic posters with detailed information about the games for each year between the poster panels. I assume there are eight cups in this set. Made by Sterling Products, Winchester, Virginia. $5.00 – 10.00 each.

Left.

1. 1896 Athens, Greece/1996 Atlanta, Georgia
2. 1904 Louisiana Purchase Exposition St. Louis U.S.A./Barcelona 1992
3. 1912 Stockholm/1988 Seoul

Right.

1. 1928 Amsterdam/1972 Munich
2. 1932 Los Angeles/1968 Mexico City
3. 1936 Berlin/1964 Tokyo
4. 1924 Paris/1976 Montreal

REVERSE VIEWS OF 1996 HISTORIC OLYMPIC POSTERS SERIES SHOWN ABOVE

Left.

1. 1996/1896
2. 1992/1904
3. 1988/1912

Right.

1. 1972/1928
2. 1968/1932
3. 1964/1936
4. 1976/1924

SIX PLASTIC STATE CUPS

Left.

1. Alaska, ©1993, a 6³/₄" plastic cup co-sponsored by Coca-Cola Classic showing Alaska's natural attractions: mountains and wildlife. Made by Louisiana Plastics in St. Louis, Missouri. $3.00 – 6.00.

2. Alaska (no date), "Great Land of the Midnight Sun," a 6³/₄" plastic cup co-sponsored by Coca-Cola Classic showing all of Alaska's natural and cultural assets, polar bears, Eskimos, totem poles, eagles, huskies, and more. Made by Louisiana Plastics in St. Louis, Missouri. $3.00 – 6.00.

3. Arizona, ©1990, a super size 6⁷/₈" plastic cup co-sponsored by Coca-Cola Classic and featuring the artwork of Barb McClain which shows Arizona's various attractions in a hand-drawn cartoonish format. Made by Sweetheart. $4.00 – 7.00.

Right.

1. Arizona, ©1992, a super size 6⁷/₈" plastic cup co-sponsored by Coca-Cola Classic showcasing Arizona's natural beauty and historical attractions. Made by Sweetheart. $3.00 – 5.00.

2. Arizona (no date), a super size 6⁷/₈" plastic cup co-sponsored by Coca-Cola Classic promoting Arizona's attractions, landscape, sports teams, vegetation, and wildlife. Made by Sterling Products in Winchester, Virginia. $3.00 – 5.00.

3. Iowa, ©1988, a large 6³/₄" plastic cup co-sponsored by Coca-Cola Classic, Sprite, and Diet Coke promoting the state of Iowa and its rivers, recreation, agriculture, etc. There's even a toll free number for tourism information at the bottom of the cup: 1-800-345-IOWA. Made by Louisiana Plastics in St. Louis, Missouri. $3.00 – 6.00.

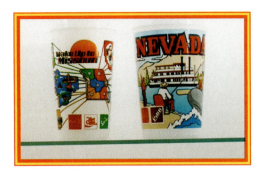 

FIVE PLASTIC STATE CUPS

Left.

1. Missouri, ©1987, a large 6³/₄" plastic cup co-sponsored by Coca-Cola Classic, Diet Coke, and Sprite encouraging us to "Wake Up to Missouri." A map of the state is keyed to "Missouri's 8 Vacationlands" which also appear in a list so we don't miss the message. $4.00 – 8.00.

2. Nevada (no date), a super size 6⁷/₈" plastic cup co-sponsored by Mr. Pibb and Coca-Cola Classic promoting Nevada's attractions, among them fishing, gambling, river rafting, rodeo, and old-fashioned railraoding. Made by Sweetheart. $5.00 – 8.00.

Right.

1. Oklahoma, ©1990, a super size 6³/₄" plastic cup co-sponsored by Coca-Cola Classic and featuring the artwork of Barb McClain which depicts Oklahoma's attractions in a colorful zippy cartoonish format. This cup, made by Sweetheart, has the Scooter Productions logo. $5.00 – 8.00.

Virginia, ©1988 "McDonald's Salute to Tourism," a series of six 6³/₄" cups promoting the attractions of the state of Virginia. Each cup is numbered and says "From a 6 Week/6 Series edition." Two major attractions are highlighted on each cup. Co-sponsored by Coca-Cola Classic and made by Louisiana Plastics in St. Louis, Missouri. $5.00 – 8.00 each.

2. Cup three: Beaches/King's Dominion

3. Cup five: Natural Bridge/Waterside, Norfolk, Virginia

1998 DISNEY ANIMAL KINGDOM CUP SET

1998 Disney's Animal Kingdom, Walt Disney World, Opens Spring 1998, a set of four unnumbered large 7" cups co-sponsored by Coca-Cola. Listings 1 and 4 below were made by Packaging Resources and have plain bases. Numbers 2 and 3 were made by Berry Plastics, Sterling and have vertical paneled bases. Customers could get each cup for 39¢ by super-sizing any Extra Value Meal. $2.00 – 3.00 each.

1. Countdown Extinction, DinoLand U.S.A.

2. Gorilla Falls, Exploration Trail

3. Kilimanjaro Safaris, Africa

4. Safari Village, Discovery River

NASCAR ALL-STAR RACE TEAM MUGS

McDonald's All-Star Race Team set of three mugs. These 6⅝" thick plastic mugs were available in the late 1980s as a mail order item. Same graphics in black on both sides. No writing on the bottom. 5.00 – 10.00 each.

1. Blue NASCAR mug
2. Green NASCAR mug
3. Yellow NASCAR mug

PLASTIC SPORTS MUGS AND BOTTLES

1. Red and white (undated), 6½" plastic beverage bottle with flex straw and cap featuring Ronald with protective helmet on a skateboard, Birdie skipping rope, Hamburglar on a scooter, and Grimace with a baseball bat. No writing on the bottom. $5.00 – 10.00.
2. 6" McDonald's Minute Maid sports tumbler with orange plastic lid and flex straw showing Minute Maid oranges skateboarding, surfing, roller skating, and playing the guitar. $6.00 – 9.00.
3. 5¾" red plastic sport bottle with white McDonald's logo and white plastic cap and clear plastic straw. No date. Made by Mueller in Prairie Du Sac, Wisconsin. U.S.A. $4.00 – 8.00.

6⁹/₁₆" sports mugs with caps and flex straws, "McDonald's" in script three times around the mugs at a 45 degree angle, French fries and cups of Coca-Cola each repeated three times around the mugs. Color of handle matches color of cap. I show two mugs here, but there are probably others which make up a set. Made by Whirley Industries. $3.00 – 5.00 each.

4. Mug with blue handle and cap.
5. Mug with purple handle and cap.

PICNIC JUG AND THREE SPORTS TUMBLERS

1. Half gallon red and white Igloo insulated beverage container with carrying handle. There's a yellow McDonald's logo on the screw-on lid. $10.00 – 15.00.

8 1/8" sport tumblers with flex straws, co-sponsored by Coca-Cola Classic, set of three. These neon-colored tall tumblers have "Enjoy Coca-Cola Classic" and "McDonald's" in underlined script vertically on opposite sides. No date or information on the bottoms. $4.00 – 8.00 each.

2. Green tumbler

3. Orange tumbler

4. Pink tumbler

SET OF THREE McDONALD'S PIZZA, LAS VEGAS SPORT MUGS: "PIZZA/McDONALD'S" VIEW

McDonald's Pizza, Las Vegas, a set of three 6¹/₂" sport mugs with flex straws, co-sponsored by Coca-Cola Classic. All the graphics are at a 45 degree angle and include "Enjoy Coca-Cola Classic," "Las Vegas," "McDonald's Pizza," and "McDonald's." Made by Whirley Industries. $6.00 – 10.00 each.

1. Pink mug
2. Green mug
3. Orange mug

SET OF THREE McDONALD'S PIZZA, LAS VEGAS SPORT MUGS: "COCA-COLA CLASSIC/LAS VEGAS" VIEW

1. Pink mug
2. Green mug
3. Orange mug

FOUR SPORTS DRINK CONTAINERS

1. "McDonald's Exercise Facility May 13 National Employee Fitness Day Commit To Get McFit," an 8³/₄" white sport bottle with cap, straw, and straw cap. Purple and blue-green decoration. "Enduro 52470" on bottom. $4.00 – 8.00.

2. "CAT Citizens Area Transit, It's You...It's CAT...It's Southern Nevada!," an 8¹/₄" sport bottle with black cap and black and pink decoration on a pearly background. On the bottom: "32 oz. Sport Quart, Whirley, Warren, PA, U.S.A." $5.00 – 8.00.

3. "Servin' Up Smiles McDonald's Style!," a 9¹/₈" yellow-green sport bottle with black decoration and black cap with green flex straw and black straw cap. The same graphic appears on both sides: a lightning bolt character tipping his hat and delivering a tray with shake, burger, and fries. Made by Pescor Plastics in Ft. Worth, Texas. $4.00 – 8.00.

4. "Can't Beat the Feeling! Enjoy Coca-Cola Classic, the Official Soft Drink of Summer"/"Good Time. Great Taste" (with large McDonald's logo in red block), an 8⁵/₈" white sport bottle with red cap and clear flex straw with red straw cap made by Louisiana Plastics. The "Good Time...Great Taste" slogan was introduced in 1984. $3.00 – 8.00.

FOUR LARGE SPORTS DRINK CONTAINERS

1. "Archway To The Dunes, Chesterton, Indiana Exit 26A," a yellow 8⅝" sport tumbler with black cap, clear plastic straw, and black straw cap. There's even a black plastic holder which holds the tumbler on the car's door via the window slot. Small black McDonald's logos encircle the top of the tumbler along with "Refills $0.50 With Any Purchase ***Chesterton Location Only." Same design both sides. Made by Alpha Products, Atlanta. $5.00 – 10.00.

2. McDonald's, "Archway To The Dunes, Chesterton, Indiana Exit 26A," an 8¾" sport tumbler with red cap which has two small flip-up lids, one for a flex straw and the other for pouring or drinking. Same design both sides. "Refills 59¢ With Any Purchase" and the recycling logo with "'Refill Containers' Protect The Environment" appear on both sides. Made by Whirley. $5.00 – 10.00.

3. "McDonald's Racing Team, Jimmy Spencer 27," a 14" red plastic drink container in the shape of an oil can. On the bottom: "Fan Fueler Drink Containers, Orange Park, FL 32073." Red funnel-shaped cap fits over a white screw-on cap. $7.00 – 12.00.

4. 1990 Comisky Park 1910 – 1990 Chicago White Sox, co-sponsored by Coca-Cola Classic. This baseball bat-shaped plastic drink container measures 11 inches to the top of the blue batting helmet. The white base is shaped like a baseball bat. On top of that is a navy blue plastic batting helmet with a Sox logo. A red straw runs down through the cap and red plastic lid. There's a red Comisky Park logo on one side with 1910 – 1990 and on the other a McDonald's logo and Coca-Cola Classic logo. Made by American Beverage Container Co. $8.00 – 14.00.

FIVE EARLY 1990s SPORTS BOTTLES

1. 1990, 9¹/₄" sport bottle with red bottom, clear straw, and red cap showing tennis player and lime-green tennis balls. $5.00 – 10.00.

2. 1990, 9¹/₄" sport bottle with purple bottom, clear straw, and purple cap showing baseball player and purple-tinted baseballs. This bottle and the one to its left are probably members of a larger set. $5.00 – 10.00.

3. 1991 Michael Jordan Fitness Fun Challenge, a 4³/₄" Happy Meal Squeeze Bottle. This little blue sport bottle with purple cap and orange straw was part of the Michael Jordan Fitness Fun Challenge Happy Meal. The idea was to get parents and children to use "the enclosed toy" to "invent new games and challenges that are active as well as fun." The bottle has a ring of embossed Arches near the top. On the bottom: "©1991 McDonald's Corp. ©Jump Inc. China, CW 4." $3.00 – 6.00.

4. 1991 Minute Maid drink bottle, a 4³/₈" bottle with clear straw for kids showing Ronald in the engine of a train with Birdie, Hamburglar, and Grimace behind him in their own train cars with McDonald's logos on the sides. "Minute Maid" is repeated six times near the base beneath the train. This is probably a Happy Meal toy. No writing on bottom. $4.00 – 7.00.

5. 1991 – 1992 Ohio State Buckeyes Big Ten Basketball Schedule Home Games, a 10" red insulated drink container with built-in flip-up straw and gray insulated insert. One side shows the Buckeyes mascot along with McDonald's and Coca-Cola Classic logos; the other side has the home game schedule, "Go Bucks! Defending Big Ten Champs!" and the Collegiate Licensed Product logo. Made by Countryside Products in Pickerington, Ohio. $5.00 – 10.00.

FOUR EARLY 1990s SPORTS DRINK CONTAINERS

1. 1992 insulated sport mug with black cap and flex straw. The black cap has two flip-lids, one for a straw and one for pouring or drinking. This mug features "McDonald's" in pink underlined script at a 45 degree angle on a grilled panel of black lines. At the bottom of the mug in small black script: "Refill this mug at participating McDonald's Restaurants for only 49¢ (plus tax). Offer good through March 31, 1993." Made by Alpha Products in Atlanta. $4.00 – 8.00.

2. 1993 "Shalimar McDonald's Shalimar, Florida, Home of the McFreez, Eglin Air Force Base, Best Base in the USAF 1993," an 8^7/$_8$" sport tumbler with red and yellow decoration and red cap with clear flex straw and white straw cap. Made by Whirley Industries in Warren, Pennsylvania. Same design both sides. $5.00 – 10.00.

3. World Cup USA 1994 plastic soccer ball sports drink container with blue plastic screw-on lid, built-in handle on back of ball, and flex straw. This unusual and playful 5^3/$_4$" soccer ball sports the 94 World Cup logo inside a large golden arch. $10.00 – 20.00.

4. Chicago Bulls basketball-shaped sports drink container with black plastic screw-on lid, red plastic straw with black cap, and built-in handle on back of ball. McDonald's logo below Bulls logo. This unusual 5^3/$_4$" ball was probably issued in 1994, as was the 1994 World Cup soccer ball. "CC Pat. Pend." appears on the bottom. $10.00 – 20.00.

FIVE SPORTS DRINK CONTAINERS

1. World Cup USA 1994, a 6³/₈" sport bottle with red cap, clear flex straw, and red straw cap. Same design both sides. Near the bottom of the bottle there's a "Property of:" line for the owner to write his or her name. $4.00 – 7.00.

2. World Cup USA 1994, a 9" sport tumbler with green cap which has two little flip lids, one for the flex straw and one for drinking without the straw. The USA's mascot is shown in four different poses surrounding the McDonald's and World Cup USA logos. There's also a small Coca-Cola Classic logo and a small World Cup USA 94 logo near the bottom. The reverse features a large graphic of the mascot with his foot on a soccer ball and holding a Coke Contour Bottle in his right hand. Made by Whirley Industries. $5.00 – 8.00.

3. "Game One September 3, 1994," an 8¹/₄" sport bottle with black cap showing the helmets of the Kentucky Wildcats and the Louisville Cardinals on a pearly background. On the reverse, there's a McDonald's logo with "What you want is what you get, ©1994 McDonald's Corporation." Bottom says "32 oz. Sport Quart, Whirely, Warren, PA, U.S.A." $5.00 – 8.00.

32 oz. "Sport Quart" thick plastic tumbler made by Whirley in Warren, Pennsylvania. This 8¹/₄" tumbler with flex straw shows French fries, McDonald's in script at a 45 degree angle, and a cup of Coca-Cola repeated three times around the tumbler. The tumbler has two stickers on it near the bottom on opposite sides. One says "39¢ Fill-up, McDonald's at Valley, June – July – August 1994 only." The other says "Call for Delivery on Campus 11 AM – 8 PM, 656-5043." This tumbler is most readily found without the plastic sticker. $5.00 – 10.00.

4. Tumbler with sticker

5. Tumbler without sticker

MISCELLANEOUS SPORTS DRINK CONTAINERS

1. 1995 McDonald's 7⅞" sports tumbler with large gold and white Arches and blue background with red ovals. Co-sponsored by Coca-Cola, red cap, and clear flex straw. $4.00 – 7.00.

2. ©1996 McDonald's Corporation, an 8¼" sport bottle with red cap and clear flex straw showing Ronald and Grimace washing a circus elephant. Made by Pescor Plastics, Ft. Worth, Texas. $4.00 – 7.00.

3. 1996 Milwaukee Region, "Raising the Bar," a 9½" gray barbell-shaped bottle with black decoration and red snap cap showing Speedee lifting a large barbell. Same design both sides. $6.00 – 12.00.

4. 1997 "Las Vegas, The Best Odds in Town," a 7⅞" sport mug with yellow cap and handle and clear flex straw showing Ronald, Hamburglar, Birdie, Grimace, McNugget Buddies, and Fry Kids performing as rock musicians with Las Vegas skyline in the background. Made by Whirley Industries, Inc., Warren, Pennsylvania, USA. $4.00 – 7.00.

5. 1998 "Natural and Refreshing Spring Water" 20 oz. bottle, an 8⅜" clear plastic bottle with red and yellow plastic dispenser valve and paper wrapper filled with, water!! This trendy container will be worth a fortune if no one but me saves one! Great item for time capsules! $1.00 – 3.00.

6. 2002, 22 oz. "Big Mouth" sports bottle showing Ronald and the McDonaldland characters (Birdie, Grimace, and Hamburglar) at an Easter egg hunt with the Easter bunny. Sitting atop this bottle is a removable yellow figural Easter bunny with a flex straw coming out of the top. There's no date on the cup and no manufacturer's name, but it came out in March of 2002. It sold for $1.59. On the bottom: "22 oz. Big Mouth." $2.00 – 3.00.

PUERTO RICAN CHRISTMAS TUMBLER SETS

Los Tres Reyes Magos Coleccion de Vasos Edicion set of four (1995).

This set of four 20 ounce tumblers featuring the Magi or Three Kings was issued in Puerto Rico in November and December of 1995. The artwork is by Samuel Diaz, a young art student at the School of Plastic Arts in San Juan who won a competition sponsored by McDonald's and Coca-Cola. Diaz's signature appears below the kings, and the McDonald's and Coca-Cola logos appear on the reverse along with a brief explanation in Spanish of the details concerning the promotion. A Puerto Rican newspaper account of this promotion informs us that more than 400,000 of these glasses were made. $8.00 – 12.00 each.

Row 1.

1. Baltasar
2. Gaspar
3. Melchor
4. Los Tres Reyes Magos

Row 2.

This second set of four 20 ounce Three Kings tumblers co-sponsored by McDonald's and Coca-Cola was designed by Raul Vizcarrondo and distributed by McDonald's in November and December of 1997. Colors and design are strikingly similar to the 1995 edition. Spanish text on the reverse tells about the origins of the promotion. $8.00 – 12.00 each.

1. Los Reyes en Puerto Rico
2. Los Reyes y las Ofrendas
3. Los Reyes en el Pesebre
4. Los Reyes y la Estrella de Belen
5. Los Reyes y la Estrella de Belen error glass missing title, artist's name, and facial outline because the color black did not print. $10.00 – 15.00.

SIX RADIO STATION MUGS

Row 1.

1. "WZPR 'The Country One' FM 100.3 WMGW 1-4-9-0 * AM" on one side of a 3¹¹/₁₆" McDonald's "My Morning Mug" (see "Breakfast Mugs" page 16, row 1, #3, for the side I don't show here). "Made in England" is embossed on bottom. $15.00 – 20.00.

2. Lite Rock 102.9 FM/Food Folks & Fun, a 3¹/₂" white ceramic coffee mug with yellow, black, and blue decoration, from Youngstown, Ohio. The "Food, Folks, and Fun" ad campaign, introduced in 1990, appears below a small black and yellow McDonald's block logo. $10.00 – 15.00.

3. Lite Rock 102.9 FM/McDonald's Today, a 3³/₈" white ceramic coffee mug with yellow, black, and blue decoration. Slightly smaller than the mug just to its left, this mug shares the same design and colors, but it has a different slogan and a larger black and yellow McDonald's block logo on the reverse. $10.00 – 15.00.

Row 2.

1. I Got Mugged By...The Waking Crew, Matt, Steve, Chuck, and Barb/96 FM WKDD of Greater Akron & Canton, a 3³/₄" white ceramic coffee mug with black decoration. $10.00 – 15.00.

2. I Got Mugged At McDonald's with K-HITS 106.9 FM, a 3⁷/₈" black ceramic mug with red and yellow decoration on one side only. The radio station in question is located in Tulsa, Oklahoma. $10.00 – 16.00.

3. "WAAL At Work!" (front) with "McDonald's, What you want is what you get" (reverse), a 3³/₄" white ceramic coffee mug with red, black, and yellow decoration. This mug comes in two sizes: 3¹/₄" and 3³/₈" mouth diameters. The whale (WAAL) musician on the smaller mug is 1³/₈" high; on the larger mug he is proportionately bigger and 1⁵/₈" high. The radio station's call letters are ¹/₈" taller on the larger mug. Shown here is the front of the larger mug. $10.00 – 15.00.

SEVEN RADIO STATION MUGS

Row 1.

1. McDonald's "What you want is what you get" (reverse of smaller WAAL At Work! mug shown on page 201, Row 2, No. 3). $10.00 – 15.00.

2. "WAAL At Work!" a 3³/₄" mug (3¹/₈" mouth diameter) made by Linyi in China with "did somebody say (McDonald's?)" thought bubble on the reverse in black writing. The WAAL whale graphic is identical to those on the two other WAAL mugs shown on page 201 and just to this mug's left, so I show here the reverse which is a definite departure from the other two WAAL mugs. $10.00 – 15.00.

3. "Y-103 FM At Work!," a 3³/₄" white ceramic mug with yellow, orange, and red decoration. A McDonald's logo appears on the reverse. No markings on bottom. Y–103 is in Youngstown, Ohio. $10.00 – 15.00.

Row 2.

1. "wake up with DAYBREAK and McDonald's" on one side of a 3³/₄" mug and "News Channel 19 Where Local News Comes First" on the other. Red, yellow, black, and blue decoration on white mug. This mug is from the Birmingham, Alabama, area. $10.00 – 15.00.

2. "Jackson WKHM 970," a 3¹/₈" Anchor Hocking milk glass mug with black and yellow decoration. This mug is from Jackson, Michigan. $10.00 – 15.00.

3. "Grand McDon. Le 16 Mai 2000, Longueuil, CHAA 103.3 FM," a 3³/₄" white ceramic mug with red decoration. The opposite side has a large Canadian McDonald's logo on it. Between the two panels near the bottom: "Promotions Trivia (450)670–8172." This mug is from Longueuil, Quebec, and was part of a promotion to help the needy. $15.00 – 20.00.

4. "McDonald's Guam" (on one side) and "Hit Radio 100, Guam's Party Station KOKU FM Hagalma, Guam, Malafunkshun" on the other. There's obviously some inside humor associated with this 5⁷/₈" white ceramic mug with red and black decoration, but it escapes me. This has to be a very limited edition mug since Guam isn't a very big place and certainly not a large market for McDonald's. $15.00 – 25.00.

RED WING POTTERY MUGS

FIVE RED WING STONEWARE MUGS

Red Wing Stoneware has been making McDonald's crockery since 1991, and the variety of items available is impressive: crocks, jugs, mugs, cookie jars, water pitchers, and even salt and pepper shakers. Dating the mugs precisely is a bit of a problem because some are dated, and some are not. Each mug has an official Red Wing Pottery stamping in blue on its bottom. The mugs are made in very limited quantities are therefore not only difficult to find but expensive. McDonald's collectors will find themselves in fierce competition with Red Wing collectors. I assume that the undated mugs are earlier than the dated ones.

Row 1: Two undated Red Wing Pottery mugs.

1. McDonald's logo in blue on 3³/₄" gray pottery mug with blue rim made by the Red Wing Stoneware Co., Red Wing, Minnesota. $30.00 – 40.00.

2. McDonald's logo in orange/red and yellow on 3³/₄" gray pottery mug with blue rim made by the Red Wing Stoneware Co., Red Wing, Minnesota. $30.00 – 40.00.

Row 2: Three dated Red Wing Pottery mugs.

1. McDonald's 1994, a 3¹/₂" pottery mug with red and blue decoration on gray made by the Red Wing Stoneware Co. in Red Wing, Minnesota. $25.00 – 35.00.

2. McDonald's 1998 Red Wing, MN, a 3³/₄" gray pottery mug with light blue rim and dark blue lettering and bright Gold Arches on the front. The "Red Wing Stoneware Co. Red Wing, Minnesota" logo appears on the bottom. $25.00 – 35.00.

3. McDonald's 2000 Red Wing, MN, a 3³/₄" gray pottery mug with red and blue decoration made by the Red Wing Stoneware Company in Red Wing, Minnesota. $25.00 – 35.00.

SIX DATED RONALD McDONALD HOUSE ISSUES

The first Ronald McDonald House was opened in Philadelphia in 1974. As of 1999, there were 206 houses in 19 countries. Information about Ronald McDonald House can be obtained by writing to: Ronald McDonald House Charities, One Kroc Drive, Oak Brook, Illinois 60523. Internet address: www.rmhc.com. E-mail: rmhuoc@aol.com.

Row 1.

1. "Every day another child says thanks," a 3⅝" brown ceramic mug with gold decoration on rim, front, and back. The front features a big Victorian-looking Ronald McDonald House, and the back has the previously mentioned caption along with "Ronald McDonald Dinner-Dance October 1982." "Made in England" appears on the bottom. $20.00 – 30.00.

2. 1983 Ronald McDonald House, a 5⅛" plastic cup showing Ronald, Hamburglar, and Grimace behind a row of very Victorian looking Ronald McDonald houses. $5.00 – 10.00.

3. Indiana Ronald McDonald House 1985, a 4" gray stoneware mug with blue decoration showing a house with a large heart on the front and a heart-shaped vehicle parked in front. In blue decoration on the bottom: "Made especially for the Indiana Ronald McDonald House By Louisville Stoneware." $15.00 – 25.00.

Row 2.

1. Indiana Ronald McDonald House 1986, a 3½" heart-shaped white ceramic mug with red and gray decoration. $10.00 – 15.00.

2. "Oktober Fest 1988" in green decoration on one side of a 4⅞" white stoneware mug and "Indiana Ronald McDonald House Volunteer Recognition" in black decoration on the other. "China" appears on the bottom. $15.00 – 25.00.

3. Safari Eighty-Nine, Indiana Ronald McDonald House Volunteer Recognition (1989), a 5¾" pedestal mug with olive, red, and black decoration. $10.00 – 15.00.

SIX DATED RONALD McDONALD HOUSE ISSUES

Row 1.

1. 1989 Ronald McDonald House 3" plastic mug with lime green sipping lid and handle showing Captain Crook and Hamburglar. $4.00 – 7.00.

1990 – 1991 Ronald McDonald Children's Charities, "Established in memory of Ray A. Kroc," a set of two 5" plastic cups featuring drawings by children. A panel on the reverse of each cup explains the mission of the Children's Charities organization and lists organizations which were awarded grants by the Baltimore/Washington Chapter of RMCC. These cups are rare items. $10.00 – 15.00 each.

2. 1990, drawings by Kate Labetti Age 4½.

3. 1991, drawings by Ashley Graling Age 6.

Row 2.

1. Ronald McDonald House, Portland (Maine), a 3¾" white ceramic mug with red and blue decoration. On the reverse, there's a drawing of the house with "Dreams Do Come True" above it and "May 26, 1995" below it. On the bottom: "S – S Made in China." $10.00 – 15.00.

2. Mac Tonight 1997, Ronald McDonald House, a 4½" white ceramic mug with red, yellow, and black decoration. The familiar crescent moon and Ray Charles with sunglasses appears on a clock face with the hands pointing at 12 and 3. Same design on both sides. Bottom says "Made in China." A curious mug considering that the Mac Tonight promotion took place in 1988 and 1989. $15.00 – 25.00.

3. 25 Years, Ronald McDonald House Charities, a 6" fountain style glass co-sponsored by Coca-Cola. The graphic shows Ronald's hand grasping a child's hand inside the outline of a house. "Coca-Cola" appears in white on the reverse. No date on glass, but Ronald McDonald House was founded in 1974, so this glass is a 1999 glass. $5.00 – 10.00.

SIX UNDATED RONALD McDONALD HOUSE ISSUES

Row 1.

1. Ronald McDonald House, a 4$^{1}/_{4}$" white plastic travel mug with red sipping lid, red and blue decoration on both sides. This mug was designed to slide into a red plastic housing (not shown) that attached to a flat surface by means of an attached piece of adhesive. $2.00 – 5.00.

2. Ronald McDonald House, Tulsa, Oklahoma, a 4$^{1}/_{2}$" white plastic travel mug with red and blue decoration and red sipping lid and base. Graphics on one side only. No date or maker. $3.00 – 7.00.

3. Ronald McDonald House, a 4$^{1}/_{4}$" white plastic travel mug with red sipping lid, red and blue decoration on one side and red plastic mounting base. $2.00 – 5.00.

Row 2.

1. Ronald McDonald House, "The House That Love Built," a 4$^{7}/_{8}$" white ceramic tankard with red and blue decoration. $20.00 – 30.00.

2. Atlanta Ronald McDonald House Golf Classic, a 4$^{1}/_{8}$" double old-fashioned glass with etched decoration and a frosted cavity in the base representing half of a golf ball. $15.00 – 20.00.

3. I Support Ronald McDonald House, a 3$^{1}/_{4}$" ceramic mug with multicolored house and yard setting. $10.00 – 15.00.

EIGHT UNDATED RONALD McDONALD HOUSE ISSUES

Row 1.

1. Ronald McDonald House, a 3¹/₂" heart-shaped white ceramic mug with red and blue decoration. The name "Scott" appears in blue on the reverse side. Heart-shaped mugs like this served various purposes for Ronald McDonald House Charities, and there are probably a great many personalized variations. $10.00 – 15.00.

2. Ronald McDonald House at Loyola, a 3³/₈" heart-shaped white ceramic mug with red decoration. This mug was issued by the Ronald McDonald House at Loyola University Medical Center, Tripp Avenue at Air Mail Road, Maywood, Ilinois (Chicago). $10.00 – 15.00.

3. Ronald McDonald House, a 3¹/₂" Luminarc clear glass mug with "Thank You!" inside a heart on the reverse, blue and red decoration. $8.00 - $12.00.

4. Celebrating ten years of love. Ronald McDonald House, Louisville, Kentucky, a 4¹/₈" old fashioned glass with red and blue decoration. $12.00 – 16.00.

Row 2.

1. Ronald McDonald House, a 5" pedestal mug with red, white, and blue decoration. This mug was found in Canada and has "Canada" stamped on its bottom. $12.00 – 18.00.

2. Ronald McDonald House, Cleveland's House that Love Built, a 3³/₄" white ceramic mug with red and blue decoration, made in China by Linyi. $8.00 – 12.00.

3. Ronald McDonald House, Durham's (North Carolina) House that Love Built, a white 3⅝" ceramic mug with red and blue decoration. $8.00 – 12.00.

4. Ronald McDonald House of Dallas, a 3³/₄" white ceramic mug with red decoration. The front shows the house with a heart-shaped sun, and on the reverse: "This is the house/that provides the home,/that cooks the meals,/that sleeps the people,/that dries the tears./This is the house/that love built." On the bottom: "Made in China." $15.00 – 20.00.

SIX SPECIFIC LOCATION PROMOTION MUGS

Row 1.

1. McDonald's, People, Pride, Progress, McTeufel Systems Inc., Mesa, Arizona, a $5^1/_2$" clear glass mug with red and yellow decoration. $15.00 – 20.00.

2. "Dial McDonald's, Minimum Order $15.00, 1532 N. 51st AVE. (602)484-0240," a $3^5/_8$" mug with red and black decoration, from Phoenix, Arizona. Made in China. $10.00 – 15.00.

3. "Hotter" repeated five times with small McDonald's logo between each, "Faster" repeated six times with small McDonald's logo between each, and below that: "Tanque Verde & Grant, Tucson, Arizona." This $3^1/_2$" white ceramic mug with blue-green decoration features the image of a running velociraptor which is shown in the same pose four times. $7.00 – 14.00.

Row 2.

1. "McDonald's of Harrison 'Triple A's,' '80 – '81 – '82," a $5^1/_2$" clear glass mug with red and yellow decoration, from Harrison, Arkansas. $10.00 – 15.00.

2. City of Richmond (British Columbia), a $3^5/_8$" white ceramic mug with blue decoration showing the city's official coat of arms, a McDonald's logo, the "No. 2 Road Bridge," and the logos of PBK Engineering Ltd., JJM Group, and Delta Catalytic. The companies listed on this mug are huge Canadian industrial contractors and consultants who worked together to build the No. 2 Road Bridge shown on the mug. JJM Construction was the general contractor, PBK was the engineering consultant, and Delta Catalytic was the paving contractor. McDonald's provided the refreshments for the the workers. The bridge was built from November 1992 to July 1993. Richmond is located just south of Vancouver, British Columbia. This is an obscure mug! $15.00 – 30.00.

3. McDonald's Riverside #3, 10141 Magnolia Ave., Riverside, California 92503, (714)359-9415, a $5^1/_2$" mug with red and yellow decoration. $15.00 – 20.00.

SIX SPECIFIC LOCATION PIECES

Row 1.

1. McDonald's Wickham Road, Melbourne, Florida, August, 1983, a 4³/₈" double old fashioned glass with red decoration. $15.00 – 25.00.

2. McDonald's Daytona Beach Florida (on front) and Spring Break 1984 (on back), a 5³/₄" red plastic mug with yellow and white decoration. On the bottom: "Betras Plastics Inc. Super Mug Spartanburg, S.C. U.S.A." 15.00 – 20.00.

3. McDonald's, 480 N. Venice By-Pass, Venice, FL 34292, a 5¹/₂" clear glass mug with red and yellow decoration. $10.00 – 15.00.

Row 2.

1. McDonald's of Red Bug Road, 1325 Tuskawilla Road, Winter Springs, Florida, a 3³/₄" red mug with black decoration, made in Japan. $10.00 – 15.00.

2. "Have you had your break today?" on one side and "Customer Appreciation Day" on the another side of a white 3³/₄" coffee mug with red and yellow decoration. A small graphic consisting of a McDonald's sign and two palm trees with small Golden Arches forming the fronds along with "Raysway, Inc." appears in red just below the "Customer Appreciation Day" panel. "Haines City, Florida" appears in red near the bottom of the mug between the two panels. "Linyi China" appears on the bottom. $8.00 – 12.00.

3. South Florida Region, a 4¹/₈" old fashioned glass with yellow and orange decoration which changes color with temperature variations. $8.00 – 12.00.

SIX SPECIFIC LOCATION MUGS

Row 1.

1. McDonald's Atlanta Region, a 3⁵/₈" ceramic mug with cobalt blue and gold decoration on the outside and white on the inside, gold rim. This mug is almost certainly an in-house promotion item. $15.00 – 25.00.

2. "GSF Big Mac Under Glass, Hawaii 1987," a 3¹/₂" white ceramic mug with black and gold decoration. This beautiful mug may have been an in-house premium of some kind, or it may have been part of a more public Hawaiian Big Mac promotion. Either way, it's an unusual mug. GSF stands for Golden State Foods, an early supplier of hamburger to California drive-ins before it became one of McDonald's major suppliers. Golden State Foods still supplies McDonald's and is considered a "giant" in the food processing industry (Love, *Behind the Arches*, 129, 133). $15.00 – 25.00.

3. McDonald's Northmac, 1920 N. Arlington Hts. Rd., Arlington Hts. (Illinois), a 5¹/₂" clear glass mug with red and yellow decoration. $15.00 – 25.00.

Row 2.

1. Union Station McDonald's, Chicago, Illinois, a 3⁵/₈" black mug with gold decoration on both sides. This mug has strong secondary appeal to railroad collectors. On the bottom: "Made in China." $20.00 – 30.00.

2. McDonald's I – 5 DeKalb, IL, a 3³/₄" white ceramic mug with red and yellow decoration. $8.00 – 12.00.

3. McDonald's, Yorkville McDonald's Rt 34 & 47 Yorkville, Illinois 60560, a 5¹/₂" mug with red and yellow decoration. $15.00 – 20.00.

SIX SPECIFIC LOCATION MUGS

Row 1.

1. McDonald's Berne, Indiana, a 3³/₄" white ceramic mug with the Swiss canton's coats of arms in bright colors. Berne takes its name from this Swiss canton. Berne, Indiana, is in the center of the state not too far from the Ohio state line. "China" embossed on bottom. $15.00 – 25.00.

2. "McDonald's Natchitoches, LA," a 3³/₄" mug with black and yellow decoration. The front just features the Arches with the town's name, but the back shows in black a magnolia blossom with "Steel Magnolia 1988" beneath it. This very special mug was issued in 1988 in the town where the movie *Steel Magnolias* was filmed. The film came out in 1989 and starred Sally Field, Dolly Parton, Shirley MacLaine, Daryl Hannah, Julia Roberts, and Olympia Dukakis. Other interesting trivia: Roger Ebert gives the film 3 stars; Natchotoches, established in 1714, is the oldest city in the Louisiana Purchase; Robert Harling is the author of the play *Steel Magnolias* which was first performed on Broadway in 1987. "China" appears in black on the bottom. $25.00 – 45.00.

3. McDonald's, 802 Pulaski Hwy., Havre de Grace, MD 21078, (301)939-0005, a 5¹/₂" clear glass mug with red and yellow decoration. $15.00 – 20.00.

Row 2.

1. McDonald's, The Spirit of Baltimore (white deco), Total Customer Satisfaction (red deco), a 3⁵/₈" cobalt blue mug with red and white decoration. The round white graphic shows the Baltimore harbour with a three-masted ship and city skyline and "Total Customer Satisfaction" in red below that. This may have been an in-house item available only to McDonald's employees in Baltimore. $10.00 – 20.00.

2. Eastern Mass. Family Night, a 4¹/₈" mug with red decoration. $10.00 – 15.00.

3. McDonald's Cancun (Mexico), a 3⁵/₈" black mug with gold decoration. $8.00 – 12.00.

SIX MICHIGAN MUGS

Row 1.

1. McDonald's, Boyne City, Michigan, August 1991, a 3^3/$_4$" cobalt blue mug with gold decoration featuring a large McDonald's logo on one side and location name and date on the other. On the bottom in white: "Do Not Use In Microwave Oven. China." $15.00 – 20.00.

2. McDonald's Cedar Springs, Michigan, a 5^1/$_4$" mug with red, yellow, and black decoration. $15.00 – 20.00.

3. "McDonald's Chesaning, Mich," on one side, "Showboat City" with river boat on the other, a 5^1/$_2$" pedestal mug with frosted decoration. $10.00 – 14.00.

Row 2.

1. "The 50's McDonald's 4145 S. Telegraph Rd. Dearborn Heights, Michigan 48125," a 3^1/$_2$" clear Luminarc mug with frosted decoration showing a jukebox and musical notes. $5.00 – 10.00.

2. McDonald's Restaurant 24020 Orchard Lake Rd., 39700 Five Mile Rd., 38400 Ten Mile Rd., 19311 Farmington Rd., 15399 Middlebelt Rd., 21050 Haggerty Rd., a 5^1/$_2$" mug with red and yellow decoration from the greater Detroit, Michigan area. $15.00 – 20.00.

3. Grand Ledge (Michigan) McDonald's June 1983, a 5^1/$_2$" clear glass mug with gray paint decoration. $15.00 – 20.00.

SIX SPECIFIC LOCATION PROMOTIONAL PIECES

Row 1.

1. Grand Rapids Region (Michigan), a 4¹/₈" old fashioned glass with frosted decoration consisting of two overlapping triangles, one showing the 1950s Speedee Systems character and the other containing the initials "QSC&V Grand Rapids Region" in frosted decoration. "QSC&V" were the principles that Ray Kroc insisted McDonald's must exemplify and uphold: quality, service, cleanliness, and value. These initials were used prominently in early McDonald's advertising and within the management structure to keep everyone focused on qualities that distinguished McDonald's from other hamburger restaurants. $15.00 – 20.00.

2. McDonald's, Trails Travel Center, I – 35 Exit 11, Albert Lea, Minnesota, a 5¹/₈" canning jar mug with yellow decoration. Embossing around the bottom warns us that this mug is "Not For Hot Products" and "Not For Home Canning." $7.00 – 11.00.

3. McDonald's of Chanhassen, 90 Lake Drive East, Chanhassen, Minnesota 55317, (612)934-8530, a 5¹/₂" clear glass mug with red and yellow decoration. $15.00 – 20.00.

Row 2.

1. McDonald's — Downtown, 415 Nicollet Mall, Minneapolis, Minnesota, a 5¹/₂" clear glass mug with red and yellow decoration. $15.00 – 20.00.

2. McDonald's Robbinsdale (Minnesota), a 3³/₄" black ceramic mug with gold decoration featuring a small city skyline including a church spire and water tower. Robbinsdale is located in greater northwest Minneapolis area. On the bottom: "CCA China." $15.00 – 25.00.

3. McDonald's of New Brighton (Minnesota), a green 3³/₄" mug with gold decoration on one side only featuring the Golden Arches inside a thought bubble. Late 1990s and probably available only to employees. $10.00 – 20.00.

SIX SPECIFIC LOCATION PROMOTIONAL ISSUES

Left.

1. McDonald's 205 Business Loop 70, Columbia, Missouri 65201, a 5½" clear glass mug with red and yellow decoration. $10.00 – 15.00.

2. McDonald's 1001 E. Lake Mead, (702)642-6730 (Nevada), a 5½" mug with red and yellow decoration. $15.00 – 20.00.

3. New York, 160 Broadway, a 3½" old fashioned glass featuring a piano with the McDonald's logo on it and elaborate gold decoration. I believe the piano is still in this historic restaurant, one of the earliest McDonald's stores in New York City. $35.00 – 45.00.

Right.

1. McDonald's, Guon Corporation, a 3¾" maroon-colored coffee mug with franchise locations in gray. Place names are as follows: Penfield Two, Panorama, Webster, Baytowne, Perington, Fairport, and Leroy. From the greater (southern) Rochester, New York, area. $10.00 – 15.00.

2. McDonald's Buono Enterprises, Brockport, East Avenue, Gates, Chili, Spencerport, a 5" mug with red decoration. From (western) greater Rochester, New York, area. $10.00 – 15.00.

3. McDonald's of Fairport, 1333 Fairport Rd., Fairport, New York (east Rochester) 14450, (716)377-1085, a 5½" mug with red and yellow decoration. $15.00 – 20.00.

SIX SPECIFIC LOCATION ISSUES

Left.

1. McDonald's Scotia, N.Y., a 3⅜" old-fashioned glass with yellow decoration. $15.00 – 20.00.

2. Ashville Market (North Carolina), 1982, a 5½" clear glass mug with red and yellow decoration. $15.00 – 25.00.

3. McDonald's Mohawk Mall 1982, a 5½" mug with red and yellow decoration. The Mohawk Mall is in Niskayuna, New York, 15 miles northwest of Albany. Built in 1970, the Mohawk Mall was one of the region's first enclosed malls. By 1998 it had only 20 stores, down from 88 in its heyday. $15.00 – 25.00.

Right.

1. McDonald's 2325 Woodville (Toledo, Ohio), 1960 – 1990, a 5½" mug with black decoration. $15.00 – 20.00.

2. McDonald's German Village, Columbus, Ohio, a 5½" mug with red and yellow decoration. $15.00 – 20.00.

3. McDonald's Restaurant, 4501 Linden Ave., Dayton, Ohio 45432, phone (513) 256-7901, a 5½" clear glass mug with red and yellow decoration. $15.00 – 20.00.

SIX SPECIFIC LOCATION PROMOTIONAL MUGS

Left.

1. McDonald's I – 35 and 122nd (Oklahoma), a 3¹/₂" Anchor Hocking white milk glass mug with red and blue graphics showing location of this McDonald's on a map of Oklahoma. $15.00 – 25.00.

2. McDonald's Glasshouse, Vinita, Oklahoma 74301 (918)256-5571, The World's Largest McDonald's, a 5¹/₂" mug with red and yellow decoration. $20.00 – 25.00.

3. World's Largest McDonald's, I – 44 Vinita, Oklahoma, a 3³/₄" white ceramic mug with blue decoration, made in China. $15.00 – 25.00.

Right.

1. World's Largest McDonald's, I – 44 Vinita, Oklahoma, a 3⁵/₈" white ceramic mug with black decoration, made in China. This mug is noticeably smaller than the blue decorated one to its left, and the graphics are slightly different. For example, the blue mug has clouds in the sky above the restaurant, and the black mug lacks these clouds. $15.00 – 25.00.

2. McDonald's of Eire and Girard (Pennsylvania), "Our Stores Shine Brighter," a 5¹/₂" pedestal mug with red decoration. $10.00 – 15.00.

3. McDonald's of Erie & Girard, Pennsylvania, "We Originate/Others Imitate," a 5⁵/₈" clear glass mug with red decoration. $10.00 – 15.00.

SIX SPECIFIC LOCATION PROMOTIONAL MUGS

Left.

1. McDonald's, Slippery Rock, PA, a 3³/₄" ceramic mug in dark blue with white decoration. From the early 1990s. $8.00 – 12.00.

2. McDonald's, Slippery Rock, PA, a 3³/₄" ceramic mug in light blue with white decoration. From the early 1990s. $8.00 – 12.00.

3. McDonald's, Hellam McDonald's, 4015 E. Market St., York, PA 17402, a 5¹/₂" clear glass mug with red and yellow decoration. $10.00 – 15.00.

Right.

1. McDonald's Mifflintown, PA. 1989, a 4¹/₈" clear glass mug with grey faux etching decoration. $10.00 – 20.00.

2. "You're very special Guayama," a 5¹/₈" Mason jar mug from Puerto Rico, red decoration. $15.00 – 25.00.

3. McDonald's, Laval Quebec, Canada, an orange 3⁵/₈" ceramic mug with red decoration from McDonald's store in Laval, a suburb of Montreal near the Laurentian mountains. "Made in England" is embossed on the bottom. $15.00 – 25.00.

SIX SPECIFIC LOCATION PROMOTIONAL MUGS

Left.

1. McDonald's 3³/₄" black ceramic mug with gold decoration saying "Jackie Joyner-Kersee appearance February 1989" and on the reverse "Power 94 FM Fresh Music Less Talk." Power 94 FM is a black radio station in Chattaoogna, Tennessee. Jackie Joyner-Kersee is a famous American track and field athlete. $15.00 – 30.00.

2. "McDonald's Texas Style I – 20 at Beltline, Mesquite, Texas," a 3¹/₂" white milk glass mug with red decoration showing (on both sides) an outline of the state of Texas, McDonald's Arches, and a longhorn steer inside of a rope oval. On the bottom: "51 Glasbake U.S.A. Microwave Safe." A nice early regional issue from the 1970s. $25.00 – 35.00.

3. McDonald's "On the 'Grow' in Sulphur Springs" (Texas), a 3⁷/₁₆" milk glass Anchor Hocking mug with maroon decoration which shows a cowboy boot with a map of Texas on it. On the bottom: "Oven Proof (Anchor logo) 312 Made in USA." An early mug from the late 1970s or early 1980s. $20.00 – 35.00.

Right.

1. McDonald's By The Seattle Center, a 5¹/₂" glass mug with red and yellow decoration. $15.00 – 20.00.

2. Milwaukee (Wisconsin) 5¹/₂" clear glass mug with black and yellow decoration promoting the attractions of Milwaukee, Wisconsin. The graphic on the front of the mug draws attention to brewing, fishing, the Milwaukee Bucks, and the Milwaukee Brewers. $20.00 – 30.00.

3. McDonald's Hwy 45, New London, Hwy 54, Waupaca, Wisconsin, a 5¹/₂" clear glass mug with red and yellow decoration. $15.00 – 20.00.

FOUR SPECIFIC LOCATION PROMOTIONAL MUGS

Left.

1. McDonald's Restaurant, Oshkosh, Wisconsin 54901, a 5¹/₂" clear glass mug with red and yellow decoration. $15.00 – 20.00.

2. McDonald's La Crosse, Prairie du Chien, Tomah (Wisconsin), a 5¹/₂" clear glass mug with red and yellow decoration. $15.00 – 20.00.

Right.

1. McDonald's Cambridge, a 3³/₄" green ceramic mug with gold decoration. Decoration showing an old arched stone bridge and a Gothic looking building suggest that this mug might be from Cambridge, England, though there are no specific markings on the mug to confirm origin. $12.00 – 20.00.

2. "McDonald's Washington Street" with McDonald's logo on a windmill, same design on both sides, blue decoration on a 4¹/₂" ceramic tankard mug. Reliable sources have told me that this tankard is from Wisconsin, but I am not certain about its origin. $15.00 – 25.00.

A SURFING CUP AND CELEBRATION! SERIES CUPS

Left.

1. 1987 Surfing Hawaii. This large cup co-sponsored by Coca-Cola shows surfers on a big wave — same decoration front and back. $4.00 – 8.00.

1988 McDonald's Celebration! series, co-sponsored by Coca-Cola Classic. The cup design comes in large and medium sizes and shows a McDonald's restaurant surrounded by balloons. On the reverse there's more balloons and a large white box outlined in black which can be personalized to present McDonald's specific location advertising. $3.00 – 7.00.

2. McDonald's/2727 28th Street S. W./Wyoming, Michigan

3. McDonald's/1516 Highway 92 West/Woodstock, Georgia

Right.

1. Your Hometown/McDonald's/Rockford, Michigan/"Grand Opening"

2. McDonald's/Across From Airport/Cheektowaga, NY

3. McDonald's/104 Your Place/Anyplace, U.S.A.

SPECIFIC LOCATION HAWAIIAN ISSUES

Left: Set of four Hawaii 25th Anniversary cups.

1993 #1 Meal Deal in Hawaii 25th Anniversary co-sponsored by Coca-Cola set of four. These plastic cups feature detailed drawings of the islands' attractions by Barb McClain's Scooter Productions ©1993. McDonald's locations are indicated by small Golden Arch logos. These cups are fun and fascinating. $5.00 – 10.00 each.

1. Hawaii

2. Kauai

3. Maui

4. Oahu

Right: Hawaiian monster drink bucket and cup.

1997 McDonald's of Mililani with My McDonald's logo, co-sponsored by Coca-Cola. This is a boldly colored and designed large heavy plastic double-walled monster drink bucket with a handle and two access lids, one for a flexible plastic straw and the other for pouring. Fitted snugly inside is a white plastic monster cup with red and yellow decoration. Designed for a long day at the beach? $7.00 – 15.00.

1. Monster bucket

2. Monster cup

SEVEN AUTO RACING ISSUES

Left.

1. 1993 Hut Stricklin McDonald's Racing Team with car #27, a 6¼" tumbler with multicolored decoration. $10.00 – 15.00.

2. Bill Elliott 1994 NASCAR McDonald's Racing Team shot glass. This 2¼" vertically paneled shot glass has a pewter emblem applied to it with yellow McDonald's Arches and yellow "94" along with "Bill Elliott" in blue capital letters, "Bill Elliot's" signature in blue, and "McDonald's Racing Team" in blue. $10.00 – 15.00.

3. Bill Elliott McDonald's Nascar 2½" shot glass showing car #94. A sticker on the bottom says: "Hunter Mfg. Group Lexington, KY 1-800-237-1869." Probable date: 1994. $6.00 – 12.00.

4. Bill Elliott McDonald's Nascar 2¼" tapered shot glass showing car #94. Embossing on the bottom says: "Hunter, China, not intended for food or beverage use." Copyright information appears in tiny writing just under the left front wheel, but the date is not clear enough to read. $6.00 – 12.00.

Right.

1. McDonald's NASCAR Racing Team, ©1995 with Bill Elliott and #94 red Thunderbird (front view) on 3¾" white ceramic mug with 3" mouth diameter. $12.00 – 16.00.

2. Bill Elliott Gotham City Special Thunderbat, McDonald's Racing Team ©1995, a 4" black ceramic mug with blue, green, white, and yellow decoration featuring front view of Elliott's Ford with Golden Arches on the hood. $14.00 – 20.00.

3. McDonald's NASCAR Racing Team ©1996 with Bill Elliott in #94 red and white Ford Thunderbird (side view). Golden Arches form the "E" in Elliott's name. 3⅝" white ceramic mug with 3½" mouth diameter and gold band around rim. $12.00 – 16.00.

NASCAR 50TH ANNIVERSARY TUMBLERS

NASCAR 50th Anniversary set of four, 1948 – 1998, ©1998 McDonald's. Bill Elliott's signature appears vertically in black on the side of the glasses between the NASCAR 50th Anniversary logo and the frontal view of the theme-specific race cars. These glasses were distributed heavily in the mid-Atlantic states and southern states, but they were available in other areas also. $5.00 – 10.00 each.

1. Coca-Cola and McDonald's logo on hood of red Ford Taurus.

2. Coca-Cola, Mac Tonight, and McDonald's logo on hood of blue Ford Taurus.

3. Coca-Cola, NASCAR, and McDonald's logo on hood of yellow Ford Taurus.

4. Coca-Cola, Ronald McDonald, and McDonald's logo on hood of red Ford Taurus.

MILWAUKEE BREWERS AND PHILADELPHIA PHILLIES TUMBLERS

1982 Milwaukee Brewers ©MSA & MLBPA, set of four with blue, yellow, and black decoration. These 5⅝" Libbey glasses were heavily distributed in the greater Milwaukee area. Each glass features photographs of two Brewers' players. $5.00 – 10.00 each.

Left.

1. Rollie Fingers and Ted Simmons
2. Paul Molitor and Pete Vuckovich
3. Gorman Thomas and Cecil Cooper
4. Robin Yount and Ben Oglivie

Right.

1993 Philadelphia Phillies, Coca-Cola Classic set of two with decoration by Zubaz, the artist-designer who was responsible for the wild tiger-striped clothing designs of the late 1980s and early 1990s. Zubaz's name does not appear on the glasses, but it did appear on store displays and other printed promotional material. Both of these glasses feature the "Phillies" name, the Major League Baseball logo, and Liberty Bell motif on a busy red, white, and blue striped background. These glasses were available in the Philadelphia area for 79¢ each with any Extra Value Meal purchase. $7.00 – 10.00 each.

1. Phillies and Liberty Bell with red and white stripes
2. Phillies and Liberty Bell with red and blue baseball seams

TOPPS BASEBALL CARD SET OF TEN TUMBLERS

1993 Topps All Time Greatest Team co-sponsored by McDonald's and Coca-Cola, set of ten. This set features the front and back of the original Topps' issues of these players' cards. Originally this set was to consist of nine players, but late in the promotion Carl Yastrzemski was added as the "DH" bringing the total to ten. The first nine glasses were available mostly in the mid Atlantic states; Yas was issued on a rather limited basis in the greater Boston/New England area, so it is harder to find than the other glasses in this set. Values: #1 – 9, $9.00 – 14.00; Yas, $15.00 – $25.00.

Left.

1. 1 of 9 Nolan Ryan, Pitcher, New York Mets, Topps Original Issue 1969.
2. 2 of 9 Johnny Bench, Catcher, Cincinnati Reds, Topps Original Issue 1970.
3. 3 of 9 Lou Gehrig, First Base, New York Yankees, Topps Original Issue 1961.
4. 4 of 9 Joe Morgan, Second Base, Cincinnati Reds, Topps Original Issue 1973.
5. 5 of 9 Cal Ripken, Shortstop, Baltimore Orioles, Topps Original Issue 1985.

Right.

1. 6 of 9 Brooks Robinson, Third Base, Baltimore Orioles, Topps Original Issue 1961.
2. 7 of 9 Roberto Clemente, Outfield, Pittsburgh Pirates, Topps Original Issue 1961.
3. 8 of 9 Willie Mays, Outfield, New York Giants, Topps Original Issue 1957.
4. 9 of 9 Babe Ruth, Outfield, New York Yankees, Topps Original Issue 1962.
5. DH #10 Carl Yastrzemski, Outfield, Boston Red Sox, Topps Original Issue 1970.

ST. LOUIS CARDINALS AND BALTIMORE ORIOLES TUMBLER SETS
Left: 1998 St. Louis Cardinals "Legendary Players" set of four.

1998 St. Louis Cardinals ©MLB and The Coca-Cola Company, "Legendary Players" set of four. These glasses were heavily distributed in the greater St. Louis area in the fall of 1998 before Mark McGwire's end of season home run statistics were known, so there is no reference to his home run record on this glass. The graphics on these glasses are quite varied and attractive. There are three informational areas on the reverse of each glass: one with a summary of the player's career, one with biographical information, and one with career highlights. $8.00 – 15.00 each.

1. Lou Brock, Outfielder.

2. Bob Gibson, Pitcher.

3. Mark McGwire, 1st Base.

4. Ozzie Smith, Shortstop.

Right: 1998 Baltimore Orioles "Greatest Moments" set of six.

1998 Baltimore Orioles Greatest Moments, a numbered set of six, sponsored by McDonald's, 5¹/₈" double old fashioned glasses. Distributed in the greater Baltimore area, these glasses feature a Baltimore Sun newspaper headline format which, small print informs us, "may not represent actual newspaper headlines." Each glass has a pasted-up storyboard commentary which complements the headline story. The glasses have a red and white block McDonald's logo near the bottom, and there is an Orioles' logo embossed in the bottom of each. If you look down at the base and turn the glass around, you can see "Baltimore Orioles Greatest Moments" inscribed around the base. Supposedly, McDonald's had to cut this promotion short because their contract with Cal Ripken expired while the promotion was still going on, so McDonald's couldn't sell glass #1, thereby causing a premature ending to the promotion. The Ripken glass will therefore probably always command a premium over the others in the series. Glass #1, $10.00 – 15.00; #2 – 6, $6.00 – 9.00.

1. One of Six, Sept. 6th, 1995, Immortal Cal.

2. Two of Six, Oct. 9th, 1966, Would You Believe It? Four Straight!

3. Three of Six, April 15th, 1954, 46,354 See Orioles Defeat Chicago, 3 to 1.

4. Four of Six, Oct. 16th, 1983, World Champions.

5. Five of Six, Oct. 6th, 1991, Memorial Stadium, Wave It Bye-Bye.

6. Six of Six, Oct. 15th, 1970, Orioles Soar To World Championship Victory.

ATLANTA FALCONS AND PHILADELPHIA EAGLES TUMBLER SETS

Left: Atlanta Falcons set of four.

Atlanta Falcons, McDonald's/Dr Pepper, set of four (1981) Libbey, 5⁵/₈". Distributed in the greater Atlanta area, these glasses appeal to McDonald's collectors, Dr. Pepper collectors, and Falcons/NFL fans. The set is dated by the fact that Bobby Butler's first year with the Falcons was 1981. $5.00 – 8.00 each.

1. William Andrews, Jeff Van Note, Mike Kenn
2. Steve Bartkowski, Alfred Jackson, Al Jenkins
3. F. Kuykendall, Joel Williams, Buddy Curry
4. R. C. Thielemann, Bobby Butler, Lynn Cain

Right: Philadelphia Eagles 1980 set of five.

Philadelphia Eagles set of five 6" tumblers made by Libbey. Each glass features two players in action. $4.00 – 6.00 each.

1. Bill Bergey, Linebacker, and John Bunting, Linebacker
2. Harold Carmichael, Wide Receiver, and Randy Logan, Safety
2. Tony Franklin, Kicker, and Stan Walters, Tackle
4. Ron Jaworski, Quarterback, and Keith Krepfle, Tight End
5. Wilbert Montgomery, Running Back, and Billy Campfield, Running Back

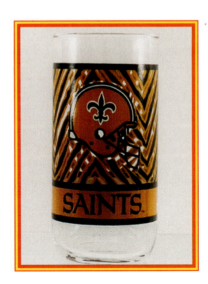

NEW ORLEANS SAINTS/ZUBAZ TUMBLER

New Orleans Saints (1993) Coca-Cola Classic, a 5³/₄" tumbler showing the Saints helmet, and black and gold striped decoration by Zubaz, the artist-designer who popularized tiger-striped clothing in the late 1980s and early 1990s. There's no date on the glass, but it's obviously contemporaneous with the 1993 pair of Phillies glasses on page 219 that preceded it in the summer of 1993. $7.00 – 10.00.

TWO PITTSBURGH STEELERS SUPER BOWL TUMBLER SETS

Row 1: Steelers Super Bowl 13 set of four and an error glass.

Pittsburgh Steelers Superbowl XIII, set of four (1978). $6.00 – 8.00 each.

1. Mike Webster, Terry Bradshaw, L. C. Greenwood
2. Donnie Shell, Rocky Bleier, Jack Ham
3. John Stallworth, Joe Greene, Mike Wagner
4. Sam Davis, Jack Lambert, John Banaszak
5. Error glass: Stallworth, Greene, and Wagner missing band of yellow McDonald's Arches around bottom. $10.00 – 15.00.

Row 2: Steelers Super Bowl 14 set of four.

Pittsburgh Steelers Superbowl XIV, set of four (1979). $5.00 – 7.00 each.

1. Sam Davis, Terry Bradshaw, Jack Ham — "Terry Bradshaw leaves the field in triumph."
2. Rocky Bleier, John Stallworth, Dirt Winston — "John Stallworth snags a long pass to set up a final touchdown."
3. Sidney Thornton, Joe Greene, Matt Bahr — "Joe Greene stops L.A. running back for no gain."
4. Jon Kolb, Jack Lambert, Mel Blount — "Jack Lambert intercepts to end an L.A. drive."

PITTSBURGH STEELERS GREATEST TEAM AND HALL OF FAME TUMBLER SETS

Left: All-Time Greatest Steelers set of four and a test glass.

McDonald's "Steelers 50 Seasons/The All-Time Greatest Steelers Team" numbered set of four double Old Fashioned glasses, 1982. Each glass lists six all-time Steeler greats, each man's position, and each man's years on the team. $6.00 – 9.00 each.

1. #1 of 4: Mullins, Brown, Lambert, Harris, Brady, and White
2. #2 of 4: Greene, Nickel, Kolb, Bleier, Shell, Ham
3. #3 of 4: Gerela, Davis, Wagner, Greenwood, Webster, Swann
4. #4 of 4: Blount, Stautner, Bradshaw, Russell, Stallworth, Butler
5. #4 of 4: test glass. This glass has a white panel on the reverse with black lettering and black McDonald's logo. It is quite different from the production version which has no panel, white lettering, and yellow McDonald's logo. $10.00 – 25.00+.

Right: 1990 Steelers Hall of Fame set of four.

McDonald's Collector Series "Steelers in the Hall of Fame"/Diet Coke/WPXI-TV Numbered set of four, 1990, Libbey, 6³/₈". These big heavy glasses were aggressively distributed in western Pennsylvania. $4.00 – 7.00 each.

1. #1 of 4: Jack Lambert, Arthur J. Rooney, Ernie Stautner
2. #2 of 4: Johnny "Blood" McNally, Franco Harris, Joe Greene
3. #3 of 4: John Henry Johnson, Terry Bradshaw, Bill Dudley
4. #4 of 4: Jack Ham, Bobby Layne, Mel Blount

SEATTLE SEAHAWKS TUMBLER SET

Seattle Seahawks Football, set of four (1979), ©MSA, 6". The Seahawks' first season was 1976. These glasses are not dated, but 1979 was Eller's last year with the Seahawks and Tuiasosopo's first, so that fixes the issue date exactly. $6.00 – 10.00 each.

1. Terry Beeson, Carl Eller, Autry Beamon
2. Dennis Boyd, Bill Gregory, Manu Tuiasosopo
3. Steve Raible, Jim Zorn, Sam McCullum
4. Sherman Smith, Steve Largent, David Sims

BAYLOR UNIVERSITY BEARS AND UNIVERSITY OF TEXAS LONGHORNS TUMBLERS

1. Baylor University Bears, a 5⅝" tumbler with green and gold decoration featuring the Baylor mascot waving a flag with a "B" on it. A large green McDonald's logo appears on the reverse. A hard to find regional issue. $20.00 – 30.00.

2. Baylor University Bears, Waco, Texas, a 5⅝" tumbler with green and gold decoration showing the Baylor mascot waving a flag with a "B" on it. This glass is virtually identical to the glass listed above and shown to its left, but "Waco, Texas" appears in green letters just below the large green McDonald's logo. $25.00 – 40.00.

3. "Hook 'Em Horns," University of Texas, a 5⅝" tumbler with light-orange and white decoration showing the Texas mascot running with a football. Large orange McDonald's logo on the reverse. $25.00 – 40.00.

4. "Hook 'Em Horns" in dark-orange and white decoration with "Austin, Texas" below the McDonald's logo on the reverse. Harder to find and more desirable than the plain Austin-less version. $40.00 – 60.00.

U.S. AND CANADIAN SUPER BOWL ISSUES

1. Superbowl XXI, January 25, 1987, Broncos vs. Giants, Rose Bowl, Pasadena, California, a 6" clear glass mug featuring two conjoined football helmets with the McDonald's logo on one and the NFL logo on the other and details about the game on the other. $15.00 – 25.00.

2. Grey Cup, Calgary, November 28, 1993, a 6⅛" Canadian fountain glass co-sponsored by Coca-Cola, frosted decoration. The Grey Cup is the Canadian Football League's equivalent of the United States' Super Bowl Trophy. The 1993 Grey Cup game was played at McMahon Stadium in Calgary between the Winnipeg Blue Bombers and the Edmondton Eskimos. The Eskimos won 33 – 23. $6.00 – 10.00.

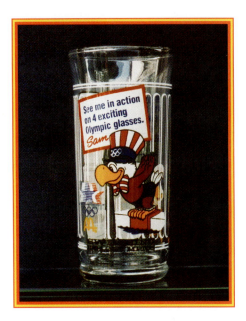

1983 OWNER, OPERATOR'S PROMOTIONAL GLASS SHOWING SAM THE OLYMPIC EAGLE ON DIVING BOARD

1983 Sam the Olympic Eagle Owner, Operator's glass. This glass was sent to selected franchise owners to encourage them to commit to the upcoming 1984 Los Angeles Summer Olympics (please refer to discussion of this practice under "Muppet Caper Manager's Glass" page 103 and "Camp Snoopy Manager's Glass" page 18). Sam is shown preparing to dive, and above him is a box which says "See me in action on 4 exciting Olympic glasses. Sam." Below Sam there's the 1984 Los Angeles Olympic logo and the McDonald's logo and the title of this glass: "Swimming 1984 Olympics." Elsewhere on the glass, there's Sam introducing the other three glasses in the proposed set (they are actually pictured) which would have included, in addition to swimming, soccer, track, and gymnastics. It may be that this proposed glass set morphed into the set of four small plastic cups which I show two of on page 186. But to continue: "McDonald's And Olympic Fans Will Want To Collect All 4" appears in blue above Sam. In yellow and vertically on the side of the glass there's this: "Commit by November 1, 1983." Unfortunately, this promotion never materialized, so this very limited production glass is in the same league with the Muppets and Camp Snoopy managers' glasses, rare and valuable. $300.00 – 500.00.

1966 ATLANTA SUMMER GAMES TUMBLERS

Atlanta 1996 Summer Olympic Games ©1995 McDonald's and Coca-Cola, set of three glasses made by Libbey and issued in Puerto Rico (Spanish language version). This set features three Olympic sports: Baloncesto (Basketball), Atletismo (Track and Field), and Futbol (Soccer). An icon of each sport appears on the front of each glass, and a history of the sport appears in Spanish on the back of each glass. These glasses seem to have been distributed in both the U.S. and Puerto Rico. They may even have been issued in Spain. $9.00 – 13.00 each.

Left.
1. Atletismo (Track and Field)
2. Baloncesto (Basketball)
3. Futbol (Soccer)

Right.

Atlanta 1996 Summer Olympics ©1995 McDonald's and Coca-Cola, set of three glasses made by Libbey and issued in the United States. This set is identical in design to the Spanish set issued in Puerto Rico, but the sports have English names on these glasses and the historical accounts of the sports are in English. Distribution of these glasses was irregular but concentrated mostly in the southeastern United States. Since the fronts of the glasses are identical to the set pictured to the left, I picture the reverse panels. $8.00 – 12.00.

1. Athletics (Track and Field) reverse panel
2. Football (Soccer) reverse panel
Not pictured: Basketball

Atlanta 1996 Summer Olympics ©1995 McDonald's and Coca-Cola, set of three made by Libbey and issued in Brazil and possibly Portugal. This glass shown here is identical in design to the U.S. and Puerto Rican sets, but the title of this glass is Basquetebol instead of Baloncesto, and the language is Portuguese. I assume that there are two others which complete the set. $10.00 – 15.00 each.

3. Basquetebol (Basketball) reverse view.
Not shown but presumably part of the set: Atletismo (Track and Field) and Futebol (Soccer).

4. Atlanta 1996 Summer Olympics ©1995 by McDonald's and Coca-Cola, a 5⅝" tumbler made by Libbey and distributed in Thailand. I'm not certain if this is a single or part of a set. The design of the glass's main panel closely resembles the other 1996 Atlanta Olympic glasses with the Olympic rings, Coca-Cola logo, and Atlanta 1996 flame logo. There's nothing on the glass to indicate that it is foreign, so it could easily be mistaken for a US issue. This glass has nine Olympic sport icons on it: tennis, kayaking, wrestling, field hockey, weightlifting, gymnastics, rowing, fencing, and basketball. My guess is that other glasses in the set show additional icons. $15.00 – 25.00.

1996 SUMMER OLYMPIC SETS FROM ITALY AND THAILAND

Left: Set of six Italian 1996 Summer Olympic glasses. Atlanta 1996 Summer Olympic Games co-sponsored by McDonald's and Coca-Cola, set of six from Italy. This set of thin-shelled 5⅞" tumblers was distributed mainly in Italy. Each glass has the official Atlanta 1996 Olympic logo as well as the Coke and McDonald's logos. There are red and green bands around the bottom of each glass, and icons representing six summer Olympic sports are featured on each glass in a predominant color. The Coke logo is surrounded by these words: "Bibita Ufficiale Dei Giochi Olimpici 1996." These glasses are difficult to find even if you live in Italy. I've identified as many of the event logos as I could. Some I am not sure of. $15.00 – 25.00 each.

1. Blue: watersports: synchronized swimming, swimming, diving, water polo, kayaking, rowing
2. Pink-purple: running, equestrian events, sailing, bicycling, baseball, marksmanship
3. Red-orange-yellow: gymnastics, tennis, fencing, archery
4. Green: basketball, soccer, volleyball, lacrosse, baseball
5. Red-pink-purple: martial arts, boxing, weightlifting, track and field, wrestling
6. Blue-green: bicycling, tennis, volleyball, soccer, track and field, diving

Right: Set of three 1996 Summer Olympic glasses from Thailand.
Atlanta 1996 Summer Olympic Games set of three (1996) from Thailand. This set of three 4⅝" glasses celebrating the 100th Olympic Games in Atlanta and co-sponsored by Coca-Cola was distributed in Thailand in 1996. Each glass has a predominant color and features big-eyed unidentifiable (Asian?) cartoon characters participating in various Olympic sports. The glasses came in white nondescript boxes which have a red McDonald's logo on the top. $25.00 – 40.00 each, add $5.00 for the box.

1. Green, boxing, tennis, basketball, kayaking
2. Red, track and field, table tennis, bicycling, baseball
3. Yellow, soccer, fencing, archery, swimming

1983 AND 1984 HOUSTON RODEO TUMBLER SETS

Left: 1983 Houston Rodeo set of four.

Houston Livestock Show and Rodeo 1983, a numbered set of four 4³/₄" double old fashioned glasses co-sponsored by Coke and McDonald's. Each of these brown, black, white, and yellow decorated glasses features two rodeo events. On one side of the glass near the bottom is a black square with "Houston" and "Coke" in it, and on the other side is a yellow and white McDonald's logo along with "McDonald's Collector Series 1983" and copyright information. $8.00 – 14.00 each.

1. First in a Series of Four: Bareback Bronc Riding/Saddle Bronc Riding
2. Second in a Series of Four: Chuckwagon Races/Women's Barrel Racing
3. Third in a Series of Four: Calf Scramble/Rodeo Clown
4. Fourth in a Series of Four: Steer Wrestling/Bull Riding

Right: 1984 Houston Rodeo set of four.

Houston Livestock Show and Rodeo 1984, a numbered set of four 4³/₄" double old fashioned glasses co-sponsored by Coke and McDonald's. This set is essentially the same as the 1983 set in general appearance, color, size, etc., but there are a few changes you need to be aware of: (1) "1984" now appears in the title of the glass instead of 1983 (2) "Second Edition Series" now appears in white letters above the yellow McDonald's logo and (3) on the third glass, "Rodeo Clown" has been replaced by "Cutting Horse." $8.00 – 14.00 each.

1. First in a Series of Four: Bareback Bronc Riding/Saddle Bronc Riding
2. Second in a Series of Four: Chuckwagon Races/Women's Barrel Racing
3. Third in a Series of Four: Cutting Horse/Calf Scramble
4. Fourth in a Series of Four: Steer Wrestling/Bull Riding

1982 AND 1994 WORLD CUP SOCCER TUMBLER SETS
Left: 1982 Espana World Cup Soccer set of four.
Espana 1982 World Cup Soccer set of four (1982). This set of four beautifully designed and colorful glasses, co-sponsored by Coca-Cola and Naranjito and decorated by Rastal, promoted the World Cup Soccer games of 1982 in Spain. The glasses appear to be of German origin since the Coke logo is in German: "Trink Coca-Cola Schutzmarke koffeinhaltig." The flags of participating nations appear on the glasses along with a soccer related action scene. These beautiful glasses are pretty difficult to find, and it's especially difficult to assemble a set. $15.00 – 25.00 each.

1. Fans on a bus going to the games; flags of Italy, Brazil, Algeria, Hungary, Kuwait, Cameroun
2. Fans in the grandstands; flags of Yugoslavia, Scotland, Honduras, Austria, Northern Ireland, El Salvador
3. Fans running onto the field; flags of New Zealand, England, CSSR, Argentina, Chile, France
4. Players and fans celebrating; flags of Spain, Belgium, Poland, Germany, Peru, UDSSR

Right: 1994 World Cup Soccer USA 1994 set of six.
World Cup Soccer USA 1994 set of six, sponsored by McDonald's and Coca-Cola. Each glass features colored portraits of two players and various facts about their careers. $10.00 – 15.00 each.

1. G. Grun and R. Smidts
2. D. Medved and M. Preud'homme
3. L. Nillis and D. Boffin
4. E. Scifo and M. Degryse
5. L. Staelens and P. Albert
6. F. Van Der Elst and P. Van Himst

SET OF ELEVEN SOCCER TUMBLERS FROM FRANCE

A set of eleven 5¼" tumblers showing players and coach of the year 2000 European soccer championship team. The glasses are unnumbered and undated, but they have the Coca-Cola wave logo on a soccer ball and Y2K McDonald's logo on the reverse. Between these logos is "Partenaires Officiels De L'Equipe De France." Another co-sponsor is Equipe De France. The glasses were packaged two per carton. I'm not sure if or how the coach's glass was packaged. It's difficult to obtain these glasses, and sets are especially difficult to complete. There's a sticker on the bottom of each glass which says: "Luminarc Verrerie Cristallerie D'Arques J. G. Durand & Cie, 62510 Arques France, www.arc-vca.com, Made in France, 0689/00." $15.00 – 25.00 each for the glasses; cartons, add $2.00.

Left.

1. #3 Bixente Lizarazu
2. #4 Patrick Vieira
3. #5 Laurent Blanc
4. #6 Youri Djorkaeff
5. #7 Didier Deschamps

Right.

1. #8 Marcel Desailly
2. #10 Zinedine Zidane
3. #15 Lilian Thuram
4. #17 Emmanuel Petit
5. #20 David Trezeguet
6. #16 Fabien Barthez (coach)

Dated or Datable Stemware (Note: Datable means that we can assign a date to the glass based on the occasion it is known to have celebrated.)

FOUR EARLY STEMWARE PIECES

1. McDonald's "Slashed Arch" toasting glass, 8¹/₄" etched. This toasting glass was issued at about the time of the opening of McDonald's 1000th store in Des Plaines, Illinois in 1968 and is considered a very rare item amongst McDonald's collectors. The logo on this glass is referred to as a "Slashed Arch" logo because it shows a line going through the arches on the left between 9 and 10 on a clock face and between 3 and 4 on the right and emulates the architectural (roof) design of early McDonald's restaurants. The left end of this line has a barb on it facing down which represents the roof design seen from the side. The Slashed Arch logo replaced the old Speedee System logo in 1962. $100.00 – 250.00+.

2. 1969 National Operators' Convention 5⁷/₈" wine goblet with faux etched gray paint decoration. The graphic is circular with the McDonald's logo in the center. This glass comes from the early years of the franchise and is considered quite rare and desirable. $100.00 – 300.00+.

3. "1500th McDonald's," a 4³/₈" champagne saucer with gold decoration commemorating the opening of McDonald's 1500th store in Concord, New Hampshire, at 113 – 117 London Road on September 27, 1970. Along with the "1500th McDonald's" script, this early and rare saucer has a large McDonald's Arches logo which virtually touches the rim. $100.00 – 200.00+.

4. "McDonald's 2000th," a 5⁵/₈" red wine goblet with gray decoration. This early and rare wine glass commemorates the opening of McDonald's 2000th store at 725 Golf Rd. in Des Plaines, Illinois, on July 26, 1972. $75.00 – 150.00+.

FOUR EARLY 1970s STEMWARE PIECES

1. McDonald's 2,500th, a 6⁷/₈" all purpose wine glass with understated yellow decoration showing the Arches as line drawings not filled in and the number "2,500th" below them. This glass celebrates the opening of the 2,500th store in Hickory Hills, Illinois, in 1973. $100.00 – 250.00+.

2. McDonald's logo in gold line drawing (Arches not filled in) on a 4³/₈" champagne saucer. This graphic is nearly identical to the one which appears on the 2,500th store opening wine glass listed above and shown to the left. I believe that this champagne saucer is the mate to the wine glass and that both glasses were produced for the 1973 store opening celebration. $100.00 – 250.00+.

3. (McDonald's) "3000th London '74," 8¹/₂" champagne flute featuring British and American flags. This glass commemorates the opening of the 3000th McDonald's store in Woolwich (London), England, in 1974. There's no McDonald's logo on this glass or any outright and obvious reference to McDonald's, so it's a real sleeper. You have to know your McDonald's glasses when it comes to this one! $100.00 – 250.00+.

4. McDonald's 20/Congratulations from Lily (1975) on 7⁵/₈" red wine glass, black and yellow decoration. $35.00 – 50.00.

FOUR STEMWARE PIECES FROM THE LATE 1970s

1. Ronald McDonald House Dinner-Dance October 15, 1977, a 6¹/₁₆" toasting or cordial glass with frosted gray decoration featuring Ronald McDonald. $20.00 – 35.00.

2. McDonald's Las Vegas 1978, a 6⁷/₈" all-purpose wine glass with gold decoration showing the Arches, from the 1978 national convention. $20.00 – 30.00.

3. "Nobody can do it like McDonald's can," New Orleans Region L.S.M., 10" hurricane glass with black decoration. This advertising slogan was introduced in 1979, so I assume the glass dates from the same period. $25.00 – 40.00.

4. McDonald's September 24, 1979, an 8⁵/₈" toasting flute with gold decoration. The date is obviously that of a major McDonald's convention. $25.00 – 40.00.

FOUR STEMWARE PIECES FROM 1979 AND 1980

1. McDonald's Christmas 1979, a 6¹/₄" all-purpose wine glass with gold decoration. $15.00 – 25.00.

2. McDonald's Albany Region 1979, an 8¹/₂" balloon wine goblet with silver/platinum decoration. $25.00 – 40.00.

3. "Store 6000," a 6¹/₂" toasting glass with faux etched gray decoration consisting of the Arches above "Store 6000." This glass commemorated the opening of McDonald's 6000th restaurant in Munich, Germany, in 1980. $100.00 – 200.00 +.

4. McDonald's Albany Region 1980, an 8¹/₂" balloon wine goblet with gold decoration. $25.00 – 40.00.

FOUR PIECES OF STEMWARE FROM THE EARLY 1980s

1. McDonald's 25th Anniversary Toronto, Canada, 1980, a 5¹/₂" brandy snifter with gold decoraton. $25.00 – 40.00.

2. McDonald's 25th Anniversary (1980), a 5¹/₂" high brandy snifter with a 3" mouth diameter and black decoration. $25.00 – 40.00.

3. McDonald's Cromwell, Connecticut, Nov. 17, 1981, a 3³/₄" brandy snifter with yellow decoration. $20.00 – 25.00.

4. McDonald's Albany Region 1981, an 8¹/₂" balloon wine goblet with silver/platinum decoration. $25.00 – 40.00.

THREE STEMWARE PIECES FROM 1982

1. McDonald's Portland, Oregon, 1982, $8^{1}/_{2}$" trumpet (pilsner) glass with brown decoration, including an Oregon rose beneath center of the Arches. $30.00 – 50.00.

2. NBMOA National Convention 1982, New York City, New York, a $6^{7}/_{8}$" all-purpose wine glass with black and yellow decoration. NBMOA stands for the National Black McDonald's Operators Association which was founded in 1972. As of 2/17/04 it had 33 chapters in 32 states with 375 members. Black operators own over 1300 McDonald's stores with sales exceeding 2 billion dollars. $15.00 – 35.00.

3. "10 Years Celebration Sidney, Feb. 1982" on one side of a $5^{5}/_{8}$" pewter tulip goblet and a McDonald's Australian logo on the other. The writing and graphics are inscribed into the pewter. Inscribed on the bottom of the base: "Oriental Pewter, Malaysia." $75.00 – 150.00+.

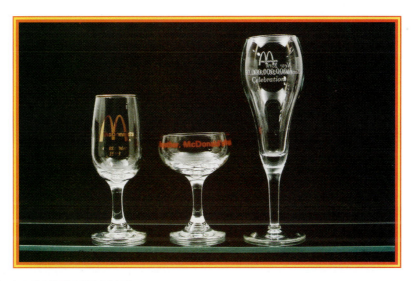

THREE STEMWARE PIECES FROM THE EARLY 1980s

1. McDonald's Christmas 1983, a $6^{1}/_{4}$" all-purpose wine glass with gold decoration. $15.00 – 30.00.

2. "Together, McDonald's and You!," a 4" dessert glass with red decoration, a party gift for fanchisees. The "McDonald's and You" ad campaign was launched in 1983. $15.00 – 30.00.

3. "McDonald's 50,000,000,000th Celebration" on one side, "New York November 20, 1984" on the other; gray (paint) decoration on $8^{5}/_{8}$" bulbous champagne/toasting glass. $20.00 – 40.00.

FOUR PIECES OF STEMWARE FROM 1984

1. Portland Oregon McDonald's 1984, maroon decoration with a single rose under center of arches, 8⁵/₈" continental champagne/toasting glass. $25.00 – 40.00.

2. McDonald's St. Petersburg Region 1984 on 5⁷/₈" wide-bowled red wine glass with gold decoration. $25.00 – 40.00.

3. Ronald McDonald House, 1974 – 1984/Philadelphia October 15, 1984, an 8¹/₂" bulbous champagne/toasting glass with frosted decoration. $25.00 – 40.00.

4. McDonald's Paris Janvier 1984, a 5¹/₂" cordial glass with yellow decoration. $25.00 – 35.00.

THREE STEMWARE PIECES FROM 1985

1. 30th Anniversary (1985), Fall River, Illinois, a 3³/₈" brandy snifter with gold decoration. $20.00 – 30.00.

2. McDonald's Christmas 1985, a 6¹/₄" all-purpose wine glass with gold decoration. $15.00 – 25.00.

3. McDonald's Celebrating 30 Years with You, Ft. Lauderdale 1985, an 8¹/₂" bulbous champagne toasting glass with applied gold glittery decoration. $25.00 – 40.00.

THREE MID 80s STEMWARE PIECES

1. Houston Region 1985, a 7" all-purpose wine glass with an unusual shape and applied gray decoration that looks like etching. $20.00 – 30.00.

2. McDonald's Las Vegas 1986, 8$\frac{1}{8}$" toasting flute with etched decoration. $15.00 – 25.00.

3. McDonald's Hellam, PA, 1986, 6$\frac{7}{8}$" toasting glass/flute with etched decoration. $20.00 – 40.00.

THREE STEMWARE PIECES FROM 1986

1. McDonald's logo in green on one side and "Gulf Shores Alabama May 6, 1986" on the other, 8$\frac{1}{2}$" bulbous champagne toasting glass. $25.00 – 40.00.

2. Grand Opening 15000 Whittier Blvd. (California) September 1986, a 6" brandy snifter with gray paint decoration meant to simulate etching. Featured above the text is a representation of a modern McDonald's restaurant. Whittier Blvd. is in East Los Angeles, California. $20.00 – 40.00.

3. McDonald's "Christmas '86," a 6$\frac{7}{8}$" all-purpose wine glass with black and yellow decoration. A city skyline is represented in a black line drawing just to the right of the McDonald's logo. $20.00 – 35.00.

FIVE 1988 STEMWARE PIECES

1. McDonald's 10,000th Store Opening April 6, 1988, McDonald's logo inside circle with Capitol and Washington Monument, 8$^1/_4$" toasting glass flute with gray (paint) decoration and six-sided stem. This glass and the one to its right were issued to owners and operators as a boxed set of two to celebrate the opening of McDonald's 10,000th store in Dale City, Virginia. $25.00 – 40.00.

2. Owner/Operator Convention April 5 – 9, 1988, below Capitol and Washington Monument scene with McDonald's logo in circle (same deco as 10,000th Store Opening glass), 8$^1/_4$" toasting glass flute with gray (paint) decoration and six-sided stem. This glass is the mate to the glass to its left. $25.00 – 40.00; both glasses in presentation box, $60.00 – 90.00.

3. McDonald's logo on one side and "Official Toasting Glass McDonald's 10,000th Restaurant, Dale City, Virginia USA, April 6, 1988" on the other, 8$^1/_8$" with gray (paint) decoration. $25.00 – 40.00.

4. 1988 Manager's Convention Hosted By McDonald's Greenville, etched decoration on 6$^5/_8$" white wine/all-purpose wine glass. North or South Carolina? I'm not sure. $25.00 – 40.00.

5. The Eddy Corporation McDonald's 25th Store 1988, gray (paint) decoration on 7$^1/_4$" toasting glass. $25.00 – 40.00.

FIVE LATE 1980s STEMWARE PIECES

1. San Diego Region Grand Opening December 2, 1988, etched decoration on 7¼" toasting glass. $25.00 – 40.00.
2. Season's Greetings McDonald's Minneapolis 1988, a 7¼" toasting glass with gray paint decoration showing a Christmas wreath and candle. The glass shown here still has the original bow on the stem, string confetti inside, and small green paper inside saying: "People, Pride, Progress, Minneapolis Region. This glass is your gift as a remembrance of our party. After dinner we will have a champagne toast to say farewell to 1988 and ring in 1989!!" $25.00 – 40.00.
3. Grand Opening, Trinity 1989, an 8⅝" toasting glass with pink decoration and pink stem. $25.00 – 40.00.
4. McDonald's North Olmsted (Ohio) Grand Opening 1989, a 7⅞" toasting glass with gold decoration. $25.00 – 40.00.
5. McDonald's Galleria Mall May 1989 Grand Opening, a 6¼" wine glass with gray print decoration. The galleria in question is the Walden Galleria in Cheektowaga, New York, a suburb of Buffalo. $20.00 – 35.00.

THREE STEMWARE PIECES FROM 1989 AND 1990

1. McDonald's Chowchilla (California) December, 1989, a 7¼" toasting glass with gray etching decoration. $15.00 – 25.00.
2. Happy Holidays McDonald's 1989, a 7⅞" wine glass with red decoration. $15.00 – 25.00.
3. McDonald's 4⅝" brandy snifter with gray decoration which says: "McDonalds (no apostrophe to show the possessive case) of Perry, Mi (Michigan) 1990." $20.00 – 30.00.

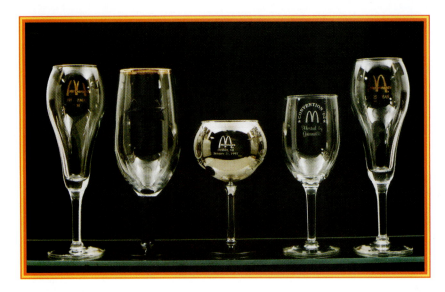

FIVE EARLY 1990s STEMWARE PIECES

1. McDonald's CHRISTMAS 1990, an 8¹/₂" toasting glass with gold decoration. $20.00 – 30.00.
2. "December 1990/Merry Christmas/Love, Caesar," an 8¹/₄" all purpose wine glass with black screen print of early McDonald's restaurant, generously decorated gold rim, and black stem and base, an unusual glass for a very special occasion. $40.00 – 60.00.
3. McDonald's, DeWitt, Michigan, January 21, 1991, in white on 5⁷/₈" polished silver wide-bowled balloon goblet wine glass. $30.00 – 50.00.
4. "Convention '92 Hosted by Greenville," a 6⁷/₈" wine glass with grey faux etching decoration. $30.00 – 50.00.
5. McDonald's CHRISTMAS 1992, an 8¹/₂" toasting glass with gold decoration. $20.00 – 30.00.

TWO WINE GLASSES AND TWO CHAMPAGNE SAUCERS

1. McDonald's Arches etched on 6" all-purpose wine glass. This could very well be a relatively early glass. $15.00 – 30.00.
2. McDonald's logo (Arches with "McDonald's" intersecting them) in yellow twelve times around top of 6" champagne saucer. $15.00 – 25.00.
3. McDonald's Arches in yellow fourteen times around the top of 6" champagne saucer along with "McDonald's" once in yellow. $15.00 – 25.00.
4. McDonald's logo in gray (paint) decoration on 7¹/₄" toasting glass flute. $10.00 – 20.00.

THREE STEMWARE PIECES

1. McDonald's Arches with Canadian maple leaf below center arch on 7⅝" all-purpose wine glass, frosted gray (paint) decoration, black stem and base, made in France by Luminarc. The simple design suggests an early date. $25.00 – 40.00.

2. McDonald's Arches on 8⅛" toasting glass flute with gray (paint) decoration. Another simply designed glass that could be early. $15.00 – 25.00.

3. "Team YASNY 25" (years), an 8" wine glass with etched decoration showing the Arches with a star with the number 25 inside it zooming around the Arches. I've not been able to identify Yasny with certainty since Internet search engines find me a bewildering array of possibilities. My best guess is that it's either a communications firm that works for McDonald's or a NASCAR related racing enterprise that has some connection with McDonald's. No date. $30.00 – 40.00.

FOUR STEMWARE PIECES

1. Chevron & McDonald's, an 8³/₄" toasting flute with etched decoration showing Chevron's logo and McDonald's block logo with etched lines above and below. This flute was intended to promote a collaborative relationship between the two companies primarily in California and perhaps at a few other locations in the southwest. Late 1990s is a possible date. $30.00 – 40.00.

2. Chevron & McDonald's, an 8¹/₂" toasting flute with red, yellow, blue, white, and black decoration showing Chevron's logo and McDonald's block logo with yellow bars above and below. The decorative design of this flute is the same as the frosted version listed above, but here we have color and a daintier flute with a rope stem. $30.00 – 50.00.

3. McDonald's Arches in center of compass: "Pursuing the Vision, 100% Customer Satisfaction," 8⁵/₈" etched toasting glass. $15.00 – 30.00.

4. McDonald's Hulen Mall, Fort Worth, Texas, a 7³/₄" wine glass with etched decoration. No date. $20.00 – 30.00.

THREE SPECIAL OCCASION CARAFES

1. Full Litre Carafe with gold decoration: Norwood III, 31 Providence Highway (Massachusetts). Carafes like this were used to pour wine into the various toasting and wine glasses shown above at special McDonald's occasions. $20.00 – 35.00.

2. Carafe, 7¹/₂" with etched McDonald's logo on the front and "West Tusc Celebrating 30 Years 1960 – 1990" on the reverse. I assume that the reference is to West Tuscaloosa, Alabama. $25.00 – 40.00.

3. One litre carafe made by Libbey of Canada, 10¹³/₁₆" high, promoting the Ronald McDonald House Celebrity Golf Classic. Etched decoration shows a waving wide-hipped Ronald. $20.00 – 35.00.

SEVEN STYROFOAM COFFEE CUPS AND A SOUP CUP

Left.

Yellow, orange, and brown decorated cups. These undated cups were a familiar sight during the 1980s and come in several sizes from small to large. Three bands of Arches encircle the cups in yellow, orange, and brown. "Please put litter in its place" appears in yellow above the bands. On some of the cups this message is punched into the cup in yellow; on others it is printed in yellow on the surface. I've also noticed that the yellow ® mark to the right of the Arches just outside the brown frame is up higher in the punched in lettering version and lower in the applied yellow lettering version. These variations that I mention are probably just a few of many inherent in this cups series. Collectors who pursue these cups need to be diligent observers. But to continue: the McDonald's logo appears in a brown frame. I show the 3⅝" and 4¼" sizes here. There were probably other larger sizes as well. $2.00 – 4.00.

1. 3⅝" cup (some, but not all, of these cups have "©1990 McD Corp" on bottom).

2. 4¼" cup (no © date on my one 4¼" cup).

3. Redesigned yellow, orange, and brown decorated cup. This cup is in the main identical to its predecessors listed above, but "Caution: Contents Hot!" now appears twice in brown small print around the top to alternate with the yellow "Please Put Litter In Its Place." "©1990 McD Corp." appears on the bottom. The cup came in various sizes. Here I show an unusual variation: a 5⅛" cup with a "Blast Back with Mac" game piece from 1989. Cups without game pieces: $2.00 - $4.00 each. Cups with game pieces: $5.00 – 10.00 each.

4. 5⅛" McDonald's Racing Team cup with three bands of logos encircling it and "Contents Hot!" and litter notices alternating twice each just above the bands. This cup belongs to the same family of cups discussed above, but instead of yellow, orange, and brown Arches, this cup has yellow, orange, and red Arches as well as the McDonald's Racing Team logo with "The Best Start In NASCAR" below it. "©1990 McD Corp." appears on the bottom. Same design both sides. These cups may come in other sizes. $4.00 – 7.00.

Right.

1. Redesigned yellow, orange, and brown decorated cup with three bands of Arches, litter and hot warnings around the top, and the McDonald's logo outlined in brown. This 3⅝" cup maintains the basic design shown on the cups shown to the left, but an orange and gold "Questions? Comments? See The Manager Or Call 1-800-244-6227" graphic has been added to one side. "©1990 McD Corp." appears on the bottom. It probably came in two larger sizes as well. $2.00 – 4.00.

Redesigned "Questions? Comments?" cups with "HOT!" repeated around the top of the cup above a band of yellow McDonald's Arches which encircle the cup. Below this band of Arches are two each of the "Caution: Contents Hot!" and "Please Put Litter In Its Place" notices. A McDonald's logo appears on one side of the cup within a red outlined box, and the "Questions? Comments? See The Manager" graphic appears of the other side in red and yellow. I show small and medium sizes here, but there was probably a large cup as well. $2.00 – 4.00.

2. 3⅝" cup.

3. 4¼" cup.

4. ©1992 McDonald's Corporation (11222), a 3¼" McDonald's Soup cup with a red and yellow McDonald's logo on each side and a graphic of a hot container of soup on each side. Red and yellow confetti flecks randomly adorn the cup. On the bottom: "Dart, Mason, Michigan." $5.00 – 10.00.

NINE STYROFOAM COFFEE CUPS

Left.

©1995 (on side), ©1990, or ©1996 (on bottom) "Caution: Hot!" coffee cup with red, yellow, and blue decoration. This is the cup that McDonald's served its coffee in during the nineties to the millennium, and, because of a jury's award to a burned coffee drinker, it goes out of its way to warn coffee drinkers that the contents are hot (as if they needed to be told!). It comes in 3½", 4¼", 5⅛", and 6" sizes. Most, but not all, of the 3⅝", 4¼", 5⅛" cups I have seen have "©1990 McD Corp" on the bottom. The one 6" cup I have has "©1996 McD Corp" on the bottom. There appear to be several design variations on the 3⅝" cup, especially in the typography. The graphics on one are slightly larger than on the other (especially apparent on the "Pitch in" litter icon), and there are other minor differences. If you decide to collect these cups, examine them carefully for minor design differences; there are numerous variations in printing and design which ultimately constitute a collector's quagmire!). $1.00 – 3.00 each.

1. 3⅝" cup with larger Arch logo, smaller block logo, and smaller litter icon, and "©1995 McDonald's Corporation" on the side.

2. 3⅝" cup with slightly smaller Arch logo, larger block logo, larger litter icon, and "©1995 McDonald's Corporation (13822)" on side.

3. 4¼" cup (1995 and 1996 dates and many design variations).

4. 5⅛" cup.

5. 6" cup.

Right.

©1996 "Caution: Hot!" coffee cups with red, yellow, and blue decoration from England. I found these cups in London in the summer of 2001. They are essentially the same as the US issues shown above, but these cups have "©1996 McDonald's Corporation" on their side and no date on the bottom. One interesting design difference is that these cups have a red ™ symbol (instead of the red ® symbol on American cups) near the bottom right of the large Arches on the cups. There is nothing on the cup to indicate a British origin. The clerk who gave me these cups assured me that there were only two sizes. $1.00 – 3.00.

1. Small 3⅝" cup (on bottom: PD 119 F79M).

2. Large 4¼" cup (on bottom: PD 30 F12M).

3. "©1997 McDonald's Corporation (13809)" on side, "©1995 McD Corp." on bottom, a 3⅝" cup with "Caution: Hot!" warnings and large Golden Arches with red, blue, and gold decoration like the cups listed above. But instead of repeating all the "Caution: Hot!" warnings and smaller arch logos around the cup, this cup has a thank-you note with balloons and confetti for the patron: "Thanks for Joining Us! Starting your Mornings for 25 Years." This cup was probably issued in medium and large sizes as well. $2.00 – 4.00.

4. "©1997 McDonald's Restaurants of Canada Limited," "Higgins & Burke Purveyors of fine coffees, since 1912, Deluxe Roast," a 3½" cup with English and French languages: "Caution: Hot! Attention: Chaud!" and "Melange Deluxe." The graphic is the same on both sides and appears to depict a South American person picking coffee beans. Comes with brown plastic lid. Made by Lily in Canada. $3.00 – 5.00.

PREMIUM BLEND AND SMILE LOGO COFFEE CUPS

Left.

©1999 McDonald's Corporation "Premium Blend" coffee cups. These redesigned cups made their debut in December 1999. They come in various sizes with various production numbers and promote and describe McDonald's "gourmet blend" coffee. ©1990 appears on bottom of the $3^5/_8$" and $5^1/_8$" cups. The 6" cup has "©1996 McD Corp" on its bottom. A later version of the 6" cup has production numbers and a recycling symbol. I first encountered these cups in New York City and New Jersey, and at the time they did not seem to be available everywhere as of the spring and summer of 2000. I presume that operators were using up their old stock and that these cups would ultimately be more widely used as has since proved to be the case. Be warned that there are likely to be many variations of these cups. Compare, for example, the positions of the borders in the two 6" cups. But that's just for starters: color and font variations are abundant. $0.50 – 1.00.

1. $3^5/_8$" cup (light orange sunburst design diamond with McDonald's logo)
2. $5^1/_8$" cup (orange sunburst design diamond with McDonald's logo)
3. 6" cup (light orange sunburst design)
4. 6" cup (orange sunburst design)

Right.

2000 "we love to see you smile" logo, two "Smile" logos, "USA Proud Partner" with Olympic rings, and "Caution: Hot!" and "Caution: Contents Hot!" warnings, a set of three coffee cups which were introduced in the spring of 2000 and which appeared (at the time) to have a promising continuance. The "Smile" slogan was introduced at McDonald's worldwide convention in Orlando, Florida, on April 17, 2000, and was officially implemented on June 30. It replaced the "Did somebody say McDonald's?" slogan which enjoyed a three-year life. The "Smile" slogan was replaced by the new tagline "I'm lovin' it" in late 2003. "©1990 McD Corp" appears on the bottom of the $4^1/_4$" and $5^1/_8$" cups. The 6" cup appears not to have a copyright date. $0.50 – 1.00.

1. $4^1/_4$" cup
2. $5^1/_8$" cup
3. 6" cup (on the bottom: 11196 A99002)

"HOW ARE WE DOIN'?"/"CAUTION: HOT!" STYROFOAM COFFEE CUPS

"©2002 McDonald's Corporation (11196) Printed In The U.S.A." on side of "Caution: Hot!" Styrofoam cup with red, blue, and yellow decoration. This cup has the typical and by now familiar Arches with red and yellow color blocks behind them as well as two small red and white block logos, but new to this cup is the "how are we doin'?" graphic with the toll-free number: 1-800-244-6227 and website address: www.mcdonalds.com. The cup comes in small (4¼"), medium (5⅛"), and large (6") sizes. The small and medium cups have "© 1990 McD Corp." on the bottom. The large cup does not have a date on its bottom. $0.50 – 1.00.

1. Small cup
2. Medium cup
3. Large cup (on bottom: 11196 – A01022)

SUNDAE, MOCHA, AND PARFAIT CUPS

FIVE CLEAR DRINKING/EATING CUPS

1. 4¼" clear plastic Iced Mocha cup from London, England (Summer 2001). The only decoration on this cup is a red band near the bottom with yellow Arches on it. The cup was used for a frozen coffee drink in England. It is undated, and there's nothing very informative on the bottom. $1.00 – 2.00.
2. ©2000 Fruit 'n Yoghurt Parfait cup with domed cap. With the cap this thin clear plastic cup stands 5½" and has the "Smile" logo and the USA Proud Partner Olympic ring logo. On the bottom: "SOLO, Urbana, IL." $1.00 – 2.00.
3. Sundae cup with McDonald's Arches embossed around rim, 3¼" clear antique glass. These are the ones that the uninformed on eBay refer to as flower pots. A lot of them survived. $2.00 – 5.00.
4. Clear plastic 3⅜" sundae cup with eight panels and a flat-domed cap. Each of the cup's panels has the Arches impressed on it. Strictly speaking, not a drink container, unless you wait for the sundae to melt! $0.25 - 0.75.
5. 1977 clear plastic sundae cup with dome cap. This 3½" clear plastic cup has the McDonald's logo on either side near the top and a dome cap with a larger McDonald's logo on its top flat surface. The bottom says: "Copyright 1977 McDonald's System Inc. Pat. Pend." It's not exactly a drinking container, but it looks enough like one to list here. Items like this are not exactly common. It takes a real optimist to save items like this! $7.00 – 10.00.

THAILAND PLASTIC AND GLASS ISSUES

2000 "Peanuts 50th Anniversary Celebration," a set of two wax-coated paper cups from Thailand which were part of a summer 2000 Peanuts Festival promotion. The cups show the characters partying. On each cup, there's a special "Peanuts 50 Celebration" logo as well as the new Arch logo and the older block McDonald's logo. $5.00 – 10.00 each.

1. 4" purple background Peanuts cup.

2. 4⁷/₈" green background Peanuts cup.

3. (2000) McCrispy Chicken Sandwich promotional glass. This frosted 3³/₄" glass features a pair of colorful Thai McDonald's cartoon character superheroes. Above them in Thai writing we have "McCrispy (Arch logo) Fried Chicken from McDonald's." The name of the character in red with a chicken's comb on his head is "Fast Fry." The character in purple who appears to have steam coming out of his head is named "Steam Marinade." Together they promote the McCrispy Chicken Sandwich. A small red box above Mr. Fast Fry contains Thai writing which announces that this is a "New Formula." There's no English writing or date on the glass, but it appears to have been issued during the summer of 2000. (A Thai citizen translated the writing on this glass for me.) $20.00 – 30.00.

4. (2000) Red, green, yellow, and blue variously sized McDonald's Arch logos on a 4¹¹/₁₆" glass. The largest logo on the glass is red with a ™ symbol beside it. On the bottom: "Thailand" in an arched pattern with "Naeco" below it. Obtained by me in early 2001 but probably dating from the year 2000. $20.00 – 30.00.

TOY CUPS

SIX PLASTIC TOY CUPS

Row 1.

1. 3¹/₂" battery-operated plastic toy cup. Not really a drinking cup, but it looks just like the Coca-Cola cups that McDonald's has been filling with soda for the past decade, so I couldn't resist including it. Shall we say that this very design is an icon as recognizable as the Arches? When you push the straw down on this cup, you hear the kinds of noises you hear when someone is dead-set on getting the last drop of liquid out of the bottom of a cup. There's no date on this toy and no Coca-Cola sponsorship. $6.00 – 10.00.

2. ©1985 2⁷/₈" plastic cup featuring Ronald McDonald in a sitting position. This is probably a Happy Meal toy. Graphic on one side only. Bottom: "©1985 McDonald's China." $7.00 – 12.00.

3. ©1987 toy transformer plastic cup. This little 1³/₄" plastic cup "Made in China W 6" looks like a little drink cup with a stubby straw coming out the top, but it's a toy that turns into a red and blue transformer character. Fun for the kids, not to drink out of. $5.00 – 8.00.

Row 2.

1. 1989 collapsible Camp McDonaldland plastic cup. This orange 2⁷/₈" cup has a plastic cap with embossed designs on the sides showing Ronald and Birdie in a canoe and Grimace and Hamburglar in a canoe. The top shows Ronald with a safari hat and binoculars. $4.00 – 7.00.

2. ©1996 toy cup with pop-up lid and red straw. The top of this plastic cup toy made in "China MT 04" opens to reveal a plastic dome in which the Hamburglar pursues three tiny hamburgers. $7.00 – 12.00.

3. 3³/₈" toy drink cup, ©1999, made in China. Not a real drinking cup, this toy cup came from Hong Kong. It has a McDonald's logo on the front and wind-up button on the reverse. When the button is wound up, a mechanical Grimace inside is activated, and eventually the cup splits apart, and Grimace walks away from the cup's two halves. $8.00 – 12.00.

EIGHT PLASTIC TRAVEL MUGS WITH SIPPING LIDS AND BASE HOUSINGS

These mugs are made of thick plastic, and they are designed to be mounted on the dashboards or center consoles of cars, boats, and campers. The mugs are designed to fit into a housing base which is attached to a flat surface with adhesive tape, and their obvious function is to hold caffeine for commuters and travelers. Canadians call these mugs "Port-A-Mugs," and Americans just refer to them as travel mugs.

Row 1.

1. $3^5/_8$" yellow and red plastic Canadian mug with sipping lid, large McDonald's logo on both sides, made by Bert-wood Marketing Inc. in Toronto, Canada. French and English writing on bottom, shown without housing base. $2.00 – 4.00.

2. Canadian McDonald's logo on both sides, Aberdeen Kamloops B.C. opposite handle, red and orange decoration on white, yellow lid and base. $2.00 – 4.00.

3. Canadian McDonald's logo in red-lined square frame on both sides, orange and red decoration on white, yellow lid and base. $2.00 – 4.00.

4. Canadian McDonald's logo in red-lined square frame on front, "The Tri-City News" on reverse in red-lined box, red and yellow decoration on white, yellow lid and base. $2.00 – 4.00.

Row 2.

1. McDonald's logo on both sides, 10295 S. Clare Ave. Clare, MI 48617 opposite handle, and black decoration on white, orange lid, handle, and base. $2.00 – 4.00.

2. McDonald's logo on both sides, 6325 W. Side Saginaw Rd., Bay City, MI 48706 opposite handle, orange and black decoration on white, orange lid, handle, and base. $2.00 – 4.00.

3. Canadian McDonald's logo in red-lined square frame on both sides, orange and red decoration on white, orange lid, base, and handle. $2.00 – 4.00.

4. McDonald's logo on front, and on reverse 17921 E. Nine Mile, East Detroit, MI, orange and black decoration on white, orange lid and base. $2.00 – 4.00.

EIGHT PLASTIC TRAVEL MUGS WITH SIPPING LIDS AND BASE HOUSINGS

Row 1.

1. Four McDonald's logos in yellow and black on white plastic, orange lid with "Whirley" on it, orange handle and base (base not shown). $2.00 – 4.00.

2. Large 2" McDonald's logo on both sides, black and yellow decoration on white, red lid and base. $2.00 – 4.00.

3. 1½" McDonald's logo on both sides, black and yellow decoration on white, red lid and base. $2.00 – 4.00.

4. McDonald's of Fremont on both sides, orange and black decoration on white, red lid and base. $2.00 – 4.00.

Row 2.

1. McDonald's logo in red block with "Central Arkansas McDonald's" below it on front, "It's a Good Time For The Great Taste" and small McDonald's logo with happy smile rising sun behind it on reverse, red and yellow decoration on white, red lid and base. The "Good time...Great Taste" ads started to appear in 1984. $3.00 – 5.00.

2. "Coffee Club" mug with pink handle and sipping lid and "What you want is what you get" logo on each side. A multicolored steaming hot cup of coffee is the featured graphic three times around the mug. Made by Whirley Industries in Warren, Pennsylvania. $2.00 – 5.00.

3. "The World's Only Floating McDonald's, St. Louis, Missouri," a 4³/₈" orange mug with black, red, and yellow graphics and red sipping lid and base. This "Trip Sip" mug picturing a McDonald's restaurant riverboat was made by Betras Plastics Inc., Spartanburg, South Carolina. This floating restaurant was launched in 1980. $5.00 – 10.00.

4. McDonald's logo in yellow and black on one side of this white mug with orange sipping lid and base, and on the other this announcement in black and orange: "Free Coffee/thru March 31, 1983/with the purchase of any/Large Sandwich/Egg McMuffin® Sandwich/Scrambled Eggs, Sausage/and Hash Browns or/Hot Cakes and Sausage;/at participating McDonald's.®" Made by Whirley Industries, Warren, Pennsylvania. An unusual travel mug since dates generally don't appear on them. $10.00 – 15.00.

FOUR PLASTIC TRAVEL MUGS WITH PLASTIC SIPPING LIDS AND BASE HOUSINGS

1. McDonald's logo in yellow and black on one side of this white mug with orange sipping lid and base, and on the other this announcement in black and orange: "Free Coffee/thru April 30, 1983/with the purchase of any Biscuit/Sandwich; Egg McMuffin® Sandwich;/Scrambled Eggs Sausage/and Hash Browns; Hotcakes;/at participating McDonalds®." Made by Whirley Industries in Warren, Pennsylvania. Another unusual dated travel mug. $10.00 – 15.00.

2. McDonald's logo in yellow and black on one side of this white mug with orange sipping lid and base (not shown), and on the other panels: (1) "Girard & Luczak & *You* mornings. Magic 96.5 WMGF FM" and (2) "Free Coffee with the purchase of any breakfast entree through March 31, 1985, at participating McDonald's in southeastern Wisconsin." Made by Whirley Industries, Warren, Pennsylvania. Uncommon combination of date and location. $10.00 – 20.00.

3. "Adam and Bob...Twice As Much In The Mornings 6 – 10 AM Daily...1590 WAKR," a 4¹/₄" plastic travel mug with black and yellow decoration. Likenesses of Adam Jones and Bob Allen appear on one side of the mug, and there's a big McDonald's logo on the reverse. WAKR is in Akron, Ohio. According to my sources, Bob Allen still does the show. $6.00 – 12.00.

4. 3³/₄" gray marbled travel mug with red cap, handle, and base. Four red and yellow block logos encircle the mug, and there's a red and yellow band around the bottom. Made by Whirley Industries in Warren, Pennsylvania. $3.00 – 5.00.

SEVEN DIFFERENT INTERNAL FUNCTION MUGS

Row 1.

1. McDonald's Annual Picnic Summer 1975, a 5½" amber mug with red decoration. $20.00 – 30.00.

2. "Security Analysts Conference/October 20 & 21, 1976," a 4" ceramic mug with yellow, black, green, and red decoration. On the reverse there's a neat bar graph which shows McDonald's net income growth from 1966 to 1975. This is a big mug with a 3½" mouth diameter, and it was probably not produced in great quantity. How many McDonald's analysts could there have been in 1976? $35.00 – 50.00.

3. "10th Annual McDonald's Family Picnic...I can, I can, I can," a one pint canning jar mug with white metal lid and red decoration. This is an early mug, judging by its design and the fact that it celebrates a low numbered picnic. $15.00 – 25.00.

4. "Security," a 3¾" white ceramic mug with gray decoration showing the Arches above an oval containing the word "Security" and a line drawing map of the world. This limited production mug would have been available only to members of McDonald's Security Department. "Made In China" appears on the bottom. $8.00 – 15.00.

Row 2.

8th Annual Old Fashioned Family Picnic, Nestlerest Park, Lake Zurich, Illinois, Sunday July 10, 1977, a 3½" white ceramic mustache mug with green and yellow decoration showing a man in stripped jacket and woman with parasol in a rowboat. This cup came with a black paper mustache on which there is white writing which says "No Mustache Of Your Own? Here's One of Ours. Have a happy day!" $25.00 – 50.00.

1. Front of Old Fashioned Picnic mug

2. Reverse of Old Fashioned Picnic mug

3. McDonald's 1983 Combined Assistants Workshop, a 5½" mug with red and yellow decoration. $15.00 – 20.00.

4. McDonald's Fourth Quarter Marketing Review 1983, a 5½" clear glass mug with red and yellow decoration. $15.00 – 20.00.

FIVE INTERNAL FUNCTION MUGS

Row 1.

1. McDonald's Madison Crew Rally 1985, a heavy 5" mug with yellow decoration. $20.00 – 25.00.

2. "Operations Training, Chicago," a 5½" amber glass mug with white decoration. Large white Arches and "Chicago" in white-outlined letters appear between "Operations" on the top and "Training" on the bottom. $15.00 – 25.00.

Row 2.

1. McDonald's Education and Training Activities, a 3¾" white ceramic mug with red, yellow, black, and gray decoration. This mug features a modern railroad engine with "McTrain" on its nose. A small McDonald's logo appears in a gap between triple red lines near the bottom of the mug. "Made In China" appears on the base. $10.00 – 20.00.

2. "We're Still The One," a 5½" clear glass mug with black decoration featuring a cartoonish TV cameraman and the logo of McDonald's "Communications Services Established 1971." As the round Communications Services logo indicates, this internal McDonald's department deals with such matters as "meetings and conventions; creative services; and publications." There are two very small Arch logos within the larger circular logo, and this mug was probably given to workshop participants during the 1980s. $15.00 – 25.00.

3. McDonald's Communication Services Dept., a 5¼" plastic mug with red decoration. $4.00 – 10.00.

Achievement awards 45
Aladdin 163
Alice in Wonderland.................................34
Anniversary mugs 11-12
Anniversary tankards 11-12
Arch Deluxe Sandwich.......................107-108
Are you Mac enough? 130
Asian sets 77-78
Australia.....................48, 124-125, 142, 235
Australian Olympic Series........................134
Australian Rugby League 185
Austria 117, 122, 127
Auto Racing 164, 191, 218
Baltimore Orioles "Greatest Moments" 221
Barware 13-14
Baseball cups 165-167
Basketball cups 168
Batman Forever 48
Batman Forever mugs.......................48, 100
Batman Returns 161
Baylor University Bears 225
Be daring, first & different 49
Beer glass 14, 35
Big Mac Sandwich 88, 108
Bill Elliott 58, 164, 218
Black History Month 123
Blast Back with Mac 64
Breakfast brigade 15
Breakfast mugs........................15-17, 201
Britney Spears 125
Brockway..69
Buzz Lightyear 36, 107
Café blend McDonald's 118
Camp McDonaldland 248
Camp Snoopy Collection Owner-Operator glass..........18-19
Camp Snoopy glasses and plastic cups 18-19
Canadian Institute of Hamburgerology 44
Canisters 78
Carafes 242
Catalog order items 49
Charity and community involvement 19
Chevron 242
Chicken Flatbread Sandwich 127
Chicken McNuggets 61, 81, 150
Christmas..20-24, 47, 61, 105, 137, 200, 234-237, 239-240
Christmas Carol 23
Christmas cups 105, 137
Cinderella...31-32
Classic fifties milkshake glasses 24-25
Coast to coast.....................................87-88
Color variations 75
Come Remember the Magic 107-108
Communications Services 253
Commuter mugs 26
Conferences 252-253

Convention mugs 27-29
Conventions and meetings 27-28, 238, 240
Cows on Parade....................................155
Cup and saucer 82
Cup holders 30
Custom Built Hamburgers 110
Decanter 13
Delivering the difference 50
Denim Collection 89
Des Plaines, Illinois 49
Dick Tracy..161
Did somebody say McDonald's?.........118, 202, 245
Disney 31-36, 48
Disney Animal Kingdom 33, 35-36, 190
Disney Animated Film Classics 31-32
Disney drinkware.................................31-36
Disney "Hatch-Match" 34
Disney Home Video Masterpiece Collection ...106
Disney Home Video set 34
Disneyland set...32
Disney Masterpiece Collection Trivia Challenge 106
Disney — Pixar Finding Nemo......................130
Disney Pixar Toy Story 2.............................109
Disney's 102 Dalmations 109, 126, 163
Disney's Atlantis — The Lost Empire 126
Disney's Lilo & Stitch 127
Dobson Products 159
Donald Duck 32-35
Dream Team II.................................170-171
Dr Pepper 222
Dukes of Hazzard 37
Dumbo..106
Embossed bottom Action Series 74
Embossed bottom California set 74
England.............78-80, 101, 116-117, 121, 127, 129, 233
Epcot 33, 36
Error glass 25, 70, 115, 200, 223
Espana 82 World Cup Soccer 230
Extra Value Meals 157
Family Night..125
Fantasia 32-34
Flintstones 48, 132, 162
Flintstones Bedrock mugs 48, 100
Flubber..108
French issues 31, 38, 187, 231, 236
Fruit 'n Yoghurt Parfait cup 246
Fun, Food, and Folks 113
Garfield...39
Garfield checkerboard design mugs 99
Garfield glass mugs 99
Garfield plastic mugs 99
George of the Jungle 108
German issues 40-41, 126
"Get into the games" paper cups 135
Golden State Foods.............................29, 210

Golf 19, 182, 206
Good morning Canada 15
Good morning Fairmont 15
Good morning Pittsburgh 15
Goofy 32-33, 35-36
Grand openings and groundbreakings 41-42, 237-239
Group II Communications 101
gsf 29, 210
Hamburger University 43-44
Happy Meal cups 119
Have you had your break today? 209
Hawaii 46, 140, 210, 217
Helping Olympic Dreams Come True 169
Hockey 182
Honey, I Shrunk the Kids 160
Hong Kong 47, 122
Hook 'em Horns 225
Houston Livestock Show and Rodeo 114
Hunchback of Notre Dame 48
Hut Stricklin 56, 164, 218
I'm lovin' it 131, 158, 245
I'm Speedee 87-88
Iced Mocha cup 246
In-house employee premiums 49-51, 76, 210
Indianapolis 500 184
Inspector Gadget 108
Italy 22, 82, 228
It's a good time for the great taste ..49, 51, 77-78, 194, 250
James and the Giant Peach 132
Japanese McDonald's 34, 61, 73, 87
Jetsons 150
Jimmy Spencer 56, 195
Junior Johnson 56, 164
Jurassic Park 162
Kente cups 159
Kentucky Derby 183-184
Keys to Quality 40
Kim Possible 157
Knoxville World's Fair 88
Kroc, Ray 6-7, 12, 45, 204, 213
Kuwait issues 62
Les Tres Reyes Magos Coleccion 200
Los Angeles Summer Olympics 49
Mac Tonight 63-64, 205, 243
Make It Mac Tonight 63
Many happy returns 16
Mary Poppins 106
Mason (Canning) Jars 21, 87, 213
Master Pizza 78, 89
McBlimp 79
McCafe Classico 127
McChoice 129
McCrispy Chicken Sandwich 247
McDonaldland Action Series 71
McDonaldland Adventure Series 72

McDonaldland Canadian Character Series 76
McDonaldland characters 65-78, 139-149
McDonald's Collector's Club 79, 88
McDonald's Guam 202
McDonald's Racing Team 56, 58-59, 164, 195, 218, 243
McFamily Night 125
McFlurry cups 121, 126
McGriddles Breakfast Sandwiches 130
McKids 146
McMoms 79
McMorning All American Breakfast 126
McMug 79
McSpresso 83
McVote '86 set 75
Mexico 16, 211
Michael Jordan 19, 132, 196
Mickey Mouse 32-36
Middle East set 62
Milk Shake cup 113
Millennium Celebration 33
Minnie Mouse 32, 35
Minute Maid Juice cups 138, 191, 196
MLBPA 165-166, 219
Monopoly glassware 90
Monopoly issues 90-97
Monopoly paper cups 91-96, 114
Mr. Pibb 154, 159, 190
Mug sets 98-101
My Chicken's McChicken 81
NASCAR 164, 191, 218, 243
NBA 125, 169-176
NBA Looney Tunes All Star Showdown 172-173
NBA plastic cups 169-176
NBMOA 235
Neopet Happy Meal 131
Netherlands issues 104-105
New Kids on the Block 151
New tastes menu 126-127, 156
NFL 178-181, 222-225
NFL cups 112, 178-181
Nothing But Net MVP 170
Nutcracker Christmas tumblers 23-24
Office coffee mug set 17
Olympic Dreams cup 133
Olympic mugs 98
Olympic Summer Games 98, 186-187
Parfait cups 246
Park City, Utah 127
Peanuts 50th Anniversary Celebration 247
Perseco 29
Pete's Dragon 106
Peter Pan 32
Philippines Character set 77
Picnic jug 192, 197, 217
Picnics 252-253

Index

Pizza 78, 89, 193
Pocahontas 106
Port-A-Mugs 249-251
Premium Fresh Salads 130
Priority One 29
Prototype McDonald's Character glasses 65-68, 73
Prototypes 23, 65-68, 73, 89
Proud Partner cup..........................127, 133, 158
Puerto Rico issues 200, 215, 227
Pure Collection 38
QSC..45
QSC & V 45, 213
Quarter Pounder with Cheese Code Name Game 109
Radio station mugs.......53, 56, 59, 81, 201-202, 216, 251
Rally 253
Reach for it 127
Red Wing Pottery mugs 203
Remember the Magic..33
Reviews..252
Roc Donald's 82, 132
Rodeo 229
Ronald McDonald House..................204-207, 233, 236
Ronald McDonald House Charities..118, 129, 204-205, 207
Salt Lake City Winter Olympics 127
Sam the Olympic Eagle 186
Sam the Olympic Eagle owner-operator's glass 226
Sample glass....................................69, 73, 75, 89
Scouting mugs 81
Sea World of Ohio..159
Security 252
Servin' up smiles 51, 194
Shot glass 14, 29
Simon Marketing 31
Slashed arch.........................12, 101, 110-111, 232
Slashed arch logo.................12, 101, 110-111, 232
"smile" logo 124, 126, 157, 245
"Smile" logo cups 124, 155, 245
Smoked glass sports mugs....................................98
Smurfs 150-151
Snow White 32
Space Jam 132
Speedee 11-12, 24-25, 87-88, 101, 110, 199, 213
Speedy Service System 88
St. Louis Cardinals "Legendary Players" 221
Steel Magnolias 1988 211
Steelers Hall of Fame set 224
Stemware...232-242
Steppin it up 79
Store managers convention...................27-29, 238
Styrofoam coffee cups 243-246
Sundae cup 114
Taking charge of number one 50
Taste Trials..125, 156

Taste Trials Game 125, 156
Test glass 69, 73, 224
Texas High School Coaches Association.................54-57
Thailand 77, 101, 228, 247
Thailand Character mugs 77, 101
The All American Meal 110
The All-Time Greatest Steelers Team 224
The customer counts..51
The Great Muppet Caper 102-103
The Great Muppet Caper owner-operator's glass 103
The Little Mermaid 106
The Simon Difference 80
Tiffany design prototype 89
Tiffany style leaded glass window design 89
Tinker Bell 36
Toledo Zoo Panda set 100
Topps All Time Greatest Team 220
Total Customer Satisfaction................................211
Touch of service..87
Toy cups 248
Training 252-253
Transformer plastic cup 248
Travel mugs 206, 249-251
Triple thick Milkshake 123, 130, 157
Trivia Challenge Game 106
Uncle O'Grimacey 143
Upromise College Savings Accelerator 127
V.I.P. Sweepstakes cups 129
Walt Disney World...............................33, 36, 109
We do it all for you 50
We love to see you smile 124, 245
We're here to help you 125
We're here when you need us 80
We're still the one 253
We've got everything under the sun 80
Who Framed Roger Rabbit...........................61, 160
Who wants to be a millionaire 126
Wine glass 14, 232-242
Winnie the Pooh 106
Workshops 28, 252-253
World Cup USA 94 ....197-198, 230
You deserve a break today 30, 80
You're up late, so we're up late 127, 135, 158
You, you're the one 80
Zubaz 219, 222
1 in a million 50
25 Years of Magic 107
100 Years of Magic 36, 109
101 Dalmations 107
1994 World Cup soccer....................136, 197-198
1996 Atlanta Olympic Games 133-134, 227-228
2000 European Soccer Championship....................231
2004 Athens Olympics 131, 158